"Fred Sanders feels the heartbeat of Wesleyan theology. His scholarship never lacks evangelical integrity or practical realism. Here is stimulating reading from a gifted teacher. Everyone who loves the gospel will resonate with the message of this book."

Robert E. Coleman, Distinguished Senior Professor of Evangelism and Discipleship, Gordon-Conwell Theological Seminary

"As Fred Sanders shows us in this accurate and edifying life and thought of Wesley, we all have much to learn from this godly evangelical founder. I pray that God will use this book to awaken his people again, filling us with his Spirit and renewing our hearts in love. I plan to use it with my students in both seminaries and churches. It is a great place for Christians to acquaint themselves with one of the most important leaders in all of church history."

Douglas A. Sweeney, Professor of Church History and the History of Christian Thought, Director of the Jonathan Edwards Center, Trinity Evangelical Divinity School

"As usual, Fred Sanders brings out treasures of his research without making us do all the digging ourselves. Though respectful of John Wesley, I've never been what you'd call a fan. But that's exactly why a book like this is so worthwhile. Challenging caricatures, Sanders offers a welcoming portrait of Wesley that is too evenhanded and well substantiated to be his own fabrication. If the purpose of this series is to display the resources of the past for the present, then *Wesley on the Christian Life* is a home run."

Michael S. Horton, J. Gresham Machen Professor of Systematic Theology and Apologetics, Westminster Seminary California

"One of the symptoms of the contemporary malaise of the Methodist movement is a growing disconnect with the actual life and teachings of our beloved founder, John Wesley. Fred Sanders has given us a wonderful gift in this practical introduction to the life and thought of Wesley. Sanders sh--- t cannot be summarized in terms of doctrinal d e sanctifying winds of the Holy Spirit through t eart. I recommend this book to all those 'restle vho need to understand this part of the churcl across the country who are longing for a guide t ed Methodist.'"

Timothy C. Tennent, Pr ___ or world Christianity, Asbury Theological Seminary

"Whether one is an admirer or a critic, all must concede that the life and thought of John Wesley have had a decisive effect on later evangelical Protestantism. Yet few of us know much about his understanding of the Christian life beyond the rather vague terms often applied to his thought, *Arminianism* and *perfectionism*. Thus, even a hard-hearted Calvinist like myself feels a debt of gratitude to Fred Sanders for this delightful, readable, learned, accessible, and sympathetic treatment of the Methodist patriarch's thinking on what it means to live as a Christian. A most lovely addition to a very fine series."

Carl R. Trueman, Paul Woolley Professor of Church History, Westminster Theological Seminary

"Readers are in for a treat here. Lively and thoughtful, appreciative but not uncritical, this book shows compellingly why even those who would not call themselves Wesleyan have a great deal to benefit from John Wesley."

Michael Reeves, author, *Delighting in the Trinity* and *The Unquenchable Flame*

WESLEY

on the Christian Life

THEOLOGIANS ON THE CHRISTIAN LIFE

EDITED BY STEPHEN J. NICHOLS AND JUSTIN TAYLOR

Bonhoeffer on the Christian Life:
From the Cross, for the World,
Stephen J. Nichols

Schaeffer on the Christian Life:
Countercultural Spirituality,
William Edgar

Warfield on the Christian Life:
Living in Light of the Gospel,
Fred G. Zaspel

WESLEY

on the Christian Life

THE HEART RENEWED IN LOVE

FRED SANDERS

CROSSWAY

WHEATON, ILLINOIS

Cover design: Josh Dennis

Cover image: Richard Solomon Artists, Mark Summers

First printing 2013

Printed in the United States of America

Unless otherwise indicated, Scripture quotations are from the King James Version of the Bible.

Scripture quotations marked ESV are from the ESV® Bible (*The Holy Bible, English Standard Version®*), copyright © 2001 by Crossway. 2011 Text Edition. Used by permission. All rights reserved.

Trade paperback ISBN: 978-1-4335-1564-4
Mobipocket ISBN: 978-1-4335-1566-8
PDF ISBN: 978-1-4335-1565-1
ePub ISBN: 978-1-4335-2487-5

Library of Congress Cataloging-in-Publication Data

Sanders, Fred (Fred R.)
 Wesley on the Christian life : the heart renewed in love / Fred Sanders.
  pages cm. — (Theologians on the Christian life)
  Includes bibliographical references and index.
  ISBN 978-1-4335-1564-4 (tp)
  1. Wesley, John, 1703–1791. I. Title.
BX8495.W5S265 2013
230'.7092—dc23   2013016026

Crossway is a publishing ministry of Good News Publishers.

VP		23	22	21	20	19	18	17	16	15	14	13
15	14	13	12	11	10	9	8	7	6	5	4	3	2	1

For Freddy:
peaceful, playful,
powerful, the fourth

CONTENTS

SERIES PREFACE

Some might call us spoiled. We live in an era of significant and substantial resources for Christians on living the Christian life. We have ready access to books, DVD series, online material, seminars—all in the interest of encouraging us in our daily walk with Christ. The laity, the people in the pew, have access to more information than scholars dreamed of having in previous centuries.

Yet for all our abundance of resources, we also lack something. We tend to lack the perspectives from the past, perspectives from a different time and place than our own. To put the matter differently, we have so many riches in our current horizon that we tend not to look to the horizons of the past.

That is unfortunate, especially when it comes to learning about and practicing discipleship. It's like owning a mansion and choosing to live in only one room. This series invites you to explore the other rooms.

As we go exploring, we will visit places and times different from our own. We will see different models, approaches, and emphases. This series does not intend for these models to be copied uncritically, and it certainly does not intend to put these figures from the past high upon a pedestal like some race of super-Christians. This series intends, however, to help us in the present listen to the past. We believe there is wisdom in the past twenty centuries of the church, wisdom for living the Christian life.

Stephen J. Nichols and Justin Taylor

INTRODUCTION

Who Listens to John Wesley Today?

Is anybody listening to the voice of John Wesley anymore? Of course Wesley is still famous enough, with a name widely recognized more than two centuries after his death. He has fame, fans, and followers. There are not only the United Methodist churches (I got saved in one) but a whole family of other Wesley-influenced denominations: the Wesleyan Church, the Free Methodist Church, the Church of the Nazarene, the African Methodist Episcopal Church, and so on. There are Methodist youth groups (I led one), Wesleyan and Methodist seminaries (I went to one of the best), and holiness camp meetings (I attended one as a teenager). There is even a Wesleyan Theological Society (I'm a member) with its own journal (I'm a subscriber), and experts in Wesleyan studies. These self-identified fans and followers of John Wesley know his message.

But Wesley's words were once heard in every church, not just the ones directly downstream from his institutional influence. His voice was once impossible to ignore, and his influence inescapable. Today, however, outside the self-identified Wesleyverse, the Wesley Literacy Quotient among evangelicals has declined alarmingly. A generation has arisen that does not know Wesley. Names, phrases, and stories that once resonated with evangelicals everywhere now signify nothing to most: Epworth, "a brand plucked from the burning," the Holy Club, Aldersgate, "my heart was strangely warmed," "the world is my parish," "earn all you can and give all you can," "offer them Christ." Aside from a few of Charles Wesley's hymns that have become permanent parts of Christian worship ("Hark, the Herald Angels Sing," "O for a Thousand Tongues to Sing," "And Can It Be That I Should Gain"), the words of the Wesleys are not being heard.

Evangelical Calvinists in particular (whether young and restless or old and dozing) too often behave as if their Reformed credentials give them a free pass to forget there ever was a John Wesley, or that he is to be reckoned one of the good guys. It was not always so. John Newton (1725–1807) was as young, restless, and Reformed as anybody, but he could testify of John Wesley, "I know of no one to whom I owe more as an instrument of divine grace."[1] Not to be outdone, Charles Spurgeon (1834–1892) ventured that "if there were wanted two apostles to be added to the number of the twelve, I do not believe that there could be found two men more fit to be so added than George Whitefield and John Wesley."[2] Spurgeon may have been indulging in a characteristic dramatic flourish, but I don't recall hearing that he surrendered his Calvinist card either before or after thus lumping together Whitefield and Wesley, respectively the great Calvinist and the great Arminian promoters of the eighteenth-century awakening. Witnesses like Newton and Spurgeon seem to prove that even Calvinists can learn from Wesley; in fact I hope this book makes it apparent that it is *especially* Calvinists who, while remaining as Reformed as they want to be, should labor to hear what this evangelical brother has to say to them across the centuries.

John Wesley intended his ministry to be an influence on all existing churches; he considered himself a spokesman for the evangelical message to all. As he said, "the original design" of his work was "not to be a distinct party, but to stir up all parties, Christians or heathens, to worship God in spirit and in truth."[3] (It should be obvious, by the way, that he would stir up the heathens to worship God by converting them to Christ.) When in 1742 he undertook a defense of the word *Methodist*, he began by saying, "I should rejoice (so little ambitious am I to be at the head of any sect or party) if the very name might never be mentioned more, but buried in eternal oblivion." In that tract, *The Character of a Methodist*, he stated his principles as clearly as possible in hopes that "perhaps some of you who hate what I am *called*, may love what I *am* by the grace of God; or rather, what 'I follow after, if that I may apprehend that for which I am apprehended of Christ Jesus.'"[4]

---

[1] Quoted in Iain H. Murray, *Wesley and Men Who Followed* (Edinburgh: Banner of Truth, 2003), 71. Note that Murray himself (b. 1931) is a great example of a recent Calvinist who unflinchingly opposes Arminianism, but is fully aware of how much spiritual blessing he has received through Wesley and the Methodists. Other examples of current Reformed thinkers who recognize what a friend they have in Wesley include J. I. Packer (see "The Glory of God and the Reviving of Religion: A Study in the Mind of Jonathan Edwards," in *A God-Entranced Vision of All Things: The Legacy of Jonathan Edwards*, ed. John Piper and Justin Taylor [Wheaton, IL: Crossway, 2004]).

[2] *C. H. Spurgeon's Autobiography*, vol. 1 (London: Passmore and Alabaster, 1899), 176.

[3] From Wesley's journal, April 12, 1789, in *The Bicentennial Edition of the Works of John Wesley*, ed. Frank Baker and Richard P. Heitzenrater (Nashville: Abingdon, 1976–), 24:128. When citing this edition, I will use the abbreviation *Works*, followed by the volume number and page number.

[4] "The Character of a Methodist" (1742), in *Works*, 9:32–46, alluding to 1 Cor. 15:10 and quoting Phil. 3:12.

Wesley understood himself well when he said his mission was "to stir up all . . . to worship God." He was above all a revivalist, an awakener of slumbering souls and torpid institutions. Surely there is a great need for his kind of stirring and awakening today. For one thing (inside the Wesleyverse), the very institutions started by Wesley have taken on the kind of coldness and lethargy that Wesley arose to stir up. Evangelicals inside of Methodism are well aware that "the Methodist movement has become what it was once a reaction against."[5] That is, believers have long since learned to look to Methodism as the mainline church, not as a movement for revival that reaches all the churches.

Second, there is a great need for Wesley's kind of stirring in our time because his message is medicinal for much that ails us all today. He perceived the inherent unity of things that we have, to our harm, learned to think of as separate, or even as opposites. He saw that holiness of heart and life was internally and necessarily linked to the free forgiveness of sins. He saw the connection between justification and sanctification, and was able to communicate it powerfully. "He was possessed of one central truth, that man is justified by faith and perfected in love."[6] He did not pick and choose from among the various benefits of union with Christ, and his preaching did not leave his listeners with that option either. He had a unified understanding of grace as both unmerited mercy and the power of God the Holy Spirit who works in us.[7] If this vast doctrine of grace could get a grip on Christians in our time, it would catalyze the same kind of awakening as when Wesley first preached it.

For these reasons, I am excited to have the opportunity to contribute a John Wesley volume to the Theologians on the Christian Life series. This book, *Wesley on the Christian Life: The Heart Renewed in Love*, undertakes two related tasks. First, it introduces John Wesley's theology and spirituality, reporting what he said and thought. Second, it recommends (with a few caveats) a generally Wesleyan approach to living a balanced Christian life.

---

[5] Statements like this can be scooped up from any renewal-minded conservative Wesleyan group. This one happens to be how the editor at the website MethodistThinker.com summarized the remarks of George Hunter, "Can the Once-Great Methodist Movement Become a Movement Again?" (presented at the United Methodist Congress on Evangelism, January 2011), accessed at http://methodistthinker.com/2011/05/26 /george-hunter-can-once-great-methodist-movement-be-a-movement-again.

[6] William Ragsdale Cannon, *The Theology of John Wesley: With Special Reference to the Doctrine of Justification* (New York: Abingdon, 1946), 7.

[7] See sermon 12, "The Witness of Our Own Spirit," Burwash, 114. Citations of Wesley's *Standard Sermons* will follow the form shown here, using not the definitive scholarly edition of the *Works*, but the influential and freely available edition of *Wesley's 52 Standard Sermons*, ed. N. Burwash (Salem, OH: Schmul, 1988). Wesley's sermons are available online at the website of the United Methodist Church's Global Ministries, http://gbgm-umc.org/umhistory/wesley/sermons.

It has one foot in the eighteenth century, reporting on what Wesley did and said and thought. But it has the other foot in evangelical existence today, arguing that what Wesley said and did then has significance for the living of the Christian life now. So although we will spend plenty of time in eighteenth-century England and I will try to be an honest reporter, nothing will be included for merely historical interest or for the sake of completeness; everything will be directed toward the application of Wesley's thought to contemporary Christian life. What we want is to hear the words of Wesley awakening us here and now.

So Many Wesleys, So Little Time

Which John Wesley will we be hearing from? The question must be raised because there are many John Wesleys to be reckoned with. It's not that he had multiple personalities or that he was intellectually inconsistent. But he was one of those historical characters that we describe as larger than life. He was magnetic, but even in his own lifetime he attracted different people differently, and he has drawn a great variety of interpreters ever since. Surveying the range of different Wesleys presented by different readers, one recent scholar observed that "Wesley's interpreters do not agree fully on how to read him. In particular, proponents on different sides of current theological debates have often cited Wesley to support their alternative positions."[8]

Some of the confusion among his interpreters is their fault. As readers of Wesley, says one, "we ignore the parts of Wesley we don't like. We revise the parts of Wesley that challenge our positions. And we repeat *ad infinitum* the parts of Wesley that we love."[9] But Wesley himself caused many of the problems. He had a particular genius for incorporating the diverse emphases of various systems of theology as he attempted to be a mere Christian. He possessed "a moderating sensibility, a tendency to avoid one-sided readings,"[10] and an instinct for getting around the theological gridlock of

---

[8] Sarah H. Lancaster, "Current Debates over Wesley's Legacy among His Progeny," in *The Cambridge Companion to John Wesley*, ed. Randy L. Maddox and Jason E. Vickers (New York: Cambridge University Press, 2010), 304.

[9] Richard P. Heitzenrater, "Twice-Told Tales," *Circuit Rider*, May/June 2003, 17. Heitzenrater's puckish article deflates a number of urban legends and misattributed quotations. In his book *The Elusive Mr. Wesley*, 2nd ed. (Nashville: Abingdon, 2003), Heitzenrater bursts several more legends, warning that "many an account of Wesley is but an editorial gloss on the man, an attempt on the part of an author to prove some point about either Wesley's thought or, more likely and less obviously, the author's own. By careful selection and editing, an author can make Wesley appear in a number of guises" (p. 25).

[10] Kenneth J. Collins, *The Theology of John Wesley: Holy Love and the Shape of Grace* (Nashville: Abingdon, 2007), 4.

competing systems. Wesley was not afraid to take definite positions on contentious, even divisive, issues. But while most leaders grow narrower as they are forced to make decision after decision, Wesley did the opposite: the result of his declaring himself on so many issues was a kind of cumulative effect by which he became more and more comprehensive. He almost seemed to be moving around intellectually just so he could be in the right places at the right times to affirm all the truths he wanted to affirm: first a Puritan background, next an Anglo-Catholic reading program, then a thunderbolt from Luther, and inundation from Pietist spiritual writers. John Wesley was hungry for truth and reality; he wanted it all, and in that pursuit he crossed lines and mixed traditions that are rarely combined.

It is a curious feature of his intellectual profile that so many kinds of Christians can find their own deepest interests represented in his legacy. As Kenneth Collins points out, "Wesley developed a theological style that not only was sophisticated in its attempt to hold a diversity of truths in tension, but also has on occasion puzzled his interpreters, both past and present, precisely because of that diversity."[11] This is precisely what we will benefit from if we hear Wesley: his ability to gather together elements of the Christian life that we have come to think of as necessarily separate.

Collins goes on to catalog[12] the numerous Wesleys that have been portrayed by the interpreters: the basically Reformed Wesley, the essentially Lutheran-Pietist Wesley, the secretly Puritan Wesley, the exotically Greek Patristic Wesley. Methodists, understandably, have a tendency to describe him retroactively as a good Methodist, though like all interpreters they have to explain why he was pleased to remain Anglican all his life. Anglican he may have been, but reasonable scholars have nevertheless described him as a secret Baptist, a crypto-Catholic, and a proto-Pentecostal. These disputes over the interpretation of his theology have become the standard fare of Wesley studies. There is a grain of truth in each of them, so that whichever Wesley a scholar may argue for, the footnotes inevitably contain the admission that other interpretations are plausible.

Somebody needs to present an Unaccommodated Wesley,[13] a vast, careful, comprehensive account that refuses on principle to align Wesley with

---

[11] Ibid.
[12] Ibid.
[13] See the attempt at strict historical description carried out by Richard A. Muller on behalf of reclaiming John Calvin from his interpreters in *The Unaccommodated Calvin: Studies in the Foundation of a Theological Tradition* (New York: Oxford University Press, 2000). The closest thing in Wesley studies is Heitzenrater, *The Elusive Mr. Wesley.*

any current systems. But in this book, I argue for a particular version of John Wesley, the one I am convinced of and whose writings have nourished me for the past twenty-five years, since the time I got saved in a Methodist youth group. The Wesley you will meet in this book is John Wesley the warmhearted evangelical Protestant. His teaching on the Christian life trades heavily on being born again, on deeply felt heart religion, on justification by faith alone, on awareness of original sin and total dependence on God's grace, on active cultivation of spiritual disciplines, and on striving for growth in knowledge and grace. His view of the Christian life is fed by the great tradition of Christian orthodoxy and is crowned by an experiential, evangelical Trinitarianism.

I am well aware of the danger of creating a John Wesley after my own image and likeness, since I hope all of those elements also characterize my own theology. I have put in place three defenses that I hope have preserved me against rendering a self-portrait and then calling it Wesley. First, the words of Wesley himself loom large in this book, enabling the reader to judge whether Wesley is saying what I claim he's saying. Second, there are several points at which I report Wesley's distinctive views even though I am conscious of disagreeing with him in the details. For example, Wesley thinks that 1 John is the most important book of the Bible (see chap. 4), but I know for certain that Ephesians holds that title. His view of the sacraments (chap. 7) is a bit too high, in my judgment; but this is his book, so he gets to have his Anglican say. I have not flagged every place where I feel myself in disagreement with Wesley, but in general the reader should assume that the views presented here are Wesley's, or at least my best effort to present them. Third, though I write as a Wesleyan theologian, I am not an especially pure example of one. For example, I'm not convinced that prevenient grace can do all the work Wesley wants it to do. I can only affirm Christian perfection in a very qualified sense. My tolerance for Calvinism is very high compared with Wesley's. Ultimately, however, I present Wesley as a warmhearted evangelical Protestant because I am persuaded by primary and secondary sources alike that the Wesley of history really was the Wesley of the evangelical Protestant faith.

Charles Wesley as Supporting Witness

A different sense in which there is a problem of "too many Wesleys" to deal with in one short book on the Christian life is that there are more Wesleys than just John. His father Samuel and his mother Susanna are both formidable theological influences, and a complete account of John's work would have to give attention to them both.[14] John's older brother, Samuel, was also a significant voice in Wesley's development. If you consider the spiritual legacy of the Wesley grandparents (all four were Puritans) and the devotional lives of the sisters in the household, the work that John Wesley did in the outer world begins to look like the most successful externalization of a family project. John Wesley was the "hit single" for the family band.

But the most important "other Wesley" is obviously his brother Charles. Four years younger than John, Charles by common consent "should be called the co-founder of the Wesleyan or Methodist tradition."[15] Charles not only co-labored with John in the work of the revival, but also actually preceded him in several important ways. It was Charles who was the most important organizer in the early days of the Holy Club at Oxford; Charles experienced his own evangelical conversion three full days before John did; and Charles was instrumental in the momentous spiritual awakening of George Whitefield, without whose contribution the evangelical awakening would have been a significantly smaller event.

Charles did more than write hymns; he was recognized in his day as a powerful evangelist. His recent biographer notes that "many of his hearers preferred the preaching of the younger Wesley to that of his more famous older brother; Charles's published sermon 'Awake Thou That Sleepest' became the most purchased piece of Wesleyana during the brothers' lifetime."[16] The brothers shared their work and mingled their ministries to such an extent that, to this day, scholars are uncertain about which brother wrote some of the sermons and some of the hymns. During the busiest seasons of the revival, it apparently didn't matter to the brothers; a Wesley sermon was a Wesley sermon, whether by John or Charles.

Why did John end up taking the lead in this shared ministry? Partly it was a matter of temperament. Charles Wesley was naturally retiring, and though he was personable and gregarious, he was not constitutionally a "public person." John certainly was. Charles "shunned the limelight

---

[14] For a short account of Samuel's abiding presence in John's thought, see Gordon Rupp, "Son of Samuel: John Wesley, Church of England Man," chap. 9 in *Just Men: Historical Pieces* (London: Epworth, 1977). For Susanna's influence, it is best to consult her own words, collected in *Susanna Wesley: The Complete Writings*, ed. Charles Wallace (New York: Oxford University Press, 1997).

[15] John R. Tyson, *Assist Me to Proclaim: The Life and Hymns of Charles Wesley* (Grand Rapids: Eerdmans, 2007), viii.

[16] Ibid.

with the same vigor that his brother John seemed to crave it."[17] Charles had a very happy marriage, had three children, and enjoyed being a father over his household. John married later, notoriously unhappily, and had no children. Charles's more fragile health required him to settle in one place as a preacher, while the cutting edge of the awakening was always itinerant preaching. But there were also philosophical differences between the brothers: Charles was a much more committed Church of England man than John and increasingly saw John's practical decisions (class meetings, lay preachers, the ordination of American bishops) as tending to undermine Anglicanism by making a "Methodist schism" inevitable. The difference between them on this point could be subtle; a recent scholar captures it by saying that Charles "was committed to the revival of *the Church of England*, whereas John was committed to the *revival* of the Church of England."[18] The practical result was that Charles was very cautious about the qualifications of lay preachers in the Methodist movement, while John could be reckless about whom he trusted with the office. For these reasons, Charles was sometimes hitting the brakes while John was almost always stomping on the gas pedal. Even if Charles was right in his cautions, John accomplished more in his zeal. And while John was especially beloved to the most energetic leaders in the second generation of Methodists, Charles had been in fights with many of them. When leadership passed into their hands, it was inevitable that they would hold John in higher regard than Charles.

So while John and Charles were not exactly alike, their work so interpenetrated that they ought to be treated together. It might be just possible to present *Wesley on the Christian Life* by focusing solely on John, omitting all references to Charles and his hymns. But what an impoverishment this would be! And how at odds with John's own method, as he seasoned his own sermons with apt bits of Charles's verses, citing them as conclusive historical proof of what the Methodists had always taught. He carried out his whole ministry to the tune of Charles's hymns, "the soundtrack for the eighteenth-century transatlantic revival."[19] Another approach would be to devote the entire book to the brothers' shared work: *John and Charles Wesley on the Christian Life*. Indeed, one of the most useful anthologies on the spirituality of the Wesleys bundles their work together in just this way.[20]

---

[17] Ibid., x.

[18] "Introduction," in Maddox and Vickers, *Cambridge Companion to John Wesley*, 8.

[19] Tyson, *Assist Me to Proclaim*, viii.

[20] *John and Charles Wesley: Selected Prayers, Hymns, Journal Notes, Sermons, Letters and Treatises*, ed. Frank Whaling (New York: Paulist, 1981). See also the excellent but long-out-of-print *Message of the Wesleys:*

The current book splits the difference, focusing on John Wesley but making use of Charles's work wherever he seems to have driven the point home more clearly or poetically. Charles also looms large in chapter 3, on heart religion, because of the importance of the hymns for stirring up the affections.

Wesley's Message for the Christian Life

Some theologians have written comprehensively on the full range of doctrines. But John Wesley was above all a preacher and a pastoral theologian, and almost everything he wrote was in the field of "practical divinity," or the Christian life. A book like *Aquinas on the Christian Life* or *Augustine on the Christian Life* would only deal with a subsection of each theologian's overall thought. But salvation and the Christian life are practically all that John Wesley ever wrote about; indeed, "it is sometimes said that, as a theologian, John Wesley specialized in the doctrine of the Christian life."[21] So this book comes close to surveying his entire theology. But it is not just Wesley 101,[22] and its focus on the Christian life dictates what has been put in and what has been left out.

For example, chapter 1 is a brief account of John Wesley's life and character, sketching the basic biographical facts of his long and eventful career, but dwelling longer on those aspects of his life which earn him a hearing as a spiritual advisor. The story leaps over entire decades but focuses on one event in particular, his evangelical conversion at Aldersgate, which is the point of departure for an extended analysis in chapter 2. Next, chapter 3 describes Wesley's orientation toward a Christianity focused on the heart, an emphasis he had in common with the German Pietists, the English Puritans, and American pastor-theologians such as Jonathan Edwards.

After these foundational matters are dealt with, the next five chapters (chaps. 4–8, the heart of the book) take up the major issues in Wesley's theology of the Christian life. Chapter 4 makes the most important interpretive argument: that John Wesley is best understood as a theologian who

---

A Reader of Instruction and Devotion, compiled and with an introduction by Philip S. Watson (New York: Macmillan, 1964).

[21] Jason E. Vickers, *Wesley: A Guide for the Perplexed* (London: T&T Clark, 2009), 94. Vickers adds that "it would be more accurate to say that he specialized in theology *for* the Christian life."

[22] For a more comprehensive introduction to Wesley, see the work of Kenneth Collins. For a more biographical approach, see Collins, *John Wesley: A Theological Journey* (Nashville: Abingdon, 2003). For a more doctrinal approach, see Collins, *The Theology of John Wesley*. A classic survey of Wesley's doctrine, largely in his own words, is Thomas Oden, *John Wesley's Scriptural Christianity: A Plain Account of His Teaching on Christian Doctrine* (Grand Rapids: Zondervan, 1994).

let the first epistle of John set the tone for his life and thought. Chapter 5 explains the role of justification by faith, not just for conversion but for the entire life of the believer and as the basis of sanctification. Chapter 6 surveys John Wesley's doctrine of grace, showing how it combines elements of forgiveness and empowerment, elements that are often thought of in disconnected ways. From this follows the idea of the means of grace (chap. 7), the channels that God has appointed for encountering us again and again to transform us. Chapter 8 examines John Wesley's vision of the perfected Christian life, the goal and purpose of everything that has gone before in the order of salvation.

After this survey of Wesley on the main elements of the Christian life, the final two chapters look around at the broader context of his theology. In chapter 9, we explore Wesley's lifelong conviction that the individual Christian life is embedded in the fuller story of God's dealings with his people, and that each Christian needs to live with an awareness of being connected to the work of God among all other Christians. The final chapter, chapter 10, shows the overarching pattern of Wesley's theology to be an encounter with the triune God and explains how the doctrine of the Trinity functioned for his spirituality.

This book's focus on the Christian life means that one of the things John Wesley is most famous for, his Arminianism, is not a major topic. It comes up a few times but never receives sustained or independent treatment. I trust the reasons for this will be evident quite early in the text, as the evangelical awakening of the eighteenth century took place on the common ground shared by evangelical Protestants. Briefly, the primary reason for omitting Arminianism from *Wesley on the Christian Life* is that most of what Wesley says about the Christian life belongs to the area in which Calvinists and Arminians agree. The cartoony Wesley existing in the public mind is a man of one idea: anti-Calvinistic free will; he is the evil opposite evoked by the cartoony Calvin with his own fixed idea, fatalistic predestination. Neither of these characters exists in reality. The real Calvin and the real Wesley have genuine disagreements, of course, and important ones. But the areas of disagreement (absolute predestination, explanations of human agency and choice) belong in the background of their treatment of the Christian life. Friction with Calvinists shows up in several chapters: a disagreement about imputed righteousness is prominent in chapter 5, prevenient grace in its Wesleyan form appears in chapter 6, and the divisive issue of perfectionism is unavoidable in chapter 8. How Calvinists and Wesleyans can cooperate in Christian work is one of the subjects of chapter 9. But the direct consideration of Calvinism and Wesleyanism as opposing systems is beyond the scope of a book on the Christian life.

Reformed people who read widely in Wesley, as opposed to reading a digest of his most biting anti-Calvinist zingers, are always surprised, and usually delighted, to find in him the same things they love in their favorite Reformed authors: a Scripture-saturated defense of original sin and justification by faith alone, a clear presentation of the gospel, a humble submission to God's sovereignty, and a radical dependence on God's grace. Scottish pastor John Duncan (1796–1870), a decided Calvinist, read the Methodist hymnal and remarked, "I wonder how Charles Wesley could write that, and be an Arminian."[23] I expect that many Reformed readers of this book will be edified and awakened by Wesley's teaching, and I hope they find themselves asking on most pages, "How could John Wesley write that and be an Arminian?" Whatever the word *Arminian* meant to most people before Wesley, there is at least the chance after John Wesley that it refers to a Christian who is doctrinally conservative and committed to the gospel.

John Wesley has a word for today. In his own time, as we will see, "parental influence, a classical education, a methodical nature and a personal crisis on the Pauline scale, all combined to make him a man with something to say."[24] He was a man of broad liberal learning, a fluency in Scripture, a keen spiritual insight, and a gift for communicating. Very little of what he taught was brand-new, but he recombined the themes of the Christian life into a combustible mixture. He saw the great unities and spoke the great verities. He also had a way of putting things that cut straight through his generation's defenses and reached into their hearts. So in what follows I have quoted him at length and have given footnotes to the most easily available editions of his books rather than to the best or standard scholarly sources. My goal is to let Wesley speak clearly, to send readers to where they can learn more from him, and to remove any obstacles that might keep readers from hearing the message that shook the world not long ago and not far away.

---

[23] John Brown, *Life of the Late John Duncan* (Edinburgh: Edmonston and Douglas, 1872), 428. A bit more snarkily, Duncan remarked, "I have a great liking for many of Wesley's Hymns; but when I read some of them, I ask, 'What's become of your Free-will now, friend?'" (p. 401).

[24] George Lawton, *John Wesley's English: A Study of His Literary Style* (London: George Allen & Unwin, 1962), 11.

CHAPTER I

JOHN WESLEY AS A SPIRITUAL GUIDE

John Wesley lived in a way that gave him credibility as a teacher on the Christian life. He has what students of rhetoric and public speaking call *ethos*: a power of persuasion based on his known character and his public accomplishments. When he spoke, forces were set in motion that changed the course of history. When we hear a quotation from Wesley, we are inclined to pay closer attention because of who said it. For example, consider the widely circulated "rule of Wesley":

> Do all the good you can,
> by all the means you can,
> in all the ways you can,
> in all the places you can,
> at all the times you can,
> to all the people you can,
> as long as you ever can.

This would be a fine anonymous exhortation, but it has more impact when attributed to John Wesley, who did so much good. Never mind that although "it sounds very Wesleyan," expert witnesses are certain that "it is not to be found in Wesley."[1] The fake quote gains gravitas from association with him. Why? Because Wesley has credibility to spare.

---

[1] Richard P. Heitzenrater, "Twice-Told Tales," *Circuit Rider*, May/June 2003, 16–17.

This chapter is a brief sketch of the biographical foundation of John Wesley's credibility as a spiritual advisor.[2] It covers Wesley's long life (1703–1791) in four broad movements: his early life, starting in his father's Epworth parsonage; his evangelical conversion at Aldersgate; his role in the great revival in the 1740s; and his decades of work as the builder and organizer of the Methodist movement. Finally, it offers some insights into Wesley's personality and character.

From Epworth

If you start John Wesley's story as far back as two generations before his birth, it looks like it will be the story of English Puritanism because all four of his grandparents were nonconformists, or Dissenters from the established Church of England. His paternal grandfather, John Westley (1636–1678), was imprisoned for refusing to use the Book of Common Prayer in worship. His maternal grandfather, Samuel Annesley (1620–1696), not only was ejected from his pastorate by the Act of Uniformity, but also later had his property confiscated when he was caught ministering in a conventicle, or unofficial small group. So when John Wesley recommended and republished select Puritan spiritual writings for a wider audience (see chap. 9), he was raiding the family bookshelf, tapping directly into a vein of his own Puritan heritage.[3]

But both of John Wesley's parents, Samuel Wesley (1662–1735) and Susanna Annesley (1669–1742), left their dissenting homes and converted to the Church of England, persuaded that it was the most faithful way of being Christian in England. So John Wesley grew up Anglican, under parents who were in the established church not by accident, but by conviction and by adult conversion. Samuel was an Anglican pastor, the rector of the church of St. Andrew at Epworth in Lincolnshire, and a poet whose publications included the quirkily titled *Maggots* (not a best seller) and an epic poem on the life of Christ ("I sing the God, who, though enthroned on high, / In human nature deigned to live and die"). Susanna was a full-time mother,

[2] The classic and comprehensive biography of John Wesley is Luke Tyerman, *The Life and Times of the Rev. John Wesley, M.A, Founder of the Methodists*, 5th ed., 3 vols. (London: Hodder and Stoughton, 1880). (I will be citing the 3rd edition, 1876.) Read it for a full immersion into the world of Wesley, at the hands of a passionate devotee. More recently and more critically, Richard P. Heitzenrater, *The Elusive Mr. Wesley*, 2nd ed. (Nashville: Abingdon, 2003), presents Wesley in his own words. Kenneth Collins, *John Wesley: A Theological Journey* (Nashville: Abingdon, 2003), strikes a fine balance between life and thought, while Allan Coppedge, *John Wesley in Theological Debate* (Wilmore, KY: Wesley Heritage, 1987), traces the development of Wesley's views through various controversies.
[3] For a fascinating bibliographical investigation, see Robert C. Monk, *John Wesley, His Puritan Heritage: A Study of the Christian Life* (Nashville: Abingdon, 1966).

giving birth to nineteen children, nine of whom died in infancy. Of the ten who survived into adulthood, seven were daughters and three were sons. Susanna provided the daily discipline and home education for all the children, though the boys were sent off to boarding school as early as age ten.

Membership in the Church of England was apparently one of the few things that Samuel and Susanna agreed about. They had serious differences of opinion about everything from household management to politics, with one of their political disagreements even resulting in a brief separation. In a letter to John (or Jackey, as his family called him), Susanna admitted to her adult son that "it is an unhappiness almost peculiar to our family that your father and I seldom think alike."[4] Still, Samuel was head of the household, and Susanna was a submissive eighteenth-century pastor's wife in her own peculiar way.

What was her own peculiar way? One story strikingly captures the relational dynamic of the Epworth parsonage and displays the Wesley spirit. While Samuel was away on a long business trip in 1711, Susanna began to hold Sunday afternoon devotional reading services in her home. These services started with her children and servants but grew to include over two hundred people. They were meant to supplement the Sunday morning services, and were in line with the kind of "religious societies" that Samuel had long encouraged as a member of the Society for Promoting Christian Knowledge. Samuel's pastoral assistant, however, felt threatened by these large audiences attending on a laywoman's reading of printed sermons. He wrote to Samuel intimating that the Epworth parsonage was beginning to look like a conventicle, the kind of unofficial church frowned upon by Anglican church order. Samuel wrote home to Susanna, suggesting that she should probably disband the meetings (recall that Susanna's father had been disciplined for holding an unsanctioned conventicle). Susanna replied that since the meetings were manifestly doing spiritual good to many souls in the village, and were directly edifying the church, it would be wrong to stop them. She agreed to submit to Samuel's authority on the issue, but announced the terms of her obedience:

> If after all this you think fit to dissolve this assembly, do not tell me you desire me to do it, for that will not satisfy my conscience; but send your positive command in such full and express terms as may absolve me from

---

[4] Luke Tyerman, *The Life and Times of the Rev. John Wesley*, 3rd ed., 3 vols. (London: Hodder and Stoughton, 1876), 1:32.

all guilt and punishment for neglecting this opportunity for doing good when you and I shall appear before the great and awful tribunal of our Lord Jesus Christ.[5]

John Wesley was only eight years old at the time, but if he was paying attention to these intense debates about spiritual matters between his father and mother, he must have learned lessons that would serve him well in the evangelical awakening, when bishops suggested to him that his methods were perhaps inappropriate. The principle of "do not advise me, but command me to desist" has been called "a cornerstone of the future of Methodism."[6]

John was fifteenth in the large family's birth order, and the middle boy between the much older Samuel (1690–1739) and the slightly younger Charles (1707–1788). Many of the Wesley children died in infancy; in fact, John was the third child to be given that name, the previous two Johns having perished early. So he was not the first John, though nobody ever called him Third John as far as I know. The most famous event from John's childhood at Epworth was the fire that destroyed the home when he was five years old. John was the last of the children to be rescued from the second floor, escaping just before the roof collapsed. There is no evidence that John or his family thought of this rescue as the hand of providence marking out John Wesley for a special future, though later Methodists often told the story that way. But John would later see a parallel between how he was "a brand plucked from the burning" in his childhood and how he was a spiritual firebrand narrowly saved from perdition by God's grace in his adulthood.

As a young boy, Wesley was one of those little household rationalists who needed to be given clear reasons for everything. Our first reported words from his lips are a sentence he uttered whenever he found himself in the difficult moral situation of being offered a snack between mealtimes: "I thank you, I will think of it." His father once remarked to his mother, "I profess, sweetheart, I think our Jack would not attend to the most pressing necessities of nature unless he could give a reason for it." Samuel also gave young John a warning about this unreasonable demand for reasonableness: "Child, you think to carry everything by dint of argument; but you will find how little is ever done in the world by close reasoning."[7] Since John Wesley

[5] The story is told in Joseph Beaumont Wakeley, *Anecdotes of the Wesleys: Illustrative of Their Character and Personal History* (London: Hodder and Stoughton, 1870), 66.
[6] Isaac Taylor, *Wesley and Methodism* (New York: Harper, 1852), 28.
[7] Tyerman, *The Life and Times of the Rev. John Wesley*, 1:18.

would go on to be famous for a certain emotional fervency in religion, it is worth noting that his basic temperament was more coolly reflective. In fact, the course of his life shows that Wesley was preeminently a man of reason, a planner, and an implementer of carefully considered decisions. When he emerged onto the world stage as a revivalist, it was partly because he had become rationally persuaded that the emotions were not being given their due consideration in religious life. Like his contemporary Jonathan Edwards, he was a man of reason whose reason told him he needed to cultivate his heart. He was smart enough to know that it's not good enough to be smart enough.

Before he was eleven, John's parents sent him to boarding school in London, where he studied until he was sixteen. He found his place in the school, wisely avoiding the older boys while assuming a leadership role among the younger. In his later estimation, it was a time of backsliding. Though he kept up the kind of devotional regimen that marked him as the offspring of Samuel and Susanna Wesley ("I still read the Scriptures and said my prayers morning and evening"), his behavior and his sentiments were entirely shaped by his social setting. It was at school that he learned to commit socially acceptable sins; the kind of sins that he knew were wrong, but which were not considered scandalous by his peers or even his teachers. He learned to judge everything on a sliding scale, comparing himself not to any objective standard, but to the people around him. "What I now hoped to be saved by," he reflected later, "was not being so bad as other people." What would later be one of his great strengths, his profound and empathetic sensitivity to people and societies, was undoing him.

In 1720, at age seventeen, Wesley went up to Christ Church, Oxford. Within four years, and years not especially marked by devoutness, he received a baccalaureate degree. Wesley excelled academically; he stayed on at Oxford, was granted a master's degree in due course, and was elected a fellow of Lincoln College. He began moving toward ordination to the priesthood and correcting his lackadaisical attitude toward religious duties:

> When I was about twenty-two, my father pressed me to enter into holy orders. At the same time, the providence of God directing me to Kempis's *Christian's Pattern*, I began to see that true religion was seated in the heart, and that God's law extended to all our thoughts as well as words and actions.[8]

---

[8] From Wesley's journal, 1738; reprinted in *John Wesley*, ed. Albert Outler (New York: Oxford University Press, 1964), 61.

For example, Wesley had been in the habit of taking Communion only about three times a year, but he now began to seek it out weekly. In 1727 he read William Law's two recent books *Christian Perfection* and *A Serious Call to a Devout and Holy Life*. These underlined what he had learned from Kempis: "I was convinced more than ever of the impossibility of being half a Christian, and determined to be all devoted to God to give Him all my soul my body and my substance." John was so earnest and public in his pursuit of the lifestyle described in the New Testament that his friends nicknamed him Primitive Christianity.

It was during this round of intense religious reading and resolution making that John, along with Charles (who had also come up to Oxford), gathered around themselves an earnest group of like-minded young men who set themselves to study the Bible, attend worship services more often and more devoutly, visit the imprisoned, and give to the poor. In the university at that time, they stuck out so much that they attracted nicknames: the Holy Club, the Sacramentarians, the Bible Moths, and the Methodists. This "Oxford Methodist" group probably included only a few dozen young men, but one of them was George Whitefield (1714–1770), whose eyes were opened when Charles Wesley gave him the book *The Life of God in the Soul of Man*, by Henry Scougal. John Wesley underwent some kind of awakening between 1725 and 1729. At least his life was transformed as he came to understand the demands of God's law. "I began not only to read, but to study, the Bible, as the one, the only standard of truth, and the only model of pure religion," he later reminisced about the year 1729.[9]

In 1735 the Wesley brothers and a few other members of the Holy Club went to North America to minister to the colonists and the Native Americans. They seem to have chosen this missionary enterprise because it was the most demanding service opportunity, and because they became convinced they could do the most good in the new world. Mr. "Primitive Christianity" was daring himself to live out the demands of Scripture in a way that matched the spiritual reality he read about among the early Christians. "I hope to learn the true sense of the gospel of Christ by preaching it to the heathen," he explained in a letter.[10]

The Georgia trip was an intense time for John, another turning point

---

[9] From section 5 of *A Plain Account of Christian Perfection*; reprinted in *John and Charles Wesley: Selected Prayers, Hymns, Journal Notes, Sermons, Letters and Treatises*, ed. Frank Whaling (New York: Paulist, 1981), 299.

[10] Letter to John Burton, October 10, 1735, quoted in William Ragsdale Cannon, *The Theology of John Wesley: With Special Reference to the Doctrine of Justification* (New York: Abingdon Press, 1946), 72.

in a life that had been metaphorically stormy and now became literally stormy. The trans-Atlantic voyage was turbulent enough to make him think death was near, and he was ashamed to realize that he—the pastor—was truly afraid to die, while some of the other Christian passengers on board were calm and composed through the storm. He was especially struck by the calm, confident faith of a group of Pietists from the German church community of Moravia. Once he arrived at the colony in Savannah, his ministry had mixed results, but was widely considered a failure. On the one hand, he saw it as a chance to exercise greater pastoral authority than he had at Oxford or as his father's assistant in Lincolnshire. He put into practice some patterns of religious life that were similar to the Holy Club's regimen, but adapted now to a whole parish. He made some decisions here that would soon bear fruit in Methodist structures:

> I now advised the serious part of the congregation to form themselves into a sort of little society, and to meet once or twice a week in order to instruct, exhort, and reprove one another. And out of these I selected a smaller number for a more intimate union with each other: in order to which I met them together at my house every Sunday in the afternoon.[11]

On the other hand, his ideas were not popular with the colonists, who thought this Oxford fellow with high church ideas (he seemed Roman Catholic) and an obsession with German Pietists (he seemed Lutheran) was out of place in the colony. He had romantic notions about witnessing to Indians. "They are as little children," he wrote before the trip, "humble, willing to learn, and eager to do the will of God."[12] These notions were, predictably, crushed upon his actually meeting the human beings themselves: "They show no inclination to learn anything, least of all Christianity," he complained in 1737. But most of all, he behaved foolishly and ran afoul of the gossips in a small colony. The colony's official log book says enough to show that something went very wrong:

Minister at Savannah
embark'd 14 Oct 1735
arrived Feb 1735–6
run away 3 Dec 1737[13]

---

[11] Wesley, "A Short History of the People Called Methodists" (1781), in *The Works of the Reverend John Wesley*, ed. John Emory, 7 vols. (New York: Emory and Waugh, 1831), 7:347.
[12] Quoted in Cannon, *The Theology of John Wesley*, 72.
[13] Quoted in Whaling, *John and Charles Wesley*, 16.

What caused the minister to "run away"? John had announced often enough to the Holy Club that he intended to remain unmarried, but in Georgia he became foolishly entangled in a romance, proposing marriage so ineptly that nobody, including the young woman he proposed to, was quite sure what had happened. When she eventually married instead a Mr. Williamson ("a person not remarkable for handsomeness, neither for greatness, neither for wit, or knowledge, or sense, and least of all for religion," remarked Wesley pertly),[14] Wesley was angry. A few months later, he decided she was in rebellion and should be barred from taking the sacrament of the Lord's Supper. Was this an act of ministerial spite, a reprisal, an abuse of power? There is no direct evidence that Wesley's motives were that low. But they might have been, and Wesley left himself dangerously defenseless. The town was prepared to believe the worst.

The details are complex and sad. The result is that Wesley returned to England with a sense that though he had done some good (and had learned German, Spanish, and Italian!) the trip was, personally and pastorally considered, an utter failure. On the voyage home, he wrote out a confession of his pride, unbelief, and forgetfulness, exclaiming, "I went to America to convert the Indians; but oh, who shall convert me? I can talk well; but let death look me in the face, and my spirit is troubled."[15] Back in England, he wrote yet another self-recrimination, saying, "Alienated as I am from the life of God, I am a child of wrath, an heir of hell." Years later he would look back over these notes and decide they could not be true; he wrote in the margins, "I am not sure of this," "I believe not," and "I had even then the faith of a servant, though not of a son."[16] Still, the original entries show what his mental and emotional condition was in 1738, and how he thought of his spiritual state.

To Aldersgate and the Revival

We have just surveyed—under one heading—everything from Wesley's childhood to his Georgia trip, including his education, his founding of the Holy Club, and his ordination. Now we turn to what happened to Wesley on May 24, 1738, the date of his evangelical conversion. It truly stands out in the middle of his life (he was thirty-five years old) as a dividing line. Ev-

---

[14] Quoted in William Henry Fitchett, *Wesley and His Century: A Study in Spiritual Forces* (New York: Eaton and Mains, 1908), 108.
[15] Tyerman, *The Life and Times of the Rev. John Wesley*, 1:166.
[16] Ibid., 1:167.

erything changed at Aldersgate. "John Wesley, on the eve of the year 1738, was the spiritual prisoner of his age. . . . John Wesley, at the close of the year 1738, was spiritually free."[17] We will spend much of the next chapter exploring what happened to Wesley on this momentous day, theologically speaking. Here we need only note the outward events and the results.

Upon arriving back in England, Wesley pursued spiritual matters intensely, preaching wherever he could, seeking spiritual advice from William Law and from the Moravian Christians who had ministered so much to him during his trip, and drawing together religious societies. In late May, on Pentecost Sunday, his brother Charles experienced an evangelical conversion. George Whitefield had already had a similar experience. With all this pressure mounting, finally in his journal for May 24, Wesley recorded these famous words:

> In the evening I went very unwillingly to a society in Aldersgate Street, where one was reading Luther's preface to the Epistle to the Romans. About a quarter before nine, while the leader was describing the change which God works in the heart through faith in Christ, I felt my heart strangely warmed. I felt I did trust in Christ alone for salvation; and an assurance was given me that He had taken away my sins, even mine, and saved me from the law of sin and death.

Indeed, it was as if a dam had broken in Wesley's soul, and all the spiritual forces of his upbringing, all his passion for Christ, and all his powers of communication came rushing out. From his conversion at Aldersgate, he went on to do all the things we know him for today. All the elements of his personal and religious striving that had been scattered and working against each other so far in his life now came together and worked toward one end.

The change in his outward behavior was not immediate or total. When he and a friend visited the Moravians to tell them what had happened, they let the friend take the Lord's Supper, but refused to administer it to John because he still seemed to them to be *homo perturbatus*, a disturbed or agitated man.[18] But where Wesley's life before 1738 gave the impression of a man searching desperately for something he had not found and perhaps wasn't sure existed, his life after 1738 had the character of a man who was tirelessly at work applying what he had learned to every corner of his life.

---

[17] Cannon, *The Theology of John Wesley*, 65.
[18] Gordon Rupp, *Religion in England 1688–1791* (Oxford: Clarendon, 1986), 358.

Meanwhile, the rest of the world was not waiting on John Wesley; other forces were moving forward that would converge in the vast evangelical revival of the eighteenth century. In particular, George Whitefield had been applying the lessons of the Holy Club in his own way in England. He had even taken the great step of preaching to crowds outdoors, and not during appointed service times. Wesley was soon to out-perform and out-organize his friend, but Whitefield took the lead in many important ways in the early stages of the revival. As one historian says, "He was the first who ever burst into that silent sea, and was converted while the two Wesleys were still fast bound in sin and nature's night, and he was the one great evangelist to share in the Revival as it embraced America, Wales, Scotland, and England."[19] Whitefield decided it was time for him to visit America and asked Wesley to pick up the British work where he was leaving off.

John Wesley does not often appear snobbish or aloof, but he was astonished when Whitefield explained to him the simple expedient of field preaching. Once he understood what was involved, he embraced it, but the action was like hugging a filthy stranger. He recorded in his journal, "at four in the afternoon I submitted to be more vile and proclaimed in the highways the glad tidings of salvation."[20] Field preaching turned out to be exactly the method required to awaken the people of England. Apparently the idea that the message of the Christian faith was something you could hear in any setting was a kind of shock to the people. Wesley said of the idea that he took it up "having been all my life (till very lately) so tenacious of every point relating to decency and order, that I should have thought the saving of souls almost a sin if it had not been done in a church."[21]

Along with field preaching, the other great method of the revival was itinerancy: not staying in one place, but moving from town to town, or from one part of the city to another, with a series of sermons. These two methods combined to make Wesley's preaching a major event wherever it happened. Huge crowds turned out to hear the message of salvation. The gatherings were usually peaceful, but the fact that they occasionally turned into riots is a good sign of how emotionally charged these events could be. Wesley's best report of a revival riot is from October 1743 in the town of Wednesbury. He was by this time well practiced in how to handle a crowd

---

[19] Ibid., 339.
[20] Ibid., 362.
[21] From Wesley's journal, cited in William Edward Hartpole Lecky, *A History of England During the Eighteenth Century (1878–1890)*, 8 vols. (New York: Appleton, 1888), 2:612.

and make himself heard. As the group around him swelled and became unruly, Wesley says:

> To attempt speaking was vain; for the noise on every side was like the roaring of the sea. So they dragged me along till we came to the town; where seeing the door of a large house open, I attempted to go in; but a man, catching me by the hair, pulled me back into the middle of the mob. They made no more stop till they had carried me through the main street, from one end of the town to the other.

In situations like this, as Wesley was jostled from place to place, he kept a cool head and looked for opportunities to get a word in. He would keep silent sometimes, speak to those immediately around him at other times, and then seize the opportunity to address the larger group.

> I continued speaking all the time to those within hearing, feeling no pain or weariness. At the west end of the town, seeing a door half open, I made toward it and would have gone in; but a gentleman in the shop would not suffer [permit] me, saying they would pull the house down to the ground. However, I stood at the door, and asked, "Are you willing to hear me speak?" Many cried out, "No, no! knock his brains out; down with him; kill him at once." Others said, "Nay, but we will hear him first." I began asking, "What evil have I done? Which of you all have I wronged in word or deed?" And continued speaking for above a quarter of an hour, till my voice suddenly failed: then the floods began to lift up their voice again; many crying out, "Bring him away! bring him away!" In the meantime my strength and my voice returned, and I broke out aloud in prayer. And now the man who just before headed the mob turned and said, "Sir, I will spend my life for you: follow me, and not one soul here shall touch a hair of your head."[22]

Such disturbances were not daily events. But excitement broke out wherever the first Methodist preachers went, as fierce opposition and deep revival swirled around each other. And the disturbances persisted for years. In October 1749, Wesley faced a particularly dangerous crowd in Bolton. As usual, he watched for the right moment and turned the tide of the crowd.

> Believing the time was now come, I walked down into the thickest of them. They had now filled all the rooms below. I called for a chair. The

---

[22] From Wesley's journal, October 1743, in *Works*, 20:99.

winds were hushed, and all was calm and still. My heart was filled with love, my eyes with tears, and my mouth with arguments. They were amazed; they were ashamed; they were melted down; they devoured every word. What a turn was this![23]

One of Wesley's secrets of success was that he thrived on the crowd, apparently drawing energy from opposition. He would say that God met him in his need and filled his heart with love, his eyes with tears, and his mouth with arguments on one occasion after another for decades.

Builder and Organizer

The term *Methodist preachers* now conjures up images of circuit riders on the American frontier, planting churches for their fast-growing denomination. But in the eighteenth-century revival, *Methodist* was a loose term for whoever preached in this new, earnest, Whitefield-and-Wesley way. Their *message* was salvation by grace through faith, as a reality that could be experienced here and now. Their *medium* was preaching, especially preaching outside of churches, whether in fields or meeting houses. When the message and the medium met, the international *movement* called Methodism happened, and it happened explosively. People demanded to hear this new thing; they demanded Methodist preachers.

Once the revival picked up momentum, Wesley and Whitefield and their coworkers were no longer promoting it so much as they were running to keep up with it. Nobody could control or manage it. But it was at this point that John Wesley stepped into a new kind of leadership role. He had natural talents as a networker and organizer, and he had learned all the right lessons from his prior successes and failures. He was the one who knew how to channel the revival into systems and patterns that would endure. Wesley had another fifty years of active life ahead of him when the revival broke out, and they were to be years full of preaching, writing, editing, and traveling. But his tasks were constantly dictated to him by the needs of the movement. As quickly as the needs arose, Wesley improvised solutions: lay preachers, class meetings, general rules, conferences, and connections. Implementing these systems and leading them by his own example would be Wesley's lifework from 1741 until his death in 1791.

---

[23] From Wesley's journal, October 1749, in Emory, *The Works of the Reverend John Wesley*, 3:469. For a fuller account of Wesley and crowd violence, see John Telford, "Encounters with the Mob," chap. 12 in *The Life of John Wesley* (New York: Eaton and Maine, 1898).

The popular demand for more evangelical preaching so far outstripped the supply of awakened Anglican ministers that Wesley took a drastic measure to fill the gap. Beginning in 1741, he appointed unordained men to preach. These lay preachers were drawn from all classes of society, and Wesley gave them authority to preach as soon as he discerned any potential in them. Thus, while the machinery of the Anglican church kept grinding along as it had been doing, an alternative delivery system emerged. Lay preachers began ministering in alternative venues. Wesley was very strict about ensuring that the lay preachers never placed themselves in direct competition with the official parish priests, and especially that they never held services at the same time as regular church. He intended for his evangelical lay ministers to awaken the people and feed them on pure doctrine, with the hope that they would be better churchmen thereafter. But Anglican leaders were understandably alarmed.

In 1747, Bishop Gibson of London wrote a circular letter to all the ministers in his diocese, warning against the Methodists. The letter made the accusation that "they persuade the people that the established worship, with a regular attendance upon it, is not sufficient to answer the ends of devotion." Bishop Gibson's letter ended with the rhetorical flourish, "Reverend Brothers, I charge you all, lift up your voice like a trumpet! And warn and arm and fortify all mankind—against a People called Methodists." John Wesley responded with an "Open Letter to the Right Reverend the Lord Bishop of London," asking first of all whether Methodists were really so dangerous as to deserve to be singled out in this way. "Could your lordship discern no other enemies of the gospel of Christ? . . . Are there no Papists, no Deists left in the land? . . . Have the Methodists (so called) monopolized all the sins, as well as all the errors of the nation?"[24]

But Wesley's main business was to respond to the charge that Methodists acted as if attending "the established worship" was not "sufficient to answer the ends of devotion." On the one hand, Wesley did not intend to set up a different church from the established church, and in that sense the normal, institutional worship services of Anglicanism were the main event. On the other hand, everybody knew (and Bishop Gibson had himself admitted in previous pastoral letters!) that the church was not getting the job done. Wesley pressed this point:

---

[24] Quoted in Rupp, *Religion in England 1688–1791*, 381.

Here are, in and near Moorfields, ten thousand poor souls for whom Christ died, rushing head-long into hell. Is Dr. Bulkeley, the parochial minister, both willing and able to help them? If so let it be done, and I have no place in these parts. . . . But if after all he has done and all he can do, they are still in the broad way to destruction, let me see if God will put a word even in my mouth.[25]

The Anglican church of the 1740s simply did not have a plan in place for meeting the spiritual needs of the people of England. It had been a long time since it even pretended to have such a plan. Wesley was completely in favor of the national church; he just intended, as a duly ordained priest of that church, to see it take up its responsibility to shepherd the souls of the nation. Speaking of the range of his own preaching ministry, Wesley had said, "I look upon all the world as my parish; thus far, I mean, that, in whatever part of it I am, I judge it meete [fitting], right, and my bounden duty, to declare unto all that are willing to hear, the glad tidings of salvation." The lay preachers and helpers were an extension of his ministry. The same impetus that drove him to field preaching drove him to appoint lay preachers to extend the gospel ministry to places the church was not even trying to reach.

Wesley provided some rudimentary training and oversight for these lay preachers, mostly in the form of exhortations and guidelines. The best are his "Twelve Rules for Helpers," sent out in 1744. These rules show Wesley as a spiritual guide extending his ministry by equipping others to join him.

1. Be diligent. Never be unemployed for a moment; never be triflingly employed. Never while away time; neither spend any more time at any place than is strictly necessary.
2. Be serious. Let your motto be, Holiness to the Lord. Avoid all lightness, jesting and foolish talking.
3. Converse sparingly and cautiously with women, particularly with young women in private.
4. Take no step towards marriage without first acquainting me with your design.
5. Believe evil of no one; unless you see it done, take heed how you credit it. Put the best construction on everything; you know the judge is always supposed to be on the prisoner's side.

---

[25] Ibid., 381. Rupp calls this passage from Wesley "some of the most moving paragraphs he ever penned."

6. Speak evil of no one; else your words especially would eat as doth a canker. Keep your thoughts within your own breast til you come to the person concerned.

7. Tell every one what you think wrong in him, and that plainly, and as soon as may be, else it will fester in your heart. Make all haste to cast the fire out of your bosom.

8. Do not affect the gentleman. You have no more to do with this character than with that of a dancing-master. A preacher of the gospel is the servant of all.

9. Be ashamed of nothing but sin; not of fetching wood (if time permit), or of drawing water; not of cleaning your own shoes, or your neighbor's.

10. Be punctual. Do everything exactly at the time; and, in general, do not mend our rules, but keep them; not for wrath but for conscience's sake.

11. You have nothing to do but to save souls. Therefore spend and be spent in this work. And go always not to those who want you, but to those who want you most.

12. Act in all things not according to your own will but as a son in the gospel. As such, it is your part to employ your time in the manner which we direct, partly in preaching and visiting the flock from house to house; partly in reading, meditation and prayer. Above all, if you labour with us in the Lord's vineyard, it is needful that you should do that part of the work which we advise, at those times and places which we judge most for His glory.[26]

Wesley trusted his lay preachers. He put basic guidelines in place for them and let them know that their ministry was in some way annexed to, and subordinate to, the ordained ministry of the official church. He expected these helpers to do the right thing. They did not always do so. Minor problems arose in various places from the beginning, but the worst examples of out-of-control lay preachers did not occur until the 1760s.

A preacher named George Bell began teaching that it was possible for his flock to be perfectly holy from then until the return of Christ. The return of Christ, he further stipulated, would be on February 28, 1762. Wesley publicly rebuked Bell, warned the Methodists in Bell's area that they had fallen into error, and did his best to pick up the pieces after the inevitable disappointment when the sun rose on March 1, 1762. A similarly divisive lay preacher was the talented Thomas Maxfield, whose "doctrines

---

[26] Outler, *John Wesley*, 145–46.

became extreme, as though he would out-Wesley Wesley."[27] In general, the pattern seemed to be that the more bright, charismatic, and powerful a lay preacher was, the more dangerous he was, and the more likely to cause trouble among the Methodists. Most lay preachers were content to be ordinary Christians exercising the priesthood of all believers, though in an especially strategic way. That was the whole point of lay preachers, a point that ambitious cranks like Bell and Maxfield missed.

Wherever the revival spread, people awoke from their spiritual slumber, and Wesley organized these awakened souls into well-ordered groups of various kinds. In doing this, he was using techniques he had been practicing since the Holy Club at Oxford. Viewing the rise of Methodism organizationally, Wesley would look back in 1781 and say that the movement had not one but three rises: first, in a very small group "when four of us met together at Oxford"; second, during the disastrous American mission trip "at Savannah, in April, 1736, when twenty or thirty persons met"; and, third, in May 1738 in London, when Wesley and Moravian leader Peter Boehler founded the Fetter Lane Society.[28] The revival gave Wesley the opportunity to use these same spiritual disciplines and community commitments in a context supercharged with spiritual renewal. It also required him to devise new systems and to experiment with new kinds of groups.

The fundamental organizational unit (beginning in 1742) was the "class meeting," an intense small group (about ten or twelve people) that met weekly and emphasized mutual accountability for spiritual growth. Into these groups Wesley directed all who "earnestly desired to flee the wrath that is to come," with the result that these groups might include seekers and recent converts, as well as more mature Christians. Each member received personal attention from a leader within the small group, rather than from an ordained minister overseeing a large number of groups. "There was no room here for lecturing or preaching; the emphasis was clearly on present and personal growth, presided over, not by a professional trainer, but by a fellow seeker."[29]

Wesley's wisdom and ingenuity in the creation of the class meeting system have been widely praised. "The greatest thing John Wesley ever gave to the world is the Methodist class-meeting," wrote Henry Ward Beecher.

---

[27] Rupp, *Religion in England 1688–1791*, 403.
[28] This is from Wesley's 1781 "Short History of the People Called Methodists," in *Works*, 9:425–50.
[29] D. Michael Henderson, *John Wesley's Class Meeting: A Model for Making Disciples* (Nappanee, IN: Evangel, 1997), 96.

And Dwight Moody would testify that "the Methodist class-meetings are the best institutions for training converts the world ever saw."[30] There were also "select bands" for the more spiritually mature. The main goal of the class meetings was to spur believers on to good works, at whatever level was appropriate to them. All the classes and bands together in a region made up the "Methodist Society" for that area. As soon as 1743, Wesley published "General Rules for the Methodist Societies," and by 1744 delegates from many of the societies gathered for the first Methodist Conference (though the conference was not legally incorporated until 1784). All the evangelical ministers of the mid-eighteenth century stood in awe of the revival that was breaking out wherever the gospel was preached. John Wesley, almost alone among these laborers, knew exactly what to do with a revival: put it into small groups.

The Methodist movement spread rapidly and had a great impact. Judging from these results, we have to say that Wesley was highly successful as an organizer and planner. If there is anything that characterizes his work as a leader, it is his many-sidedness. He never made the mistake of thinking there was any single solution to every problem. He knew that people were complex and needed to be supported in complex ways. His comprehensiveness is summed up in a quotation that may be apocryphal, but nicely encapsulates his wisdom:

> Preach our doctrine, inculcate experience, urge practice, enforce discipline. If you preach doctrine alone, the people will be antinomians; if you preach experience only, they will become enthusiasts; if you preach practice only, they will become Pharisees; and if you preach all of these and do not enforce discipline, Methodism will be like a highly cultivated garden without a fence, exposed to the ravages of the wild boar of the forest.[31]

In all of his organizing, Wesley constantly endeavored to keep the Methodist revival within the bounds of the Anglican Church. He was always a Church of England man, and although he knew and respected several Dissenters and Baptists, he was not interested in leading people out of the established church into a dissenting movement. His brother Charles

---

[30] Both of these quotations are from ibid. Henderson's book is the best discussion of John Wesley's strategy and how it applies to ministry through small groups in the contemporary church.

[31] This is a caption under a picture in Nicolson Square Church, Edinburgh. Franz Hildebrandt cites the caption in *Christianity according to the Wesleys* (London: Epworth, 1956), 11–12, noting that there is no other record indicating that Wesley actually said these words. Nevertheless, they epitomize Wesley.

constantly warned him that authorizing lay preachers and organizing Methodist Societies was bound to lead to a breakaway group sooner or later. Several histories of Anglicanism refer to the events of the late 1700s as "the Methodist Schism." Americans might be more inclined to think of it as the birth of a new denomination. In fact, the American situation played an important role in making a new denomination possible and even necessary.

The evangelical awakening happened in England and America beginning around 1740, just as the American colonies were transforming themselves into a nation. Historians even argue that the awakening itself played a role in the formation of a unified American outlook; a revival in 1740 followed by national independence in 1776 was probably not a coincidence. The celebrity status of George Whitefield as an itinerant preacher canvassing up and down the entire colonial seaboard was also likely a unifying factor. But there were many other causes that also fed into the American Revolution, and once the revolution happened, evangelical Anglicans in the United States found themselves in a difficult situation amid conflicting loyalties. Some early Americans found a way to remain loyal to the established Church of England while declaring political independence from her king. But colonial diversity and the absence of a federally established church in the new nation also opened up a new possibility: a non-Anglican church carrying out the ministry of the awakening; Methodism as a denomination, in other words, rather than as a renewal movement within a national church.

What Wesley rejected in the old world he endorsed in the new. In 1784 Wesley ordained preachers for the United States, and even bishops (Coke and Asbury), which led to the formation of the Methodist Episcopal Church within the year. Methodism as a church distinct from Anglicanism grew rapidly in America, sent out missionaries around the world, and soon even counter-colonized England, planting Methodist churches on Anglican soil. But these events occurred after Wesley's lifetime.

John Wesley died in 1791 in London at the age of 87. His death was peaceful, a model of the way a man should pass out of this world if he knows his accounts with God are already settled. If my short telling of Wesley's life has been something of a hagiography, the reader may be thinking, "Of course he died like a saint." But Wesley's serene and resigned death should not be taken for granted. Recall that he was terrified of the storm on the Atlantic in 1738 precisely because he was afraid to die, and he was afraid to die precisely because he was afraid to face God. What John Wesley learned, and taught others, was to face God right now on the basis of the grace of Jesus Christ. The old evening prayer of Bishop Thomas Ken says,

> Teach me to live, that I may dread
> the grave as little as my bed.

That was how John Wesley came at last to die. Wesley thought that a movement could be judged by how well it did at preparing its people for this final trial. On this count we have to judge both his movement and his personal life favorably. "The world may not like our Methodists and Evangelical people, but the world cannot deny that they die well."[32]

Character of the First Methodist

We have had to omit much from this brief account of John Wesley's busy life, but what we have seen ought to be enough to show that he is worth listening to as a teacher on the Christian life. Before we turn to his teaching on the subject, it will be helpful to give a summary of his status as a theologian, his personality, and his character.

First, his status as a theologian. John Wesley was a theologian, but he was by temperament an especially unsystematic theologian. For some time, it was fashionable for commentators to deny that Wesley was a theologian at all. Then came a wave of defenders saying that he was a "folk theologian," a "pastoral theologian," or an "intuitive theologian." These defenses are on the right track. I think it is best to say that Wesley was a theologian who intended to be consistent, but who preferred to express himself in a series of occasional pieces rather than in a comprehensive statement of beliefs. He was more like Luther, who produced a brilliant series of theses, sermons, tracts, pamphlets, attacks, defenses, and occasional treatises, than like Calvin, who drafted an impressively comprehensive introduction to theology at age twenty-six and then commented on nearly every book of the Bible. It will not do to say that Wesley was so busy that he never had a chance to compose a more systematic statement. When he threw himself into a lifestyle of traveling, preaching, and organizing, his life and his literary legacy both took on the same shape. That shape was a focused response to a given situation in a series of brilliant

---

[32] Quoted in Lecky, *A History of England During the Eighteenth Century*, 2:695.

improvisations making use of available material. His life and his theology were isomorphic in this way.

As a result, if you want to read Wesley at his best, you do not consult a systematic theology—you read a lot of sermons. In fact, Wesley's sermons, along with his Bible notes, even became an actual doctrinal norm for later Methodists. In 1763, Wesley and his co-laborers framed a "Model Deed" to ensure that the content of Methodist preaching would remain somewhat standardized. One of the provisions was that ministers should "preach no other doctrine than is contained in Mr. Wesley's Explanatory Notes upon the New Testament and four volumes of sermons."[33]

If Marshall McLuhan was right when he quipped that "the medium is the message," then you can tell a lot about any movement by the form of its main documents. Ignore the actual theology for a moment and just look at the medium that conveys it: Calvinists excel at making confessions and catechisms; Catholics have papal encyclicals and canon law; Anglicans have a Book of Common Prayer and the Thirty-Nine Articles; dispensationalists have study Bibles and time-line diagrams. In each case, there is a fit between the genius of the group and the document or deposit that enshrines that genius. Methodists have a hymnal, the *Explanatory Notes upon the New Testament*, and a set of *Standard Sermons*, all from the Wesleys; these are the carriers of their theology.

It is tempting to think that Wesley's followers, lacking a real systematic theology, are trying to force a heap of songs, notes, and sermons to do the work of doctrine. But that misses the point that the songs, notes, and sermons are direct expressions and carriers of spiritual life. Systematic theology is a service discipline; it helps the worship, Bible reading, and preaching of the church stay faithful and consistent. When he left notes, songs, and sermons to his followers, Wesley was not leaving something sub-theological, but something more immediate than a systematic theology. In some denominations, the standard approach is to get hold of the theology and then ask, "Will it preach?" Wesleyans, by contrast, seem to have got hold of the sermon and then asked, "Will it theologize?"

Following out the guidelines of the notes, the hymnal, and the *Standard Sermons*, it is easy enough to sketch a Wesleyan systematic theology; though the Wesleyan movement has never been as theologically prolific as the Reformed or Lutheran traditions, several good Wesleyan systematic

---

[33] Outler, *John Wesley*, 87.

theologies do exist.[34] But the best of them take note that Wesley got them started on the path to right theology by providing them with right worship, right Bible reading, and right preaching. Someone has said of Protestantism that it is inherently wordy: conceived in an argument, born in theses, and weaned on a catechism. The part of Protestantism under Wesley's influence is different. It is also proud to be wordy ("my mouth was filled with arguments"), but the words rhyme. The movement seems to have been conceived in a revival, born at a hymn-sing, and weaned on Bible notes.

When it comes to John Wesley's personality and character, two closely related elements need to be noted: he was a hard worker, and he had tremendous confidence. At age twenty-three, he wrote to Charles, "Leisure and I have taken leave of one another. I propose to be busy as long as I live, if my health is so long indulged me."[35] He carried out that resolution. Bishop J. C. Ryle (1816–1900) noted Wesley's "extraordinary diligence, self-denial, and economy of time," remarking that "it puts one almost out of breath to read the good man's Journals, and to mark the quantity of work that he crowded into one year."[36] And his health was indeed "long indulged" him, so he remained physically vigorous for decades of productive work. One historian notes that Wesley

> was gifted with a frame of iron and with spirits that never flagged. . . . During the greater part of his career he was accustomed to preach about 800 sermons a year, and it was computed that in the fifty years of his itinerant life he travelled a quarter of a million of miles, and preached more than 40,000 sermons.[37]

Other scholars have computed Wesley's miles-and-sermons statistics somewhat differently, but everybody agrees the number is staggering.

Was Wesley too busy, and did he work too hard? "Nobody would have been more scornful of the idea that he needed what would now be called a 'sabbatical,'" wrote Gordon Rupp, yet in his judgment, "nobody needed one

---

[34] For a survey, see Thomas Langford, *Practical Divinity: Theology in the Wesleyan Tradition*, rev. ed. (Nashville: Abingdon, 1998). In my opinion, the greatest theologian in the Wesleyan tradition was William Burt Pope. For a short sketch, see his essay on "Methodist Doctrine," in *The Wesley Memorial Volume: Or, Wesley and the Methodist Movement, Judged by Nearly One Hundred and Fifty Writers, Living or Dead*, ed. J. O. A. Clark (New York: Phillips & Hunt, 1881), 168–90. More comprehensively, see Pope's three-volume *Compendium of Christian Theology*.
[35] Tyerman, *The Life and Times of the Rev. John Wesley*, 1:46.
[36] J. C. Ryle, *Christian Leaders of the Last Century; or, England a Hundred Years Ago* (London: T. Nelson, 1869), 83.
[37] Lecky, *A History of England During the Eighteenth Century*, 2:682.

more" than Wesley.[38] Dr. Samuel Johnson relished any opportunity to visit with Wesley, but complained that it was impossible to have a leisurely visit with such a dynamo: "He is never at leisure. He is always obliged to go at a certain hour. This is very disagreeable to a man who likes to fold his legs and have out his talk, as I do."[39]

From Wesley's point of view, though, he was maintaining a reasonable schedule and was very careful not to let himself become overburdened or harried. In a 1777 letter, he said, "Though I am always in haste, I am never in a hurry; because I never undertake any more work than I can go through with perfect calmness of spirit."[40] The difference he drew between haste and hurry is the difference between a sinful attitude of harried workaholism and the serenity of obedient service. It is also the key to thinking of Wesley as a role model or guide in the area of productivity. We should never try to match his productivity! Gifted with an unusual amount of natural energy and drive, Wesley set an impossibly high standard of getting things done. He was in an elite class of healthy, hardworking, high-capacity productive people. What we should imitate, however, are his principles and his attitude toward work, devoting all our time and energy to serving God and man. But we should not try to match his productivity. As the also-industrious Charles Wesley wrote, in a hymn intended to form the outlooks of the young orphans in Georgia, since Christ himself worked,

> Then let us in His footsteps tread,
> And gladly act our part;
> On earth employ our hands and head.
> But give Him all our heart.

Indeed, having said goodbye to leisure as a young man, John Wesley was simply carrying out the first of his rules for assistants: "Be diligent. Never be unemployed for a moment; never be triflingly employed. Never while away time; neither spend any more time at any place than is strictly necessary." We should only add to that his own description, "always in haste . . . never in a hurry," and "with perfect calmness of spirit."

---

[38] Rupp, *Religion in England 1688–1791*, 428.
[39] James Boswell, *The Life of Samuel Johnson*, new ed., with notes and appendices by Alexander Napier, vol. 3 (London: George Bell, 1889), 247.
[40] Letter to "a member of the society," December 10, 1777, in Emory, *The Works of the Reverend John Wesley*, 6:784.

Closely related to his productivity was his self-confidence, what one biographer called "his usual imperturbable confidence."[41] Though Wesley was capable of self-doubt and could receive correction and criticism from others, his approach was to charge ahead over the top of naysayers and discouragement. A good example of Wesley's unflappability is from a journal entry on April 22, 1779. That day, he read a passage in Tobias Smollett's *History of England* that attacked, derided, and dismissed the revival work that he and Whitefield had spent their lives on:

> Imposture and fanaticism still hang upon the skirts of religion. Weak minds were seduced by the delusions of a superstition, styled Methodism, raised upon the affectation of superior sanctity, and pretensions to divine illumination. Many thousands were infected with this enthusiasm by the endeavours of a few obscure preachers, such as Whitefield, and the two Wesleys, who found means to lay the whole kingdom under contribution.

Imagine reading a history book that treated your life's work in this way. Rather than being discouraged, Wesley was certain that by writing in this way, Dr. Smollett had undermined his own credibility, not Wesley's: "Poor Dr. Smollett! Thus to transmit to all succeeding generations a whole heap of notorious falsehoods! Meantime, what faith can be given to his History? What credit can any man of reason give to any fact upon his authority?"[42]

In this brief review of Wesley's life and character, I have emphasized the things that make Wesley a credible theological guide on the subject of the Christian life. But even in a sympathetic report like this, there is no reason to idolize him. He did have some character flaws, and his life was marred by unfortunate lapses of judgment. The phrase that I often heard about him when studying in a Wesleyan seminary was, "He was a man of God, but he had feet of clay." Perhaps nowhere are his characteristic weaknesses so evident as in his disastrous marriage.

John Wesley as Husband

In 1751, John Wesley slipped on the ice on London Bridge, hurting his ankle so badly that his next few sermons had to be delivered sitting down or kneeling. He chose to convalesce at the home of a widow, Mary (or Molly,

---

[41] Lecky, *A History of England During the Eighteenth Century*, 2:606.
[42] The Smollett quotation and Wesley's response are both from an April 1779 journal entry, in *Works*, 4:34.

as she was called) Vazeille. In just over a week, they were married. What led to this precipitous wedding?

John Wesley had spiritual oversight over many preachers, and he gave them all good advice about marriage: it had to be subordinate to ministry, it probably wasn't the best option for serious preachers, and at any rate, any preacher considering marriage should seek discernment and accountability from his closest friends in ministry. For Wesley himself, following this advice would have meant conferring with his brother Charles at least, and with many other leaders and friends in the movement he was spearheading. But once before, Charles had intervened decisively to keep John from getting married, and John evidently knew that he would have to get married quickly and without giving Charles a chance to prevent it.

So Wesley broke his own rules when he married Molly, and got what he deserved. Early Methodist historians painted Molly as an unstable woman of sour disposition and a flaring temper, and posed questions like, "How did so wise and great a man come to make so unhappy a choice?" She does seem a bit crazed with jealousy, but then again, when Molly opened the mail, she found letters from Wesley's many—female—admirers. And she found in his coat pocket a letter of spiritual advice to a woman that included the warm words: "The conversing with you, either by speaking or writing, is an unspeakable blessing to me. I cannot think of you without thinking of God. Others often lead me to Him; but it is, as it were, going round about: you bring me straight into His presence." That's enough to get some dishes flying around anybody's house. How did so wise and great a man manage to be so foolish?

John Wesley's marriage really was the great tragedy of his life, a dark cloud with no silver lining. Gordon Rupp says, "The marriage was a disaster. One must grieve for John Wesley and pity his wife."[43] Molly stormed out of the marriage several times, and eventually she stayed gone. Wesley's diary entry for June 23, 1771, is famously cold: "For what cause I know not, my wife set out for Newcastle, purposing 'never to return.' *Non eam reliqui; non dimisi; non revocabo*"—that is, "I did not forsake her; I did not dismiss her; I will not recall her." Ten years later, in October 1781, Wesley arrived in London and was notified that his wife had died, more than thirty years after that fateful slip on London Bridge. The couple had no children. They had endured two decades of conflict and one of total separation.

---

[43] Rupp, *Religion in England 1688–1791*, 401.

All of John Wesley's friends knew that by temperament, by calling, and by position, he was equipped to be one of the great examples of consecrated singleness in the history of the church. It was obvious to all that he had an apostolic gift of spiritual fatherhood over souls. It was equally clear that his single-minded focus on ministry made the Methodist revival the place where he channeled his affections and energy, with an exclusivity that both imitated monogamy and excluded it. But while all of Wesley's advisors recognized this, Wesley himself seemed willfully blind to it. He insisted on marrying, against the definite counsel of his spiritual advisors. So instead of an example of wise celibacy, we have in John Wesley a cautionary tale about a terrible husband, terribly mismatched to a terrible wife. Wesley was protected from great transgressions and (despite scurrilous slanders spread against his name) was not guilty of any real scandal. Nevertheless, he was a man of God with feet of clay. He had other personal failings, but none were so protracted and compromising as his failed marriage. He also had his own share of idiosyncrasies of temperament and character. When we learn from Wesley's example and from his teaching on the Christian life, we are learning not from a flawless role model, but from a man whose errors and transgressions are painfully obvious.

"There are few greater Englishmen than John Wesley," wrote the literary historian A. R. Humphreys, "and to compress his achievement into a paragraph is like trying to see the world in a grain of sand and eternity in an hour."[44] We have compressed his life and character into one short chapter, and are now ready to hear what he has to say about his grandest subject, the Christian life.

---

[44] A. R. Humphreys, *The Augustan World: Society, Thought, and Letters in Eighteenth-Century England* (New York: Harper & Row, 1963), 145.

CHAPTER 2

BORN AGAIN (AND THE PASTOR WHO WASN'T)

One of the names that Wesley used for describing nominal, sinful, and lukewarm Christians was a name that caused him a lot of trouble: "almost Christians." He charged them to become "not only almost, but altogether Christians." An "almost Christian," as Wesley's hearers could tell, was really a "not Christian." How dare he? In Christian England, it was a provocation to tell churchgoers that they were not Christians. But Wesley was not just trying out shocking ways of speaking to get his audience's attention. He meant it.

He meant it first of all because he was reflecting on his own experience. For years he had been convinced that it was impossible to be "half a Christian." Since reading the challenge of William Law's *Serious Call to a Devout and Holy Life*, he had resolved to give to God "all my soul, my body, and my substance." And then at Aldersgate in 1738 he broke through to an understanding of saving faith. Looking back from Aldersgate, he declared that he was now altogether a Christian, where previously he had been "only almost" a Christian. Wesley immortalized the phrase "The Almost Christian" in the classic 1741 sermon with that title (sermon 2 in the *Standard Sermons*). There he made a long list of all the virtues a person could have without being truly Christian: heathen honesty, works of mercy, a form of godliness ("the outside of a real Christian"), church attendance, private prayer, and deep sincerity. But he testified personally that these were not enough: "Suffer [permit] me then, to speak freely of myself. . . . I did go thus far for many years, as many of this place can testify. . . . Yet my own conscience beareth me witness in the Holy Ghost, that all this time I was but almost a Christian."[1]

Wesley was not arguing merely from his own experience when he declared to his fellow Anglicans of the 1700s that they, too, were only almost Christians; his experience was undergirded by two prior judgments. First was his theological conviction that the message of salvation is all-important, and has to be stated in terms of free forgiveness and regeneration: "If any doctrines within the whole compass of Christianity may be properly termed fundamental, they are doubtless these two—the doctrine of justification, and that of the new birth."[2] And second was his pastoral judgment that the church of his age was filled with unregenerate members, shepherded by a frightful number of unregenerate pastors. So Wesley's own experience, his theological convictions, and his understanding of the times flowed together providentially at the headwaters of the revival. We should look at each in turn.

A Heart Strangely Warmed

Something happened to John Wesley on May 24, 1738, at Aldersgate—but what? The Wesley who came "most unwillingly" to listen to a public reading of Luther's *Preface to Romans* was a thirty-five-year-old Anglican priest with experience in foreign missions. For over a decade he had been convinced that it was impossible to be half-Christian and had committed himself to a spiritual regimen of monastic strictness. With all that he knew and all that he had seen and heard, what was the word that reached him on that night?

Though Wesley does not tell us exactly which sentences from Luther's *Preface to Romans* penetrated his mind, he does say that it was from part of the book in which Luther "was describing the change which God works in the heart through faith in Christ." This could apply to any number of passages in the work, but perhaps it was this one: "Doing the works of the Law," wrote Luther, "and fulfilling the law, are two very different things."

---

[1] Sermon 2, "The Almost Christian," in *Wesley's 52 Standard Sermons*, ed. N. Burwash (Salem, OH: Schmul, 1988), 15.
[2] Sermon 45, "The New Birth," Burwash, 458.

On the one hand, the works of the law include "everything that one does or can do," and it is never enough. But faith, according to Luther, is the only thing with power to fulfill the law:

> Faith is a living, daring confidence in God's grace, so sure and certain that a man would stake his life on it a thousand times. This confidence in God's grace, and knowledge of it, makes a man glad and bold and happy in dealing with God and with all his creatures, and this is the work of the Holy Ghost in faith. Hence a man is ready and glad, without compulsion, to do good to everyone, to serve everyone, to suffer everything, in love and praise of God, who has shown him this grace, and thus it is impossible to separate works from faith, as impossible as to separate heat and light from fire.[3]

It was this Lutheran teaching about a heart changed by "living, daring confidence in God's grace" that got through to Wesley, reorienting his spiritual quest and instantly solving the theological and spiritual problems he had either inherited or invented. For several months, Wesley had been wrestling with the Lutheran teaching as communicated to him by Peter Boehler and the other Moravians. Looking back on his development, Wesley would testify just how great his confusion about salvation had been:

> It was many years after I was ordained deacon before I was convinced of the great truths above recited. During all that time I was utterly ignorant of the nature and condition of justification. Sometimes I confounded it with sanctification (particularly when I was in Georgia); at other times I had some confused notion about the forgiveness of sins, but then I took it for granted the time of this must be either the hour of death or the day of judgment. I was equally ignorant of the nature of saving faith, apprehending it to mean no more than a firm assent to all the propositions contained in the Old and New Testaments.[4]

It seems that Wesley had very recently come to a true doctrinal understanding of justification by faith. What happened to him at Aldersgate was that

---

[3] Quoted in Philip S. Watson, *The Message of the Wesleys: A Reader of Instruction and Devotion* (Grand Rapids: Francis Asbury, 1984), 9. Watson (a Luther scholar who was Methodist) was a keen interpreter who noted the emphasis that Luther placed on good works. "That is why the Wesleys' evangelical conversion, or pentecostal experience, or call it what you will, was not the end but only a new beginning" (p. 10).
[4] From "A Farther Appeal to Men of Reason and Religion," in Luke Tyerman, *The Life and Times of the Rev. John Wesley*, 3rd ed., 3 vols. (London: Hodder and Stoughton, 1876), 1:54.

he suddenly ("about a quarter before nine") experienced its application to his own soul.

Over the course of the previous weeks, Wesley had finally adopted classic Protestant views, and the arguments of Luther had cleared away some peculiar eighteenth-century Anglican mistiness. By his own confession he reached this stage of his ministry "utterly ignorant of the nature and condition of justification." Somehow all the reading and praying and seeking he had done up until this point in his life had only served to entrench him ever more doggedly in a false understanding of how a person is accepted by God. He was sure the answer must be personal holiness, and everything he read and experienced seemed to confirm this to him. "There was a basic principle in Wesley's thought at this period in his life," writes William Cannon,

> the principle that man must be saved through moral goodness, through universal obedience, and through the rigid fulfillment of all the commandments of God. This principle defined his conception of justification and, like a magnet, drew unto itself all elements which helped to confirm, clarify, and more especially to achieve its aim.[5]

The magnet image is apt: Wesley's mind was magnetized by the law of God, and it drew to itself all the legalistic elements in his environment. Even when he read a good gospel-centered book, he only drew from it the legal bits. We know that Wesley read plenty of properly Protestant teaching in his earlier life. The Anglican and Puritan sources he immersed himself in included plenty of sound teaching on justification by grace alone through faith alone. Indeed, after Aldersgate, Wesley would rifle through the Anglican church's official Homilies, Articles, and prayer book to confirm that his new understanding was in fact not new to the church, but only new to him. It was an easy task, since the classic Anglican sources are packed with the gospel of justification by faith.[6] But first the magnetic polarity of Wesley's own soul had to be reversed. Until the principle of grace was activated in his own strangely cold heart, Wesley systematically read for the message of legal performance. Until then, all the books kept pitching grace, but Wesley kept catching law.

---

[5] William Ragsdale Cannon, *The Theology of John Wesley: With Special Reference to the Doctrine of Justification* (New York: Abingdon, 1946), 63.
[6] For details on justification by faith in the formative period of Protestant Anglicanism, consult C. FitzSimons Allison, *The Rise of Moralism: The Proclamation of the Gospel from Hooker to Baxter* (New York: Seabury Press, 1966).

And though he always read voraciously, the three most important books in Wesley's spiritual quest so far—Jeremy Taylor's two-volume *Holy Living and Holy Dying* (read in 1725, at age twenty-three), Thomas à Kempis's *The Imitation of Christ* (read in 1726), and William Law's *Serious Call to a Devout and Holy Life* (read around 1727)—were books particularly well suited to feed a legalistic appetite.[7] Cannon describes what Wesley took from each of these authors in his early period:

> From Jeremy Taylor he learned that he could achieve goodness only by dedicating his whole life to God. Thomas a Kempis taught him that obedience must be centered in the heart. And William Law instructed him in the way of self-denial as the absolute fulfillment of God's law. Thus these men influenced Wesley at this period in his life, not in that they changed or even modified his basic conception of salvation or justification before God, but rather in that they taught him how to achieve morally and spiritually the conditions which that conception imposed.[8]

As a result, as he approached the turning point of Aldersgate, Wesley was asking his lifelong question, "How can I keep the law of God?" And he was gradually coming to understand the right answer when Luther's characteristically sharp way of putting it got through to him: "While he was describing the change which God works in the heart through faith in Christ, I felt my heart strangely warmed." Wesley, asking how to fulfill the law, learned from Luther that "doing the works of the Law and fulfilling the law are two very different things." The only way to fulfill the law is by faith, that "living, daring confidence in God's grace" that "makes a man glad and bold and happy in dealing with God and all his creatures." Wesley had worked very hard at obeying the law, but Luther's "glad and bold and happy" did not describe his efforts. Wesley had founded the Holy Club at Oxford, but as someone has remarked, that Oxford Holy Club was no Happy Club. Indeed, trying to live the Christian life without understanding justification by faith had nearly made a wreck of Wesley. At Aldersgate, Wesley was still asking, "How can I keep God's law," and he finally accepted the answer: "by faith." He found the gospel of justification as the God-ordained means to the end of holy living.

Was John Wesley saved before this experience? Historians and theologians have struggled long with the question, or questions, raised by

---

[7] Wesley reports his encounters with these three writers in the opening section of *A Plain Account of Christian Perfection*, 1777.
[8] Cannon, *The Theology of John Wesley*, 63.

Wesley's experience at Aldersgate. If it was a conversion experience, it was hardly a conversion to Christianity, for pastor and missionary John Wesley was obviously already an adherent of the Christian religion. Was it a conversion then from outward, formal Christianity, to a higher form of "real Christianity," or from dead faith to living faith? Words like these are closer to the truth, but we must do justice to how fervently pious the pre-Aldersgate Wesley was. Even better, some have argued that Aldersgate was the moment when Wesley received, not salvation itself, but an experience of the assurance of salvation. Or was it a momentous transition from a legalistic view of salvation to a biblical and evangelical view? This is even closer to the truth because by his own testimony Wesley did not accurately understand the gospel during the earlier phase of his ministry.

Yet Wesley had actually already made this evangelical adjustment to his understanding of salvation a few months before. Since returning from Georgia, he had been steadily losing one argument after another in London with the Moravian missionary Peter Boehler, whose presentation of justification by faith, power over sin, and assurance of salvation at first seemed to Wesley "a new gospel." Wesley tried to refute Boehler, but admitted that "when I set aside the glosses of men and simply considered the words of God, comparing them together and endeavouring to illustrate the obscure by the plainer passages, I found they all made against me."[9] Listening to the personal testimonies of three Moravians, Wesley announced that he "was now thoroughly convinced" of the truth of the doctrine and began seeking a personal appropriation of it. He began asking God to give him this faith.

In other words, the May 24, 1738, experience at Aldersgate is especially tricky to understand because, as one scholar summarizes, "it was not there that Wesley initially resolved to lead a holy life; it was not there that he received his compassion to save souls; it was not there that he underwent his theological revolution. All these vital elements of his life were gained before that date."[10] What Wesley insisted on, emphasized, and underlined, was the personal application of faith in that moment. Note the threefold italics (emphasis in the original) with which he stresses the personal character of the event: "I felt my heart strangely warmed. I felt I did trust in Christ alone for salvation; and an assurance was given me that He

---

[9] From Wesley's journal, quoted in Richard P. Heitzenrater, *The Elusive Mr. Wesley*, 2d ed. (Nashville: Abingdon, 2003), 97.

[10] Colin W. Williams, *John Wesley's Theology Today* (New York: Abingdon, 1960), 102. Williams is summarizing the argument of A. S. Yates, whom he follows in arguing that what Wesley gained at Aldersgate is best described as assurance of personal salvation.

had taken away *my* sins, even *mine*, and saved *me* from the law of sin and death." Luther remarked somewhere that "much of religion turns on being able to use possessive pronouns. Take from me the word 'my' and you take from me God."[11] John Wesley certainly came to terms with the possessive pronouns of salvation on this date!

Immediately after Aldersgate, as we have seen, Wesley began announcing that he had until recently been only almost Christian. Is there any reason to doubt his own testimony? Yes, a little. Always a close watcher of his own spiritual ups and downs, Wesley was prone to overstate the significance of some transitions in his life. It may be that, in the excitement of this great experience, and in his eagerness to understand and communicate the important change, Wesley began oversimplifying the biographical and experiential events in order to make the theological point. We will join him in making that point shortly and stand by the position that Aldersgate was John Wesley's evangelical conversion.

But first let us admit that Wesley could revisit his life story and read it differently. We have already seen him write, in spiritual agony on the voyage home from Georgia, "alienated as I am from the life of God, I am a child of wrath, an heir of hell," only to question himself later with the (undated) marginal note, "I am not sure of this." And about seven months after Aldersgate, he wrote a strange journal entry that begins, "My friends affirm *I am mad*, because I said 'I was not a Christian a year ago.' I affirm I am not a Christian now," and continues with admissions that he could feel a lack of love for God, a lack of joy, and the absence of peace, before concluding definitively, "I am not a Christian."[12] This journal entry may have been a thought project of some kind, musing on the high calling of the Christian life. But as late as 1766, he wrote in a letter to Charles, "I do not feel the wrath of God abiding on me; nor can I believe it does. And yet (this is the mystery) I do not love God. I never did. Therefore I never believed in the Christian sense of the word."[13] Again, outbursts like this may reveal more about Wesley's occasional bouts of emotional despondency than about his considered spiritual judgments, never mind his theology. More telling is the fact that in later years, depending on what theme he wanted to highlight, Wesley could trace the arc of his Christian life in a way that started in

---

[11] Quoted in J. C. Ryle, *Holiness: Its Nature, Hindrances, Difficulties, and Roots* (Darlington: Evangelical Press, 1979), 314.
[12] Heitzenrater, *The Elusive Mr. Wesley*, 99–100.
[13] Ibid., 189.

his awakening to a lively sense of God's demands for holiness in 1725 and made little reference to 1738 as a turning point (see for instance his *Plain Account of Christian Perfection*).

The contradictory statements are enough to drive conscientious historians to distraction. Richard Heitzenrater surveys all of Wesley's statements about his spiritual development and summarizes, "Thus in 1725, he thought he was a Christian; for a while after 1738, he thought he had not truly been a Christian in 1725; by the 1770s, he was willing to admit that perhaps his middle views were wrong, and that he could understand himself as having been in some real sense a Christian in 1725."[14] And Kenneth Collins, writing about justification by faith, affirms that "Wesley both knew and did not know this vital doctrine before 1738," carefully distinguishing the possible meanings of the verb "to know."[15]

Perhaps we should think of Wesley as being like Apollos at the turning point marked by his encounter with Priscilla and Aquila in Acts 18:24–26: he was "an eloquent man, competent in the Scriptures," who "had been instructed in the way of the Lord. And being fervent in spirit, he spoke and taught accurately the things concerning Jesus, though he knew only the baptism of John" (ESV). When Priscilla and Aquila heard Apollos speaking boldly in the synagogue at Ephesus, they must have known something was not quite right, because "they took him aside and explained to him the way of God more accurately." Before his evangelical awakening at Aldersgate, Wesley was eloquent, competent in the Scriptures, instructed in the way of the Lord, and fervent in spirit. Unlike Apollos, he knew considerably more than "the baptism of John," but something was not right in his bold preaching. Luther (through Boehler) took him aside and gave him a more accurate understanding.

It turns out that Wesley's actual experience at Aldersgate is not a solid enough foundation for constructing any understanding of the Christian life. But that is as it should be. Wesley would not build anything on experience, and neither should his interpreters. Something important took place in Wesley's life on that evening as he listened to Luther's words, and a lot of life-changing theology migrated from Wesley's head to his heart, from his theological reflections to his experience. Doctrines that had slowly developed, arguments that had been intermittently won and lost, and decisions

---

[14] Ibid., 35.
[15] Kenneth Collins, *Wesley on Salvation: A Study in the Standard Sermons* (Grand Rapids: Francis Asbury, 1989), 44–45.

that had been gradually rendered were all telescoped into a breakthrough moment. The conclusion we are left with is that Aldersgate was a milestone in the application of evangelical truth to John Wesley's heart, and we should lift our eyes up from that strangely warmed heart to the theological realities that transformed it that night. Historian Gordon Rupp came to the same conclusion, a doctrinal conclusion, as he grappled with the question of whether Wesley was saved at Aldersgate. To call it simply Wesley's conversion risks lumping too many things together:

> Drastic it was, but I think John Wesley never talked of it as his "conversion," and in fact what nineteenth-century Evangelicals described as one experience of "conversion" was for the Methodists a complexity in which at least three of what they called "our doctrines": justification by faith, the new birth, and the witness of the Spirit, were all involved.[16]

Wesley said that before Aldersgate he was "utterly ignorant of the nature and condition of justification," had "some confused notion about the forgiveness of sins," assumed that nobody could know they were forgiven until "either the hour of death or the day of judgment," and was "ignorant of the nature of saving faith." But he suddenly woke up to these truths, experienced their power, and began preaching them. Aldersgate may or may not have been his conversion (God knows), but it was certainly his personal evangelical awakening, and it sparked England's. We can call it his conversion to real Christianity, if by Christianity we mean what John Wesley meant by it: not a set of external forms and relations, but a personal experience in which God brings it home to you that he has brought you into a restored fellowship with him through Christ. For the rest of his life, Wesley was on guard against merely formal religion, or merely nominal Christianity. Going through the motions of church and being called a Christian are not the same as actually being saved.

Salvation by Faith

Equipped with his post-Aldersgate understanding of justification, of forgiveness, of assurance, and of saving faith, Wesley launched into the preaching ministry for which he is famous. The great monument of his new message is "Salvation by Faith," which is printed as sermon 1 in the

---

[16] Gordon Rupp, *Religion in England 1688–1791* (Oxford: Clarendon, 1986), 326–27.

authoritative *Standard Sermons*. Wesley preached "Salvation by Faith" in St. Mary's, the University Church of Oxford, on June 11, 1738. "His new experience was thus only eighteen days old when he uttered this great manifesto before the University," says commentator E. H. Sugden,[17] who also noted that "on this day John Wesley blew the first trumpet-call of the Evangelical Revival." The Scripture text was Ephesians 2:8, "by grace are ye saved through faith." This was a favorite text of Wesley's, and he would take up the same verse twenty-seven years later as the basis of his most comprehensive sermon, number 43, "The Scripture Way of Salvation."

In "Salvation by Faith," John Wesley pressed home the evangelical view of salvation with force and clarity. His opening words are about grace itself; we will examine them at the proper place in chapter 6, below. Most of sermon 1, however, is not about grace as the source of salvation, but about faith as the condition of salvation. He explains to his listeners the nature of faith with words that are more like a prayer or a hymn than a dictionary entry. Faith, says Wesley, is

> not only an assent to the whole Gospel of Christ, but also a full reliance on the blood of Christ; a trust in the merits of his life, death, and resurrection; a recumbency upon him as our atonement and our life, *as given for us*, and *living in us*. It is a sure confidence which a man hath in God, that through the merits of Christ, *his* sins are forgiven, and *he* reconciled to the favour of God; and, in consequence, hereof, a closing with him, and cleaving to him, as our "wisdom, righteousness, sanctification, and redemption," or, in one word, our salvation.[18]

Wesley's definition of faith is incisive as well as expansive. It cuts to the heart of the matter, but takes in everything. It directs the eye to the one thing necessary—Christ crucified—but places it in context of the "whole Gospel" of his "life, death, and resurrection" as the one who is both "given for us" and also "living in us." It specifies the heart's personal reliance on the Savior ("recumbency . . . sure confidence . . . closing with him . . . cleaving to him") as well as the great, historic truths of the gospel ("assent").

What Wesley announced to his listeners from this moment on was a classic evangelical definition of faith that ranks alongside other classics like Calvin's: "A firm and certain knowledge of God's benevolence towards

---

[17] E. H. Sugden, *Wesley's Standard Sermons* (London: Epworth, 1921), 35. The date for this sermon is widely misreported as the following Sunday, June 18, but see Sugden's remarks on page 35.
[18] Sermon 1, "Salvation by Faith," Burwash, 5, his emphasis.

us, founded upon the truth of the freely given promise in Christ, both revealed to our minds and sealed upon our hearts through the Holy Spirit."[19] Or the Heidelberg Catechism's:

> True faith is not only a certain knowledge, whereby I hold for truth all that God has revealed to us in his word, but also an assured confidence, which the Holy Ghost works by the gospel in my heart; that not only to others, but to me also, remission of sin, everlasting righteousness and salvation, are freely given by God, merely of grace, only for the sake of Christ's merits.[20]

If Wesley was advancing beyond these earlier Protestant statements in any way, it was only by insisting so emphatically on personal application that he provoked his hearers to self-examination.

But advancing beyond classic Protestant teaching was not the point; Wesley had just recently caught up with Protestant theology and was now in the business of announcing it with a fervor that eighteenth-century England desperately needed. In the build-up of the sermon "Salvation by Faith," he announces true, saving faith with a voice to wake the dead.

He begins the sermon by walking his audience through all the kinds of faith that are not saving. First there is "the faith of a heathen," the sort of belief that acknowledges God, immortality, and moral obligation. Such faith is good, but it is not the faith mentioned in Ephesians 2:8, the kind through which salvation by grace happens. It is not enough to believe in God alone: "Christ, and God through Christ, are the proper objects" of saving faith. Theism is not faith. Nor is saving faith to be confused with the "faith of a devil, though he goes much further than that of a heathen" in that devils are capable of affirming a large number of specifically Christian theological truths.[21] But a devil affirms these simply as "a train of ideas in the head" rather than as "a disposition of the heart." Saving faith, by contrast, "is not barely a speculative, rational thing, a cold, lifeless assent." Orthodoxy is not faith. For his final contrast, Wesley focuses on "the apostles themselves . . . while Christ was yet upon the earth."[22] These disciples were in the very presence of Christ and were empowered by him to preach and to

---

[19] John Calvin, *Institutes of the Christian Religion*, ed. John T. McNeill, trans. Ford Lewis Battles, 2 vols. (Philadelphia: Westminster, 1960), 3.2.7.
[20] Heidelberg Catechism, in answer to question 21, "What is true faith?"
[21] Sermon 1, "Salvation by Faith," Burwash, 5.
[22] Ibid., 4.

heal, but as Wesley points out, until their faith in Christ included "the necessity and merit of his death, and the power of his resurrection," it was not properly Christian faith. Following Jesus without submitting to his death and resurrection is not faith. Christian faith, saving faith, is recumbency (total reliance, coming to rest) upon Christ as our atonement and our life, as given for us and living in us.

This is the way Wesley awakened his audience from their slumber and confronted them with the biblical view of faith. Once again, some of his persuasiveness came from the fact that he had so recently been asleep himself. Only recently had he completed the long journey to the evangelical view of faith. Wesley had long entertained inadequate notions of faith and had a history of trading up to better ones. As a young man of twenty-two, Wesley had written in a letter to his mother, Susanna, that he agreed with the philosopher who said, "Faith is a species of belief, and belief is defined [as] 'an assent to a proposition upon rational grounds.'"[23] Susanna's response was sharp:

> Dear Jackey,
>
> Divine faith is an assent to whatever God has revealed to us, because He has revealed it. And this is that virtue of faith which is one of the two conditions of our salvation by Jesus Christ. But this matter is so fully and accurately explained by Bishop Pearson ("I Believe") that I shall say no more of it.[24]

Slapped down intellectually by his mother, Wesley recanted immediately. "I perceived on reflection," he wrote of his initial definition of faith, that it was guilty of

> trespass against the very first law of defining, as not being adequate to the thing defined.... I am, therefore, at length come over entirely to your opinion, that saving faith (including practice) is an assent to what God has revealed because He has revealed it and not because the truth of it may be evinced by reason.[25]

But though Susanna convinced him to upgrade from mere rationalism to accepting the authority of revelation, her idea of faith was still inadequate.

[23] Tyerman, *The Life and Times of the Rev. John Wesley*, 1:39.
[24] Ibid., 1:39–40.
[25] Ibid., 1:40.

She provided the right clue, however, when she indicated to Jackey that he ought to be reading his Anglican theology better ("This matter is so fully and accurately explained by Bishop Pearson").[26]

Wesley's initial jolt was from Luther (via Boehler and the Moravians), but he did finally consult his own Anglican resources, and there he found Cranmer's "Homily on the Salvation of Man," with a definition of faith that is strikingly similar to what we have heard from Wesley:

> For the right and true Christian faith is, not only to believe that holy Scripture, and all the aforesaid articles of our faith are true, but also to have a sure trust and confidence in GOD'S merciful promises, to be saved from everlasting damnation by Christ: whereof doth follow a loving heart to obey his commandments. And this true Christian faith neither any devil hath, nor yet any man, which in the outward profession of his mouth, and in his outward receiving of the Sacraments, in coming to the Church, and in all other outward appearances, seems to be a Christian man, and yet in his living and deeds shows the contrary.[27]

Not only does Cranmer's classic Reformation-era sermon contrast saving faith with the faith of a devil, but it also contrasts it with mere outward profession. Wesley echoed this definition in his own account of faith in sermon 1, and he would also quote it at length, with striking effect, as the punch line of sermon 2, "The Almost Christian."[28] Wesley threw the challenge, and the very words, of Cranmer's Reformation in the face of his Oxford hearers: "Whosoever has this faith, thus working by love, is not almost only, but altogether, a Christian."[29]

Then Who Else Might Be Unsaved?

When John and Charles Wesley went very, very public with their announcement that they once were lost (last week) but now were found, that they were blind but now (this week) could see, there was general alarm among their friends and family. Rev. John Hutton of Westminster, for example, had for some time looked up to John Wesley as a guide (he is "my son's

---

[26] The reference is to Bishop John Pearson's influential *Exposition of the Creed* (1663).

[27] This is from Cranmer's "Homily on the Salvation of Man," in the collection known as the *Elizabethan Homilies*.

[28] Rupp sketches this line of argument in *Religion in England 1688–1791*, 345.

[29] Sermon 2, "The Almost Christian," Burwash, 16. Note just above this sentence the three-hundred-word quotation from the "Homily on the Salvation of Man," which is the crux of Wesley's own sermon.

Pope," exclaimed Hutton's mother in a letter to the elder Samuel Wesley). Imagine Hutton's shock when, the Sunday after Aldersgate, John Wesley attended a religious gathering hosted by Hutton and "told the people that five days before he was not a Christian . . . and the way for them all to be Christians was to believe and own that they were not now Christians." Hutton's response was flustered: "If you was not a Christian ever since I knew you, you was a great hypocrite, for you made us all believe you was one."[30] No doubt Wesley summoned Hutton to self-examination on the spot. For Wesley, the whole point was that if he could be so deceived about the state of his own heart and about the real meaning of Christian faith, then anybody at any level of Christian culture could also be struggling under equally dangerous misconceptions. And if Wesley could throw his own testimony into their path as a provocation and an occasion for coming to more accurate knowledge of the Scripture way of salvation, then he would not hesitate to do so.

Charles Wesley, whose own evangelical conversion had taken place on Pentecost Sunday, a few days before John's moment at Aldersgate, was even more eloquent than John about how hard it was to wake from the almost-Christian slumber. He testified that the better people seemed outwardly, the harder it would be for them to admit their need to be born again. In his Oxford sermon "Awake Thou That Sleepest,"[31] he warned that "if this sleeper be not outwardly vicious, his sleep is usually the deepest of all," and especially if he is "a quiet, rational, inoffensive, good natured professor of the religion of his fathers."[32] Charles, as usual turning everything into hymns, did so with his conversion. In the conversion hymn "My Gracious, Loving Lord, to Thee What Shall I Say?" he contrasted his former life of outward religion with the renewal he had experienced:

> A goodly, formal saint
> I long appeared in sight,
> By self and Satan taught to paint
> My tomb, my nature, white.
> The Pharisee within
> Still undisturbed remained

---

[30] Quoted in Rupp, *Religion in England 1688–1791*, 357–58.
[31] "Awake Thou That Sleepest" is sermon 3 in the *Standard Sermons* of John Wesley, though the heading clearly indicates Charles as the author. As we noted in the introduction, the two worked very closely together.
[32] "Awake Thou That Sleepest," Burwash, 19. Here "professor" has the older sense of "one who professes."

The strong man, armed with guilt of sin,
Safe in his palace reigned.

But O! the jealous God
In my behalf came down;
Jesus himself the stronger showed.
And claimed me for his own:
My spirit he alarmed,
And brought into distress;
He shook and bound the strong man armed
In his self-righteousness.

Charles uses warfare language to describe the encounter between the one who seems to be a "goodly, formal saint" and "the jealous God." He pictures himself as a strong Pharisee erecting defenses of self-righteousness against Jesus, who must show himself stronger, alarm and distress the soul, and shake and bind the strong man. Jesus is victor. As with John Wesley, the message of Charles is equal parts testimony and challenge: I was like this, and you may be so now.

Susanna Wesley, who had raised both boys in a Christian home and had watched closely over their spiritual development, was at first, understandably, annoyed by their new testimony. In December 1738 she wrote to Charles, "I think you are fallen into an odd way of thinking." Surely John and Charles were making too much of their recent spiritual experiences. Perhaps they had, after all, only come to a better understanding that they had been Christians all along.

> You say that till within a few months you had no spiritual life, nor any justifying faith. Now this is as if a man should affirm he was not alive in his infancy, because when an infant he did not know he was alive. All, then, that I can gather from your letter is that till a little while ago you were not so well satisfied of your being a Christian as you are now.

Nevertheless, Susanna apparently could tell that they had at least a livelier understanding of justification by faith, and so she went on, "I heartily rejoice that you have now attained to a strong and lively hope in God's mercy through Christ. Not that I can think you were totally without saving faith before; but it is one thing to have faith, and another thing to be sensible we have it."[33] And a few years later, Susanna herself came to a fuller understanding of faith, which caused her to look back on her earlier life as a time of "legal night," suggesting that her own understanding of the gospel underwent a dramatic change.[34]

John and Charles Wesley both looked utterly Christian on the outside, but they testified that they had in fact been laboring all these years under a misconception. Everywhere they looked, they saw nominally Christian people spiritually asleep in the churches. The Wesleys began confronting them in person and continued to do so for the rest of their lives. In 1755, John noted in his journal that a visitor had come to stay with them, "who is accounted both a sensible and a religious man. What a proof of the Fall! Even with all the advantages of a liberal education, this person, I will be bold to say, knows just as much of heart religion, of scriptural Christianity, the religion of love, as a child three years old of algebra." And in 1781, he wrote an admonishing letter to his nephew, "You are good-humored, mild, and harmless; but unless you are born again, you cannot see the kingdom of God! But ask, and you shall receive, for it is nigh at hand."[35] Harmlessness, or not hurting anybody, was a special target of Wesley's ire when it was offered as a substitute for actual Christian faith. Nothing was more harmful than that kind of harmlessness! "Observe well: Religion is not harmlessness; which a careful observer of mankind properly terms hellish harmlessness, as it sends thousands to the bottomless pit."[36]

Evangelicals have sometimes been known to throw around the distinction between the saved and the unsaved within the church too casually. Missionary David Brainerd was expelled from college for saying that one of the tutors had "no more grace than a chair"; and George Whitefield insulted a bishop by writing that if he was a Christian, then Muhammad was a Christian. These are regrettable lapses into snottiness, and both men had reason to repent of their tones, if not their truth claims. But the distinction between saved and unsaved is clear, and even when it is stated more carefully, as it usually was by Wesley, it is quite alarming to

---

[33] John Whitehead, The Life of the Rev. John Wesley (London: Stephen Couchman, 1793), 44.
[34] See the comments of John Brown, "Well might we exclaim—if this be 'night,' what a glorious condition must that be which a Wesley would call 'day'!" John Wesley's Theology: The Principle of Its Vitality, and Its Progressive Stages of Development (London: Jackson, Walford, and Hodder, 1865), 16.
[35] Quoted in Kenneth Collins, The Theology of John Wesley: Holy Love and the Shape of Grace (Nashville: Abingdon, 2007), 206.
[36] Sermon 113, "The Difference between Walking by Sight, and Walking by Faith," in The Works of the Rev. John Wesley, vol. 7 (London: Wesleyan Conference Office, 1872), 263. I do not know which "careful observer of mankind" coined the phrase "hellish harmlessness," but Charles Wesley rhymed it with "riot and excess" in his hymn "For Those Who Begin to Be Awakened."

see the distinction run right down the middle of groups of self-professed believers.

But the decisive step, in Wesley's day and in every era of Christendom, was to take this message into the pulpit and challenge churches with the message of salvation. There was already a tradition in England of preaching conversion messages to church members, but that tradition had become marginal to the Anglican establishment, and associated only with Puritans. Richard Baxter's *Call to the Unconverted* (1657) announced to nominal Christians, "The numbers of unconverted Souls among you call for my most earnest Compassions and hasty Diligence to pluck them out of burning." And Joseph Alleine's *Alarm to Unconverted Sinners* (1672) pressed the need both for authentic conversion and for a holy way of life:

> Whether it be your Baptism, or whatever else you pretend, I tell you, from the Living God, that, if any of you be prayerless persons, or unclean, or malicious, or covetous, or riotous, or a Scoffer, or a Lover of evil Company, in a word, if you are not holy, strict, and self-denying Christians, you cannot be saved, except you be transformed by a farther work upon you, and renewed again by repentance.[37]

Wesley took up this Puritan tradition and brought it into the mainstream of the Anglican church life of his day. It is still a message that needs to be heard, and needs to be preached with a combination of boldness and pastoral tact. John Piper made the exact same point recently in a book about regeneration, standing against the claim that born-again Christians could have "lifestyles of worldliness and sin that are indistinguishable from the unregenerate." But he also admitted that to deny that possibility was "not rosy news for the church," because "it implies that there are millions of church attenders who are not born again."[38] That was the situation John Wesley found himself in, and he set out to change it.

Scriptural Christianity against the False Prophets

The novelist Franz Kafka, notorious for his deeply disturbing writing, once declared, "If the book we are reading does not wake us, as with a fist ham-

---

[37] Both of these are quoted in Robert C. Monk, *John Wesley, His Puritan Heritage: A Study of the Christian Life* (Nashville: Abingdon, 1966), 145.

[38] John Piper, *Finally Alive: What Happens When We Are Born Again* (Fearn, Scotland: Christian Focus, 2009), 21.

mering on our skulls, why then do we read it? . . . What we must have are those books which come upon us like ill fortune, and distress us deeply, like the death of one we love better than ourselves, like suicide. A book must be an ice-axe to break the sea frozen inside us."[39] With a few changes, we could imagine John Wesley making the same pronouncements about preaching. At least he preached like a man who was intent on breaking up a frozen interior sea with the ice axe of a sermon. "I design plain truth for plain people," he said in the preface to his *Standard Sermons*. Like the later Charles Simeon, who sometimes said to his congregation, "Permit me to address you as dying men," John Wesley spoke with eternity in his mind's eye.

> I am a creature of a day, passing through life, as an arrow through the air.
> I am a spirit come from God, and returning to God: just hovering over the
> great gulf; till a few moments hence, I am no more seen! I drop into an
> unchangeable eternity! I want to know one thing, the way to heaven: how
> to land safe on that happy shore.

It was in this spirit that he brought his message to an England that thought it was already Christian by birthright. Without being insensitive, and without becoming sectarian, Wesley knew he had to break through people's defenses.

Sermon 4 in the *Standard Sermons*, "Scriptural Christianity," is the classic moment of John Wesley's challenge to the church. It is a brilliant tour de force of a sermon, for which Wesley was never invited to preach at Oxford again. As a fellow of Lincoln College, he was supposed to preach a certain number of times, but after this August 1744 sermon, the authorities preferred to excuse him from the obligation and to pay for his substitute to preach. The text is Acts 4:31, "And they were all filled with the Holy Ghost." The first half of the sermon is a robust, concrete description of the lives and characters of the Spirit-filled primitive Christians. Ignoring the extraordinary gifts of the Spirit, Wesley invited his listeners to

> take a nearer view of these his ordinary fruits, which we are assured will
> remain throughout all ages;—of that great work of God among the chil-
> dren of men, which we are used to express by one word, Christianity; not

---

[39] Quoted in George Steiner, *George Steiner: A Reader* (New York: Oxford University Press, 1984), 36.

as it implies a set of opinions, a system of doctrines, but as it refers to men's hearts and lives.[40]

Item by item, Wesley lists the characteristics of these first Christians. They had experienced the new birth. They had assurance of salvation and confidence toward God. They were full of joy, animated by love of God and their neighbors. They were humble, and they hurt nobody. They made regular use of all the means of grace, and each one had a soul "athirst to do good."

"Such," declared Wesley, "was Christianity in its rise. Such was a Christian in ancient days." And in the second half of the sermon, Wesley turns to "a plain, practical application" by asking a few pointed questions. "Where," he inquires, "does this Christianity now exist? Where, I pray, do the Christians live?" If there is not a place where the inhabitants show the marks of the first Christians, then Wesley draws the conclusion, "Why then, let us confess we have never yet seen a Christian country upon earth." From there he turns to each class of persons in his audience: magistrates, teachers, ministers, and students. The questions at each level are stark and soul-searching. Two classic questions he poses to the students: "You waste away day after day, either in reading what has no tendency to Christianity, or in gaming, or in—you know not what?" and "May it not be one of the consequences of this, that so many of you are a generation of triflers; triflers with God, with one another, and with your own souls?"[41]

J. C. Ryle said of "Scriptural Christianity," "The reader will probably agree with me that this is a remarkable sermon, and one of a class that is not frequently heard in University pulpits."[42] Though it got Wesley barred from preaching at St. Mary's in Oxford, he had already counted the cost, weighed his words carefully, and decided that this was the right way to address his generation. The contrast between real Christianity and false Christianity had to be drawn. Charles, naturally, made a hymn out of it:

Ye different sects, who all declare,
Lo, here is Christ, and Christ is there
Your stronger proofs divinely give,
And show me where the Christians live!

---

[40] Sermon 4, "Scriptural Christianity," Burwash, 29.
[41] Ibid., 38.
[42] J. C. Ryle, *Christian Leaders of the Last Century; or, England a Hundred Years Ago* (London: T. Nelson, 1869) 99–100.

And John duly inserted this stanza of Charles's into the footnote on Acts chapter 2 in his *Explanatory Notes on the New Testament*.

In another sermon, Wesley had an even harsher word to address to the unregenerate clergy, and above all to the kind of pastor who knowingly allowed his congregation to imagine that by being harmless they were being holy. In sermon 32, explaining Jesus's warning to "beware of false prophets," Wesley asks who these words should be applied to. Who misleads the sheep, pointing to a broad and easy path, and claiming it is the road to heaven? Wesley answers his question:

> Ten thousand wise and honourable men; even all those, of whatever denomination, who encourage the proud, the trifler, the passionate, the lover of the world, the man of pleasure, the unjust or unkind, the easy, careless, harmless, useless creature, the man who suffers no reproach for righteousness' sake, to imagine he is in the way to heaven. These are false prophets in the highest sense of the word. These are traitors both to God and man. These are no other than the first-born of Satan; the eldest sons of Apollyon, the Destroyer. These are far above the rank of ordinary cutthroats; for they murder the souls of men. They are continually peopling the realms of night; and whenever they follow the poor souls whom they have destroyed, "hell shall be moved from beneath to meet them at their coming!"[43]

As the evangelical awakening spread, and John Wesley began preaching in the fields, appointing lay preachers to take the gospel message to the crowds, and forming the class meetings, his practices were questioned by other ministers. His justification for these irregular methods should now be fully apparent. Not only were millions being left unreached by the ordinary channels of church ministry, but also millions more were sitting in churches hearing nothing but moral platitudes. They were missing the message of the gospel, the announcement of justification by faith alone. In a 1755 letter to Rev. Thomas Adams, Wesley said he saw it as his "bounden duty" to take these steps: "It is from a full conviction of this, that we preach abroad, use extemporary prayer, form those who appear to be awakened into societies, and permit laymen, whom we believe God has called, to

---

[43] Sermon 32, which is the twelfth in the series "Upon Our Lord's Sermon on the Mount," Burwash, 328.

preach." And he concluded, "Soul-damning clergymen lay me under more difficulties than soul-saving laymen."[44]

In our generation, it is easy to picture John Wesley rejecting his church and joining, or starting, a new denomination. Though Wesley had that option, and many assumed he would follow that course, he never seriously considered it. He was Anglican, and he spent the rest of his life preaching evangelical truth in the established church. His reasons were no doubt complex, but part of his motivation probably had to do with the recognition that any church can become a spiritually inert warehouse of unregenerate members and ministers. The Baptists and assorted nonconformists of his day were also capable of drifting and defection. By staying put, Wesley made it clear that his message for the nominal Christians of his church was a message for the nominal Christians of every church: you must be born again.

---

[44] Letter to Rev. Thomas Adams, October 31, 1755, in *The Letters of John Wesley*, ed. John Telford, 8 vols. (London: Epworth, 1931), 3:151.

CHAPTER 3

HEART RELIGION

"Heart religion" may sound quaint to modern ears, but it was the favorite term that Wesley and the other evangelicals used to describe what mattered most to them. Christianity was for them not just a set of ideas to be entertained or a set of practices to be engaged in; it was a matter of the whole soul, the entire person, the complex bundle of emotional responses to everything we encounter, the seat of selfhood in relation to God: the heart. "True religion, in great part, consists in the affections," said Jonathan Edwards in his masterpiece *The Religious Affections*, and in this he and his contemporary John Wesley were in full agreement. One of the marks of Christian maturity is increasingly strong emotional responses to God, and a stronger grasp of the fact that to be holy is to be happy. Heart religion has been shamed by its supporters and blamed by its opponents, but no cries of pietism, romanticism, or sentimentalism should scare us away from it. Christianity is a religion of the heart, and Wesley's approach to the Christian life was directly through the territory of a holiness that was also happiness.

This chapter presents Wesley's view of heart religion and defends it against common misunderstandings. Indeed, if John Wesley is the standard, there is nothing so rational, so practical, and so outward-looking as the religion of the heart.

The Need for Revival

To understand the impact of Wesley's message, I said we would look at his own experience (Aldersgate), the theology that led up to it (salvation by grace through faith), and his reading of the historical moment he was born into. That historical moment, eighteenth-century England, was a time of spiritual decline. This was not just the judgment of a few red-hot, self-appointed critics, but was widely recognized by religious leaders and social commentators. In 1738, the very year of Wesley's evangelical awakening, Bishop Thomas Secker sent out a call to his clergy with this dark diagnosis: "An open and professed disregard to religion is become, through a variety of unhappy causes, the distinguishing character of the present age." Secker was a high-ranking Anglican statesman; he had just moved the previous year from being bishop of Bristol to bishop of Oxford, and would later become archbishop of Canterbury. "Christianity is now ridiculed and railed at with very little reserve, and the teachers of it without any at all," he warned. Pastors and priests were a laughingstock for the general public, and Secker worried that the growth of the irreligious spirit was preparing England for a great disaster:

> This evil is grown to a great height in the metropolis of the nation; is daily spreading through every part of it; and, bad in itself as any can be, must of necessity bring in all others after it. Indeed, it hath already brought in such dissoluteness and contempt of principle in the highest part of the world, and such profligate intemperance and fearlessness of committing crimes in the lower, as must, if this torrent of impiety stop not, become absolutely fatal: and God knows, far from stopping, it receives, through the ill designs of some persons and the inconsiderateness of others, a continual increase.[1]

Leaders like Secker, however insightfully they could diagnose the disease, were unable to prescribe a realistic cure. What was called for, they thought, was a kind of preaching best described as moral essays from the pulpit. The sermons of Bishop Joseph Butler (1692–1752) are an example of this kind of ministry at its best. Butler could take up any text of Paul the apostle and turn it into wise and learned discourses "Upon Human Nature, or Man Considered as a Moral Agent," "Upon the Social Nature of Man," "Upon the Natural Supremacy of Conscience." Butler's sermons are fine in their own way, and as a thinker, he made valuable contributions to ethics and apologetics. But when it came to understanding the times and knowing

---

[1] Thomas Secker, *Charge to the Clergy*, 1738; reprinted in Richard Watson, *A Collection of Theological Tracts*, vol. 6 (Cambridge: J. Archdracon, 1785), 2.

what ought to be done (1 Chron. 12:32), John Wesley was a quantum leap ahead of men like Butler. Wesley knew that the main danger of the times was "formality . . . mere outside religion," and announced in 1746 that it had "almost driven heart religion out of the world."[2] Butler, in sharp contrast, told his clergy in 1751 that "it is highly seasonable now to instruct the people in the importance of external religion," and he especially pointed out that church buildings ought to be made attractive.[3] This was the exact opposite of Wesley's diagnosis.

Though they cried out against the spiritual decline, the religious leaders who held the reins of power in the mid-1700s recoiled in disgust at the evangelical awakening. Apparently leaders like Secker and Butler thought that something less extreme than Methodism ought to stop the "torrent of impiety" that was swamping England. "The surprising thing," notes one history of the period, is that Secker "did not perceive that the sort of decent mediocrity which was his ideal was not sufficiently stimulating to remedy the evils which he deplored."[4] Apparently these gentlemen believed that their society could continue to remain perfectly calm and composed while changing its course from hell to heaven. But if the problem was truly drastic, the solution also needed to be drastic. Wesley knew what was called for, and alongside Whitefield, he and the other evangelicals moved forward with their program of renewing heart religion and reviving the church.

The age was a kind of spiritual depression, to be sure. But sketching the Wesleyan revival against the backdrop of the spiritual torpor of the eighteenth century has one danger. It would be easy to make it seem that there was a general lack of excitement and that what the evangelical awakening brought was some much-needed fervor about something, anything. Wesley's critics in fact made this charge. But Wesley argued otherwise. He always led with the content of Christian doctrine and drew the conclusion that the proper, reasonable response to this doctrine should be a strong emotional one. An unemotional response to the doctrines of sin and forgiveness was an irrational response, a response that failed to correspond to the subject.

Even an unsympathetic historian of the revival, W. E. H. Lecky, saw that doctrine was the key to it. How unsympathetic was Lecky? He deplored

---

[2] Wesley, preface to *Standard Sermons*, in *Wesley's 52 Standard Sermons*, ed. N. Burwash (Salem, OH: Schmul, 1988), xx.
[3] "Charge to the Clergy of Durham, 1751," in *Sermons by Joseph Butler* (Boston: Hillard, Gray, Little, and Wilkins, 1827), 325.
[4] John H. Overton and Frederic Relton, *The English Church from the Accession of George I to the End of the Eighteenth Century* (London: Macmillan, 1906), 121.

the "extraordinary revival of the grossest superstition" during these years, and declared that it was "a natural consequence of the essentially emotional character of Methodism that its disciples should imagine that every strong feeling or impulse within them was a direct inspiration from God or Satan."[5] But Lecky saw that Methodism succeeded among the people because "it satisfied some of the strongest and most enduring wants of our nature which found no gratification in the popular theology," and it met those felt needs because

> it revived a large class of religious doctrines which had been long almost wholly neglected. The utter depravity of human nature, the lost condition of every man who is born into the world, the vicarious atonement of Christ, the necessity to salvation of a new birth, of faith, of the constant and sustaining action of the Divine Spirit upon the believer's soul, are doctrines which in the eyes of the modern Evangelical constitute at once the most vital and the most influential portions of Christianity, but they are doctrines which during the greater part of the eighteenth century were seldom heard from a Church of England pulpit. The moral essays which were the prevailing fashion, however well suited they might be to cultivate the moral taste, or to supply rational motives to virtue, rarely awoke any strong emotions of hope, fear, or love, and were utterly incapable of transforming the character and arresting and reclaiming the thoroughly depraved.[6]

Behind the emotional upheaval, Lecky admitted, was a set of theological teachings. The revival was not excitement for its own sake, but excitement for the sake of evangelical theological claims. Wesley preached original sin, the atonement, the new birth, and the indwelling of the Holy Spirit. If these teachings are true, then it is not crazy to respond to them from the heart. It would be crazy not to.

The gently moralizing bishops of the day were perplexed. Bishop Secker heard that audiences responded immediately to evangelistic sermons, and he puzzled over Wesley's "doctrine of momentaneous illapse." Bishop Butler heard Whitefield say he was sent by God, and Butler worried aloud to Wesley, "Sir, the pretending to extraordinary revelations and gifts of the Holy Ghost is a horrid thing, a very horrid thing." But in their

---

[5] William Edward Hartpole Lecky, *A History of England During the Eighteenth Century (1878–1890)*, 8 vols. (New York: Appleton, 1888), 2:590.
[6] Ibid., 2:593.

concern to keep everything decent and in order, these learned men were missing the point precisely by missing the heart. Wesley's contribution, said one writer, "may be compressed into a single sentence. He restored Christianity to its place as a living force in the personal creed of men and in the life of the nation." Not content with that "single sentence," the author goes on to note that this was "a change profound and wonderful, carrying in itself the pledge and the secret of a thousand other changes!"[7] Indeed, Wesley "quickened the conscience, not merely of his own followers, but of the Church which had cast him out, and of the whole nation to which he belonged. Christianity, not merely as a creed, but as a conscience, was in this way re-born under British skies."[8]

Regeneration and Justification

It would be enlightening to trace all those evangelical doctrines that fueled the revival, but there is one in particular that demands our attention, because it is the hinge on which Wesley's message turned. That is the doctrine of the new birth, the gracious act in which God instantaneously renews a human heart. Nearly everything Wesley taught flowed from his understanding of the new birth, because the new birth (or regeneration) is where the great salvation proclaimed in the gospel actually enters into human experience. It is "a vast inward change, a change wrought in the soul, by the operation of the Holy Ghost."[9] And it is crucial that we see how Wesley related this doctrine, a doctrine about a change that takes place in the human subject, to the great objective truths of salvation in Christ.

Sermon 45, entitled simply "The New Birth," begins with the important distinction: "If any doctrines within the whole compass of Christianity may be properly termed fundamental, they are doubtless these two; the doctrine of justification, and that of the new birth."[10] Note carefully how Wesley goes on to relate these two doctrines. He is not famous for his careful theological distinctions, but on this point he is ruthlessly, incisively careful. Justification and regeneration must be distinguished from each other precisely so they can be held together; they must be understood to be different if they are to be recognized as inseparable. Justification, says

---

[7] William Henry Fitchett, *Wesley and His Century: A Study in Spiritual Forces* (New York: Eaton and Mains, 1908), 283.
[8] Ibid., 284.
[9] Sermon 19, "The Great Privilege of Those That Are Born of God," Burwash, 183.
[10] Sermon 45, "The New Birth," Burwash, 459.

Wesley, is a doctrine "relating to that great work which God does for us, in forgiving our sins," while regeneration relates to "the great work which God does in us, in renewing our fallen nature." Justification is *for* us, regeneration *in* us.

The two certainly belong together: "on the one hand, . . . whosoever is justified, is also born of God, and on the other, . . . whosoever is born of God, is also justified"; in fact, it is certain "that both these gifts of God are given to every believer in one and the same moment." Both happen at once: "In one point of time his sins are blotted out, and he is born again of God."[11] They occur simultaneously in the "order of time," but logically, conceptually, or in the "order of thinking," justification comes first. "We first conceive his wrath to be turned away, and then his Spirit to work in our hearts."[12]

For this reason, Wesley cautions against confusing them, an error he says is all too common. "But though it be allowed, that justification and the new birth are, in point of time, inseparable from each other, yet they are easily distinguished, as being not the same, but things of a widely different nature." And following out the "for us" versus "in us" logic, Wesley distinguishes them further:

> Justification implies only a relative, the new birth a real, change. God, in justifying us, does something for us; in begetting us again, he does the work in us. The former changes our outward relation to God, so that of enemies we become children; by the latter our inmost souls are changed, so that of sinners we become saints. The one restores us to the favour, the other to the image, of God. The one is the taking away of the guilt, the other the taking away of the power, of sin.[13]

The distinction is perhaps even clearer if we think of regeneration as initial sanctification. The same irreversible order applies to the relationship between justification and sanctification, as Wesley points out in sermon 5, "Justification by Faith." Justification is primarily a matter of being forgiven.

> It is not being made actually just and righteous. This is sanctification; which is, indeed, in some degree the immediate fruit of justification; but nevertheless, is a distinct gift of God, and of a totally different nature. The

---

[11] Sermon 19, "The Great Privilege of Those That Are Born of God," Burwash, 183.
[12] Sermon 45, "The New Birth," Burwash, 459.
[13] Sermon 19, "The Great Privilege of Those That Are Born of God," Burwash, 183.

one implies, what God "does for us" through his Son; the other, what he "works in us" by his Spirit.[14]

Regeneration is the first moment of that sanctification, the instant when God, working in us by his Spirit, places holiness in us and makes a change to our actual state. A justified sinner is forgiven, but his character has not been changed by the act of justification, which God does for him through his Son. The regenerate person, however, has a character that has been changed by God's intervention. He has been "made actually just and righteous," at least in principle and as the beginning point of a process that, as it continues to develop, will be recognized outwardly as sanctification. Justification is the imputing of righteousness to the believer, and regeneration is the implanting of righteousness into that same believer. Both happen at once, but they are different things. They belong together as the concerted actions of the one God, who "implants righteousness in every one to whom he has imputed it."[15] They belong together as the concerted action of God the Father, who takes action for us through his Son, and in us by his Spirit.

Born Again to Holiness and Happiness

Wesley was equally excited about both sides of the distinction. We have already seen how passionately he preached justification by grace through faith (chap. 2), and we will see that he drew further practical implications from justification (chap. 6). Justification is a lightning bolt that strikes and completes its work in a flash of divine power. But regeneration is an impartation of life that begins in an instant, then makes progress and grows toward its fulfillment. As a result, regeneration is the doctrine that gave Wesley the widest scope for his preaching on the Christian life. The new life begun at regeneration is a life with a new principle, new possibilities, new power and energy, and a new relationship with God. It yields not just new experiences, but new capacities for new experiences. Wesley often described these capacities as new senses. Before being born again, you have the ordinary five biological senses. But after rebirth, you become aware of new realities that cannot be apprehended by those senses. What has happened? "A new class of senses opened in your soul," explains Wesley, "not depending on organs of flesh and blood, to be *the evidence* of things not

---

[14] Sermon 5, "Justification by Faith," Burwash, 45.
[15] Sermon 20, "The Lord Our Righteousness," Burwash, 197.

seen, as your bodily senses are of visible things; to be the avenues to the invisible world, to discern spiritual objects and to furnish you with ideas of what the outward eye hath not seen, neither the ear heard."[16] Spiritual things are spiritually apprehended through spiritual senses.

The language of spiritual senses is partly metaphorical, and Wesley avoided stretching it too far or claiming that Christians have ten sense organs (five natural and five spiritual). To apply the notion of spiritual senses to his hearers, Wesley made great use of the parallel between the first birth and the second. "To consider the circumstances of the natural birth, is the most easy way to understand the spiritual."[17] He was struck by the way a matured fetus is perfectly formed and fully equipped for life outside the womb, but remains blind, deaf, and dumb. The baby in the womb has eyes and ears, but cannot use them to interact with the outer world. He partakes of oxygen ("subsists indeed by the air"), but without breathing it in or feeling its influence on him directly.

> But no sooner is the child born into the world, than he exists in quite a different manner. He now feels the air with which he is surrounded, and which pours into him from every side, as fast as he alternately breathes it back, to sustain the flame of life: and hence springs a continual increase of strength, of motion, and of sensation; all the bodily senses being now awakened, and furnished with their proper objects.[18]

The parallel almost preaches itself: being born again introduces the believer into a whole new world of knowing and experiencing God.

> He lives a life which the world knoweth not of, a "life which is hid with Christ in God." God is continually breathing, as it were, upon the soul; and his soul is breathing unto God. Grace is descending into his heart; and prayer and praise ascending to heaven: And by this intercourse between God and man, this fellowship with the Father and the Son, as by a kind of spiritual respiration, the life of God in the soul is sustained; and the child of God grows up, till he comes to the "full measure of the stature of Christ."[19]

---

[16] *An Earnest Appeal to Men of Reason and Religion*, par. 32, quoted in Rex D. Matthews, "With the Eyes of Faith: Spiritual Experience and the Knowledge of God in the Theology of John Wesley," in *Wesleyan Theology Today*, ed. Theodore Runyan (Nashville: Kingswood, 1985), 412.
[17] Sermon 19, "The Great Privilege of Those That Are Born of God," Burwash, 183.
[18] Ibid., 184.
[19] Sermon 45, "The New Birth," Burwash, 463.

This is the new life: grace descending and praise ascending, or the Spirit inspiring and the soul responding, as spiritual life is "received by faith" and immediately "rendered back by love, by prayer, and thanksgiving."[20] "Here then is the sum of the perfect law," said Wesley in one of his earliest sermons: "Let the spirit return to God that gave it, with the whole train of its affections."[21]

Wesley never tired of elaborating the blessings of the new birth, or of describing the new life that God opens for believers in this "vast inward change, a change wrought in the soul, by the operation of the Holy Ghost; a change in the whole manner of our existence."[22] If individuals were born again, Wesley taught, they would know it. They would have communion with God, and would have the promises of the new covenant fulfilled in their own hearts, observably. He preached the doctrine this way at the conclusion of sermon 2, "The Almost Christian," charging his audience to answer "the great question of all," which is in fact at least fifteen questions driving at the same point:

> Is the love of God shed abroad in your heart? Can you cry out, "My God, and my All"? Do you desire nothing but him? Are you happy in God? Is he your glory, your delight, your crown of rejoicing? And is this command- ment written in your heart, "That he who loveth God love his brother also"? Do you then love your neighbour as yourself? Do you love every man, even your enemies, even the enemies of God, as your own soul? As Christ loved you? Yea, dost thou believe that Christ loved thee, and gave himself for thee? Hast thou faith in his blood? Believest thou the Lamb of God hath taken away thy sins, and cast them as a stone into the depth of the sea? that he hath blotted out the handwriting that was against thee, taking it out of the way, nailing it to his cross? Hast thou indeed redemp- tion through his blood, even the remission of thy sins? And doth his Spirit bear witness with thy spirit, that thou art a child of God?[23]

It may seem as if Wesley is preaching too high a doctrine of the Chris- tian life. In his rapturous account of the life of those who are born of God, he can talk as if everybody with saving faith needed to have an immediate

---

[20] This is from the other great "spiritual respiration" passage in the *Standard Sermons*, sermon 19, "The Great Privilege of Those That Are Born of God," Burwash, 185.
[21] Sermon 17, "Circumcision of the Heart," Burwash, 171. This sermon was preached in 1733, five years before Aldersgate. But the mature Wesley included it in the *Standard Sermons* in 1771, in the section warn- ing against antinomianism. The line quoted is a kind of poetic expansion of Eccles. 12:8.
[22] Sermon 19, "The Great Privilege of Those That Are Born of God," Burwash, 183.
[23] Sermon 2, "The Almost Christian," Burwash, 17.

experience of all these blessings. But Wesley's attention never stopped at the level of a Christian's experience. His focus was always above and beyond that, on the spiritual blessing itself in all its fullness and integrity. He would carve the words "Not as though I had already attained" (Phil. 3:12) above his description of a real Christian life. He was not setting up an experience as a standard. He was trying to do justice to the greatness of salvation and keep his eye fixed on the purposes of God in saving us. The salvation announced in the New Testament is not simply a matter of affirming the right doctrines, or of attending church, or of doing good works. Spiritual reality is not lodged in those places, but resides in the heart.

This is the point of heart religion: not to put an impossible pressure on the experience (or even on the emotional life) of the believer, but to press home the need for spiritual reality. Heart religion is not about worshiping the heart, but about worshiping God from the heart. In the phrase "heart religion," *heart* is a contrast term; it is opposed to formal religion, intellectualized religion, and moralistic religion. What is formal religion? It is religion focused on externals, on "forms or ceremonies." Wesley was not against outward decorum and a beautiful liturgy. He genuinely loved the Anglican liturgy and the Book of Common Prayer. But forms are only forms. "Supposing these [forms] to be ever so decent and significant, ever so expressive of inward things," Wesley said, they would still not avail. "The religion of Christ rises infinitely higher, and lies immensely deeper, than all these." The value of external forms is derivative, and in times of need they are even expendable. "Let no man dream that they have any intrinsic worth; or that religion cannot subsist without them."[24] Wesley was not anti-liturgical, but he knew from experience how liturgy could serve as a place to hide from God.

Similarly, Wesley was not anti-intellectual, anti-theological, or anti-creedal, but here too he had personal experience with the way a clever mind can invest too heavily in doctrinal orthodoxy and twist it into a strategy for avoiding the presence of God. Wesley might even go so far as to say that orthodox creeds are necessary, but he would always insist that they were not sufficient:

> Although true religion naturally leads to every good word and work, yet the real nature thereof lies deeper still, even in "the hidden man of the

---

[24] Sermon 7, "Way to the Kingdom," Burwash, 63.

heart." I say of *the heart*. For neither does religion consist in *orthodoxy*, or *right opinions*; which, although they are not properly outward things, are not in the heart, but the understanding. A man may be orthodox in every point. . . . He may think justly concerning the incarnation of our Lord, concerning the ever blessed Trinity and every other doctrine, contained in the oracles of God; He may assent to all the three creeds,—that called the Apostles, the Nicene, and the Athanasian; and yet it is possible he may have no religion at all. . . . He may be almost as orthodox,—as the devil (though indeed, not altogether; for every man errs in something; whereas we cannot well conceive him to hold any erroneous opinion;) and may, all the while, be as great a stranger as he to the religion of the heart.[25]

Heart religion is a commitment to spiritual reality, an aversion to anything that falls short of reality, a shrewdness about all the places a religious person can hide from God, and a recognition that the heart is the organ of engagement with what is real.

Observe well: This is religion, and this alone; this alone is true Christian religion; not this or that opinion, or system of opinions, be they ever so true, ever so scriptural. It is true, this is commonly called faith. But those who suppose it to be religion are given up to a strong delusion to believe a lie, and if they suppose it to be a sure passport to heaven are in the high road to hell.[26]

Against formalism and intellectualism, against the "strong delusion" of mistaking ideas for saving faith, against a shallow moralism that substituted good works for true religion, Wesley and the other preachers of the evangelical revival stood in protest. "Go thou higher and deeper than all this! Let thy religion be the religion of the heart."[27]

A Heart Problem, a Heart Solution

Another reason that true religion has to be heart religion is that the human problem is a heart problem. We heard the historian Lecky account for the rise of Methodism by saying that Wesley's preaching brought back into circulation "a large class of religious doctrines which had been long almost wholly neglected," and that among these were "the utter depravity of

---

[25] Ibid.
[26] Sermon 113, "The Difference between Walking by Sight, and Walking by Faith," in *Works*, 7:260.
[27] Sermon 25, "Upon our Lord's Sermon on the Mount, Discourse V," Burwash, 262.

human nature," and "the lost condition of every man who is born into the world." It is crucial to remember that Wesley took the doctrine of original sin and trumpeted it to an eighteenth century that preferred to believe in the essential goodness of humanity, the inevitable march of progress, and the bright future of decent people rightly governed. Wesley begged to differ. Even the otherwise sound churchmen of his day preached a message that was too weak and too soft, too much like a series of recommendations for how to behave better. "According to them, religion is only a well ordered train of words and actions," and not a thing of the heart. The weakness of their preaching was rooted in their failure to understand how bad humanity really was. In thinking of the Christian message as advice about moral reform, Wesley noted, "they speak consistently with themselves; for if the inside be not full of wickedness, if this be clean already, what remains, but to 'cleanse the outside of the cup'? Outward reformation, if their supposition be just, is indeed the one thing needful."[28]

"But ye have not so learned the oracles of God," Wesley insisted. The Bible says otherwise. We are not basically good, with a few external failings. We are radically fallen, as Wesley emphasized in his sermon "Original Sin." Wesley taught that original sin is "the fundamental point which differences heathenism from Christianity." In contrast to all forms of paganism, even the highest and noblest forms, Christianity alone has an accurate understanding of the depth and extent of human sin, of "the entire depravation of the whole human nature, of every man born into the world, in every faculty of his soul, not so much by those particular vices which reign in particular persons, as by the general flood of atheism and idolatry, of pride, self will, and love of the world."[29] Though humanity was created good, wickedness has set in and corrupted it to the very core. "Is man by nature filled with all manner of evil? Is he void of all good?" asked Wesley. "Allow this, and you are so far a Christian. Deny it, and you are but a heathen still."[30] The human predicament goes to the heart of man.

"Know your disease!" warned Wesley, and he immediately matched it with "Know your cure!" If deep depravity is the human predicament, then radical salvation is the solution. "By nature ye are wholly corrupted; by grace ye shall be wholly renewed."[31] From the nature of sin, then, Wesley

---

[28] Sermon 44, "Original Sin," Burwash, 457.
[29] Ibid., 456.
[30] Ibid.
[31] Ibid., 457.

deduces the nature of true religion. The proper nature of religion is *therapeia psuches*, soul healing, "God's method of *healing a soul* which is thus diseased." And that cure affects all the elements of the soul corrupted by sin: our atheism and our idolatry, our pride and our self-will, as well as our love of the world:

> Hereby the great Physician of souls applies medicines to heal this sickness; to restore human nature, totally corrupted in all its faculties. God heals all our Atheism by the knowledge of Himself, and of Jesus Christ whom he hath sent; by giving us faith, a divine evidence and conviction of God, and of the things of God,—in particular, of this important truth, "Christ loved *me*"—and "gave himself for *me*." By repentance and lowliness of heart, the deadly disease of pride is healed; that of self-will by resignation, a meek and thankful submission to the will of God; and for the love of the world in all its branches, the love of God is the sovereign remedy. Now, this is properly religion, "faith" thus "working by love"; working the genuine meek humility, entire deadness to the world, with a loving, thankful acquiescence in, and conformity to, the whole will and word of God.[32]

If we were only a little bit sick, we would need only a little bit of salvation. But being desperately disordered and sick all the way to the heart, we stand in need of true religion, heart religion.

Happy Methodists and the Joy of Puritanism

In 1739, as the revival was drawing great attention and curiosity, Wesley published a short statement called "The Character of a Methodist" to explain what all this noise regarding heart religion was about. Remember that at this early stage, the term *Methodist* was a label appended by the outside world to the goings-on of the Wesleys, George Whitefield, and a group of co-revivalists that included Calvinists and Arminians alike. When the outside world looked into this diverse movement and called it Methodist, it was grasping for a label for the upsurge of heart religion. A modern parallel might be the secular news media in the 1970s attempting to understand what was unique about "born-again" Christians as opposed to, apparently, other kinds of Christians; or more recently asking, "Who are these evangelicals?" So Wesley obligingly set forth a brief defense of the

---

[32] Ibid., 456.

movement under the now-misleading title "The Character of a Methodist." If we retitled it today, we might call it "The Character of Those Who Believe in Heart Religion."

A Methodist, says Wesley, is not distinguished by particular doctrinal opinions ("as to all opinions which do not strike at the root of Christianity, we think and let think") or by a special terminology or vocabulary. Methodists cannot be identified by distinctive "actions, customs, or usages"; their uniqueness, he says, "does not lie in the form of our apparel" or "in the posture of our body." Finally, a common charge against the participants in the evangelical revival was that they overemphasized one particular part of Christianity at the expense of all the others. Wesley replies that the Methodist is not "distinguished by laying the whole stress of religion on any single part of it."

> If you say, "Yes, he is; for he thinks 'we are saved by faith alone' ": I answer, You do not understand the terms. By salvation he means holiness of heart and life. And this he affirms to spring from true faith alone. Can even a nominal Christian deny it? Is this placing a part of religion for the whole?[33]

With these negatives, Wesley is leading up to a positive answer about the character of a Methodist. By now that answer ought to be obvious: if the distinguishing feature is not in doctrines, works, external forms, or even emphasis, then where is it? It is in the heart. The word occurs four times in his answer; in fact, the occurrence of the word *heart* is the link between the diverse Scriptures Wesley pulls together to make up his definition:

> I answer: A Methodist is one who has "the love of God shed abroad in his heart by the Holy Ghost given unto him"; one who "loves the Lord his God with all his heart, and with all his soul, and with all his mind, and with all his strength." God is the joy of his heart, and the desire of his soul; which is constantly crying out, "Whom have I in heaven but thee? and there is none upon earth that I desire beside thee! My God and my all! Thou art the strength of my heart, and my portion for ever!"

And then Wesley takes the next step, striking a note that may sound odd to our ears. "He is therefore happy," say Wesley. "Happy in God, yea, always

---

[33] "The Character of a Methodist" (1742), in *Works*, 9:32–46 (here and below).

happy, as having in him 'a well of water springing up into everlasting life,' and overflowing his soul with peace and joy." The Christian that Wesley is describing, the one changed by God's grace from the inside out, has real, effective heart religion at work in him. And *therefore*, being holy, he is happy. Christian happiness is a necessary consequence of the heart religion Wesley has been describing. Salvation is present salvation, know-so salvation, conscious salvation that intersects our experience and expresses itself in attitudes, tempers, and feelings. You can't have peace without knowing you have peace, or joy without recognizing it. The blessed man of Psalm 32:1, whose sins are forgiven, is blessed ("or rather happy," as Wesley suggests translating it) because he knows and experiences this forgiveness.[34]

George Whitefield took a stand for the same point in his 1739 sermon "The Common Privilege of All Believers" when he said that "letter-learned preachers . . . talk professedly against inward feelings." Furthermore, they "say we can have God's Spirit without feeling it, which is in reality to deny the thing itself. And had I a mind to hinder the progress of the gospel and to establish the kingdom of darkness, I would go about telling people they might have the Spirit of God and yet not feel it."[35] You can't be born again without knowing it, without feeling it, the evangelicals preached.

"True religion, or a heart right toward God and man, implies happiness, as well as holiness."[36] Wesley is in earnest about this happiness; the language of happiness permeates his writings. In recent times, happiness has come to sound like a shallow feeling, especially in response to good circumstances. A modern speaker trying to describe a profound feeling would be more likely to use a word like *joy* and perhaps contrast it with happiness: joy is deep, happiness is shallow. But in the eighteenth century, the word *happiness* carried a much deeper significance. Popular philosophers used it in a way that resonated with classical Greek and Roman ideas about the purpose of life. When they talked about "human happiness," they were calling to mind the purpose for which man was originally created, and envisioning the complete fulfillment of that purpose. The Declaration of Independence (1776) listed the pursuit of happiness along with life and liberty as basic human rights that came from God. The founders were obviously not thinking about picnics or entertainment when they

---

[34] Sermon 7, "Way to the Kingdom," Burwash, 65.
[35] George Whitefield, "The Common Privilege of All Believers"; reprinted in Timothy L. Smith, *Whitefield and Wesley on the New Birth* (Grand Rapids: Francis Asbury, 1986), 96.
[36] Sermon 7, "Way to the Kingdom," Burwash, 64.

made this list. Wesley would never have distinguished between a shallow, merely emotional happiness, on the one hand, and a deep, settled joy, on the other, because the word *happiness* did not connote frivolity or shallowness to him. *Happy* is a good word in his vocabulary, and he uses it freely, interchangeably with the word *joy*. "Happiness," Gordon Rupp points out, "is a great key word in the first Methodist hymn-book, which began with a section entitled 'Of the Pleasantness and excellence of religion.'"[37]

Rupp and many other interpreters of Wesley are inclined to find in Wesley's emphasis on happiness something new and unprecedented in his age. They identify it as a distinguishing mark that especially sets him apart from the Puritans of the generations before him, contrasting Wesley's "optimism of grace" with their pessimism about humanity. But having traced the connection between heart religion, holy affections, and happiness, we are in a position to see things differently. In fact, it is precisely in his emphasis on the unity of holiness and happiness that Wesley stands closest to the Puritan tradition.

The connection between Puritan spirituality and Wesleyan Methodism can be hard for us to discern at this distance, since both terms have taken on extra (and unfair) connotations for us. There is a modern bias that directs us to think of Puritanism as the opposite of happiness, and of Puritans as the frozen chosen, baptized in vinegar and weaned on a pickle. It was the scathing wit of H. L. Mencken that defined Puritanism as "the haunting fear that someone, somewhere, may be happy." As a result of these willful distortions, as C. S. Lewis points out, "nearly every association which now clings to the word *puritan* has to be eliminated when we are thinking of the early Protestants. Whatever they were, they were not sour, gloomy, or severe; nor did their enemies bring any such charge against them."[38]

In reality the typical Puritan book was not some argumentative doctrinal tome, but a devotional book with a title like *Union and Communion*, *Instructions about Heartwork*, *The Bruised Reed*, *Keeping the Heart*, or *The Fountain of Life Opened Up*. One thing Puritans insisted on was the removal of merely traditional items that had been previously presented as divinely ordained, especially liturgical clutter that threatened to obscure the clear teaching of heart religion. Think of Wesley's insistence on true religion

---

[37] Gordon Rupp, "The Future of the Methodist Tradition," *The London Quarterly and Holborn Review* 184 (1959): 268.

[38] C. S. Lewis, *English Literature in the Sixteenth Century* (Oxford: Clarendon, 1954), 34.

residing in the heart, rather than in outward forms and ceremonies, and some similarities become more apparent. In fact, with his insistence that "formality" or "mere outside religion" had "almost driven heart religion out of the world," why didn't Wesley take a more Puritan stance, even leading his followers out of the corrupt established church of his day?

The main reason is that John Wesley, son of parents who had converted to Anglicanism as adults, was just a committed Church of England man. Rupp points out that sixteenth-century Puritanism had been engaged in a life-and-death struggle to reform the Church of England more thoroughly. The epic conflict had been costly on both sides, and had resulted in "the violent repudiation of Puritanism." But later, in the eighteenth century, Methodism arose as a kind of renewal of the Puritan impulse safely ensconced within the established church. Wesley's own grandparents had suffered the loss of freedom and of property for working outside the accepted guidelines of the religious settlement. "Now," says Rupp, "Wesley did what the Puritans had failed to do and neither the government nor the bishops interfered." In fact the whole catalog of Methodist measures is practically taken over from the Puritan agenda:

> Here again, many of the things which Methodists did and said seemed like echoes of that Puritanism which the Church of England had rejected and which had bred in it a distaste for "enthusiasm." The Puritans had used itinerant preachers, lay preachers, field preaching; in their smaller conventicles they exercised a stricter Christian discipline than that of formal Christianity. They had been exponents, in a vast and impressive literature of spiritual and moral and dogmatic theology, of doctrines of "inward religion," of a personal walk with God, of conversion, assurance, perfection. John Wesley himself owed more than he ever knew to this Puritan tradition of his own ancestors; the very language of his theology and many of his categories are conditioned by seventeenth-century Puritan controversies.[39]

Rupp goes on to point out that when Wesley put together a fifty-volume collection of highly recommended spiritual writings under the title *The Christian Library*, "the Puritans are the largest company, even though Puritanism was a largely Calvinist tradition."[40]

---

[39] Rupp, "The Future of the Methodist Tradition," 267.
[40] Ibid.

Perhaps it is the Calvinist-Arminian divide that keeps us from recognizing that Wesley's spirituality is so deeply indebted to Puritan spirituality. But the fact is that Wesley's approach to the Christian life is a Puritan approach. This accounts for why he sounds so much like his contemporary Jonathan Edwards in his insistence on religious affections. For that matter, it is why he sounds like John Owen in his insistence on holiness of heart and life, or, in our own day, why he sounds so much like J. I. Packer and John Piper. We can miss these similarities if we think the most important dividing line among Protestants is the line between Calvinists and Arminians. Instead, think of the dividing line as Wesley and Whitefield did: put all the Puritans on one side, earnestly pursuing holiness, keeping short accounts with God, and jealously norming their lives by the gospel. On the other side put those who are only concerned to be doctrinally correct, liturgically proper, or socially acceptable. When we turn to the relationship between grace and law (in chap. 6), we will see a striking agreement between Wesley and the Puritan Reformed. Here we only need to note the great similarities of those who pursue heart religion earnestly, and their great difference from all attempts to ground the Christian life elsewhere.

Sing Lustily and with Good Courage

Methodists sing. They always have, and we can hope they always will. There are many historical and cultural reasons why the traditions that descended from the evangelical revival became singing traditions, but the main reason is obvious. Heart religion wants to sing. Jonathan Edwards argued that since strong affections are the essence of true religion, it follows that "such means are to be desired as have much of a tendency to move the affections."[41] When Christians gather, it does not need to be a high-energy pep rally or a melodramatic plucking at the heartstrings. Surely we have had enough of that sort of thing. But abuse does not disqualify legitimate use, and Christian worship needs to stir up the affections and allow for their corporate expression. All aspects of church life (our reading, preaching, receiving of Communion and baptism, our prayer and worship) should be carried out in a way that stirs us up and deeply affects our hearts with the truth. For this end, nothing is so well suited as music, and especially congregational singing. It is "a means of raising or quickening the spirit of

---

[41] Jonathan Edwards, *The Religious Affections* (Edinburgh: Banner of Truth, 1961), 50.

devotion, of confirming [a person's] faith, of enlivening his hope, and of kindling or increasing his love to God and man."[42] This is precisely how Wesley approached the practice of congregational hymn singing: he was rationally persuaded, after due deliberation, that the appropriate thing to do was to stir the heart through the most effective implement, the hymn.

The Methodists were not the first to use the congregational hymn in their meetings. There was an ancient Christian tradition, of course, and even among their contemporaries, the Methodists were influenced by the Moravians and by the great Congregationalist Isaac Watts (1674–1748), the true "Father of English Hymnody." But the revival took up all the best hymns from these sources, added countless more to them, and moved forward in united song. "With the assurance that hymn singing was practiced by Jesus (cf. Mark 14:26; Matthew 26:30) and urged by St. Paul (cf. Ephesians 5:19; Colossians 3:16), Methodists sang hymns in all their services of worship."[43]

Of course it was Charles Wesley who dominated this field. For his part, John took an early lead by translating great German hymns for Methodist use. But Charles was an unstoppable fountain of song. Just the bare statistics of his productivity are staggering. "He wrote between six thousand and nine thousand hymns and sacred poems (depending upon what one is willing to call a hymn or poem), and more than four hundred of these continue in contemporary Christian hymnals."[44] Some of the nine thousand were clunkers, but most were good, many were great, and some are classics. Charles could hymnify anything, from earthquakes to toothaches, from salvation history to the triune mystery. "He seems almost to have thought in rhyme."[45] The Wesleyan hymnals are among the most important of the publications from the movement, and while a few of the hymnals are monumental classics, we should not forget that smaller hymn collections came out at a rate of more than one per year: "They published some fifty-seven collections of hymns during fifty-three years, culminating in the famous hymn-book of 1780."[46]

---

[42] From Wesley's preface to the 1780 *Collection of Hymns for the Use of the People Called Methodists*; quoted in Thomas Walter Herbert, *John Wesley as Editor and Author* (Princeton, NJ: Princeton University Press, 1940), 64.
[43] Karen B. Westerfield Tucker, "Wesley's Emphases on Worship and the Means of Grace," in *The Cambridge Companion to John Wesley*, ed. Randy L. Maddox and Jason E. Vickers (Cambridge: Cambridge University Press, 2010), 231.
[44] John R. Tyson, *Assist Me to Proclaim: The Life and Hymns of Charles Wesley* (Grand Rapids: Eerdmans, 2007), viii.
[45] Gordon Rupp, *Religion in England 1688–1791* (Oxford: Clarendon, 1986), 410.
[46] Ibid., 409.

The Wesley hymns are remarkable instruments for shaping the affections. Some worship happens through songs that are not much more than vehicles of expressing what is in the heart, but Wesley hymns are so theologically rich that they also serve as instruments of instruction. One scholar notes that "the hymns that the Methodists sang, like all effective hymns must be, were emotional, but their content throughout was scriptural and doctrinal. They did not merely stir emotion, but caused their singers to contemplate religious truth and meditate upon it."[47] One of the secrets of the hymns is the sheer density of Scriptural allusion. Charles Wesley seems to have memorized the Bible and to have had it always on the tip of his tongue. A really dense Wesley hymn can somehow manage to fit three Scripture references in two lines. It zips along without clutter, but if you stop to unpack how much is being said, suggested, and alluded to, it takes a full page of exposition that exhausts the reader but not the hymn. Take a verse at random from any hymn. Here is a hymn to the Holy Spirit from 1746:

> No man can truly say
> That Jesus is the Lord
> Unless thou take the veil away,
> And breathe the living word;
> Then, only then we feel
> Our interest in his blood,
> And cry with joy unspeakable,
> Thou art my Lord, my God!

Footnoting these lines is an advanced exercise in Bible literacy. Here we have explicit reference to at least four passages (1 Cor. 12:3; 2 Cor. 3:16; 1 Pet. 1:8; John 20:28), with the possibility of many more tingling at the edges. (Is "breathe the living word" a reference to Heb. 4:12? What biblical moment does "feel our interest in his blood" call to mind?) "Many writers have put individual hymns under the microscope and demonstrated the extent to which they are saturated in Scripture, with sometimes half a dozen allusions from very diverse portions in a single verse."[48] That depth and density is amazing enough, but the marvel of Charles Wesley's craftsmanship is that the result is singable, even memorable, rather than sounding like a heavy-handed, didactic concordance drill.

---

[47] J. Ernest Rattenbury, *The Evangelical Doctrines of Charles Wesley's Hymns* (London: Epworth, 1941), 84.
[48] Rupp, *Religion in England 1688–1791*, 410.

There is so much to say in praise of Wesley's hymns that perhaps it is best to let someone say something extravagant. Bernard L. Manning (1892–1941) praised Charles Wesley's hymnal as "a work of supreme devotional art by a religious genius." Some of Manning's praise is almost embarrassing. He calls the Wesley hymnal "in its own way . . . perfect, unapproachable, elemental in its perfection. You cannot alter it except to mar it." *Perhaps* this is a bit much. But he also points out that Charles Wesley happened to stand at a unique place in history to make his contribution to Christian song. English poetry and English music were ripe for this kind of work.

> It was Charles Wesley's good fortune, or (if you like) it was in the providence of God, that he was set to express the Catholic faith as it was being newly received in the Evangelical movement at a moment when prevailing taste and prevailing literary habits combined to give him a perfect literary instrument for hymn-writing.[49]

And Manning correctly identifies how Wesley brought together three things rarely combined so well in church music:

> There have been other writers of dogmatic hymns (we think of the Greek Church); there have been other writers of hymns revealing a personal experience of religion (we think of the nineteenth century); there have been other writers of mystical religious poetry (we think of the seventeenth century). It is Wesley's glory that he united these three strains—dogma, experience, mysticism—in verse so simple that it could be understood, and so smooth that it could be used, by plain men. You can find a union of these qualities in the greatest Latin hymns of the Medieval Church, but hardly (I believe) anywhere else. These three qualities, among others, give such a life to the hymns that they can never grow old while Christians experience God's grace.[50]

John Wesley recognized how important the hymns were to the success of the revival and the progress of heart religion. He "treated them as statements of Methodist theology of equal importance with those of his own sermons and treatises." In fact, as J. Ernest Rattenbury goes on to argue, "In certain ways they have proved to be more important, for, unlike

---

[49] Bernard Lord Manning, *The Hymns of Wesley and Watts: Five Informal Papers* (London: Epworth, 1942), 30.
[50] Ibid.

John's reasoned writings, they were read and sung by all Methodist people and so penetrated their hearts, illuminated their minds and expressed in striking and memorable phrase the saving truths which were believed and preached."[51] So John pointed to the hymns as the place where the life of the regenerate believer was cultivated and expressed. He wrote insightful prefaces to many of the hymnbooks. In the preface to the great 1780 *Collection of Hymns for the Use of the People Called Methodists*, John declared that the hymnal was "a little body of experimental and practical divinity" that set forth "scriptural Christianity" organized "according to the experiences of real Christians." He went on to ask rhetorically:

> In what other publication of the kind have you so distinct and full an account of Scriptural Christianity? Such a declaration of the heights and depths of Religion, speculative and practical? So strong cautions against the most plausible Errors: particularly those that are now most prevalent? And so clear directions for making your calling and election sure; for perfecting holiness in the fear of God?[52]

Even with great hymns, however, a congregation needed to sing them well, and the Wesleys had plenty of experience with the highs and the lows of public singing, as you can tell by reading between the lines of John's "Directions for Congregational Singing." In order to render public singing "more acceptable to God, as well as more profitable to yourself and others," Wesley admonished congregations to "be careful to observe the following directions." His language is archaic ("lustily" now means "libidinously," but in the eighteenth century it meant "vigorously and energetically"), but surely anyone who has sung in groups recognizes the timelessness of his advice:

1. Sing all. See that you join with the congregation as frequently as you can. Let not a slight degree of weakness or weariness hinder you. If it is a cross to you, take it up, and you will find a blessing.
2. Sing lustily, and with a good courage. Beware of singing as if you were half dead, or half asleep; but lift up your voice with strength. Be no more afraid of your voice now, nor more ashamed of its being heard, than when you sung the songs of Satan.
3. Sing modestly. Do not bawl, so as to be heard above, or distinct from, the rest of the congregation, that you may not destroy the harmony;

---

[51] Rattenbury, *Evangelical Doctrines of Charles Wesley's Hymns*, 63.
[52] Cited in ibid., 68–69.

but strive to unite your voices together, so as to make one clear melodious sound.

4. Sing in time. Whatever time is sung, be sure to keep with it. Do not run before, nor stay behind it; but attend closely to the leading voices and move therewith as exactly as you can. And take care you sing not too slow. This drawling way naturally steals on all who are lazy; and it is high time to drive it out from among us, and sing all our tunes just as quick as we did at first.

5. Above all, sing spiritually. Have an eye to God in every word you sing. Aim to pleasing Him more than yourself, or any other creature. In order to do this, attend strictly to the sense of what you sing; and see that your heart is not carried away with the sound, but offered to God continually; so shall your singing be such as the Lord will approve of here, and reward when he cometh in the clouds of heaven.[53]

Wesley must have heard plenty of half-dead, bawling, drawling congregational song in his days, and he was keen to make the singing as good as it could be. The performance had to be good enough to accomplish its goal. That goal was not perfect music for its own sake, but a continual offering of the heart to God.

Ordering the Affections in a System of Zeal

Wesley was not a natural systematizer, but there was at least one occasion when he became positively excited about the idea of showing the organic, systematic structure of Christian faith. He was a preacher and a world changer, not a theological ponderer or chart maker. But perhaps he knew that as a purveyor of heart religion, he had a duty to be especially clear and rational. So he took up the task of showing how the various parts of Christian love, or zeal, were related to each other, with a special interest in their relative rankings.

He was preaching "On Zeal" (sermon 92, not one of the *Standard Sermons*) from the text Galatians 4:18, which in the King James translation reads, "It is good to be zealously affected always in a good thing," and it dawned on him that our loves, the things we are zealous for, need to be ordered according to the goods they are directed toward. Our zeal should be directly proportional to the things God has regard for. "In a Christian be-

---

[53] These instructions were first printed in Wesley's 1761 hymnal *Sacred Melody; or, A Choice Collection of Psalm and Hymn Tunes with a Short Introduction.*

liever," he argued, "love sits upon the throne which is erected in the inmost soul; namely, love of God and man, which fills the whole heart, and reigns without a rival." His next move was to begin showing how all the other goods are ordered around that enthronement of love in the inmost soul:

> In a circle near the throne are all holy tempers;—longsuffering, gentleness, meekness, fidelity, temperance; and if any other were comprised in "the mind which was in Christ Jesus." In an exterior circle are all the works of mercy, whether to the souls or bodies of men. By these we exercise all holy tempers—by these we continually improve them, so that all these are real means of grace, although this is not commonly adverted to. Next to these are those that are usually termed works of piety—reading and hearing the word, public, family, private prayer, receiving the Lord's supper, fasting or abstinence. Lastly, that his followers may the more effectually provoke one another to love, holy tempers, and good works, our blessed Lord has united them together in one body, the church, dispersed all over the earth—a little emblem of which, of the church universal, we have in every particular Christian congregation.[54]

Wesley evidently took the hierarchical ordering seriously: "This," he affirms, "is the entire, connected system of Christianity: and thus the several parts of it rise one above another, from that lowest point, the assembling ourselves together, to the highest—love enthroned in the heart. And hence it is easy to learn the comparative value of every branch of religion."

At the center of the system is love. The first movement outward from that circle is the most important: love of God and man will manifest itself in "holy tempers," among which Wesley lists fruits of the Spirit. No doubt he would also insist on the "train of affections" and emotions as well, but here he leaves out things like joy in favor of emphasizing the most peaceable of the tempers ("the mind that was in Christ"). His reason for doing this was probably that he is preaching about zeal and wants to make the point that zeal is not the same as being wild and intemperate in pursuing the good. So Wesley begins from the heart and moves out to tempers.

One of the most interesting transitions in this system is the direct path from the holy tempers to works of mercy. You might expect Wesley to move from tempers to spirituality, but instead he goes to works of service: "In an

---

[54] Sermon 117, "On Zeal," in *The Works of John Wesley*, ed. John Emory (New York: Waugh and Mason, 1835), 290.

exterior circle are all the works of mercy, whether to the souls or bodies of men." Wesley must have in mind here the traditional medieval lists of the "corporal works of mercy" (feed the hungry, clothe the naked, visit the sick, bury the dead, etc.) and the "spiritual works of mercy" (instruct the ignorant, forgive offenses, comfort the afflicted, pray for others). Wesley, somewhat unusually, calls them "real means of grace," since by these actions we "exercise all holy tempers" and "continually improve them." The works of mercy are outlets for the necessary self-expression of the holy tempers that arise from a heart transformed by love.

Only then does Wesley move out further to things "that are usually termed works of piety," or spiritual disciplines like "reading and hearing the word, public, family, private prayer, receiving the Lord's supper, fasting or abstinence." For this priority of service over spiritual formation, Wesley cites scriptural passages like "God will have mercy and not sacrifice," and even lays down the principle: "Whenever, therefore, one interferes with the other, works of mercy are to be preferred. Even reading, hearing, prayer are to be omitted, or to be postponed, 'at charity's almighty call'; when we are called to relieve the distress of our neighbour, whether in body or soul." And last of all, Wesley comes to the church, which "our blessed Lord has united . . . together in one body" so that believers can "provoke one another to love, holy tempers, and good works." And within the church he makes yet another distinction, with the universal church, on one hand, being most important, and a local gathering of believers, on the other, being less important.

How should zeal work, then? It should be proportioned to the level of good in each of these: every Christian should love and pray for "that particular church or Christian society whereof he himself is a member," but even more for "the church universal." But Wesley goes on to warn, "he should be more zealous for the ordinances of Christ than for the church itself; for prayer in public and private; for the Lord's supper, for reading, hearing, and meditating on his word; and for the much-neglected duty of fasting." These are at a higher order of good than the church, which exists for the purpose of making these things happen. But these spiritual disciplines, or "ordinances of Christ," rank lower than the works of mercy, the good works that we should be zealous for.

> But as zealous as we are for all good works, we should still be more zeal-
> ous for holy tempers; for planting and promoting, both in our own souls,

and in all we have any intercourse with, lowliness of mind, meekness, gentleness, longsuffering, contentedness, resignation unto the will of God, deadness to the world and the things of the world, as the only means of being truly alive to God. For these proofs and fruits of living faith we cannot be too zealous.[55]

But at the center is love itself: "the end of the commandment, the fulfilling of the law." For Wesley and his system of zeal, "the church, the ordinances, outward works of every kind, yea, all other holy tempers, are inferior to this, and rise in value only as they approach nearer and nearer to it."

Wesley's Last Letter: To Wilberforce

One of the surprising things about Wesley's system of zeal is that it moves so directly from the heart renewed in love out to good works in the world. We have come to expect heart religion to yield an inwardly focused spirituality, but if Wesley is to be our standard for heart religion (and who better?), then heart religion is a practical thing that drives real social change. As evidence, we could point to any number of effects that the Wesleyan revival had on England. It used to be popular to say that Wesley's impact on England was so great that it preserved England from experiencing a cataclysm like the French Revolution. But that argument is dubious and ought to be handled with care. Even if it could be proven, after all, it might just mean that the heart religion of the revival was a successful distraction, or a pacifier that kept the working classes from rising up against their oppressors.[56] But Wesley's work did in fact alter the moral climate of eighteenth-century England, and heart religion had its impact on the wider world.[57] Probably the best direct evidence for this can be seen in Wesley's effectiveness as an advocate for social justice on a number of fronts, particularly in his influence on the abolition of slavery.

Wesley condemned slavery repeatedly from the pulpit and used his

---

[55] Ibid.

[56] The argument that "Wesley stopped the English version of the French Revolution" is called by scholars the Halevy thesis, from a 1906 book by Élie Halévy translated into English as *The Birth of Methodism in England*, ed. and trans. Bernard Sammel (Chicago: University of Chicago Press, 1971), 51. For full discussion, see Gerald W. Olsen, ed., *Religion and Revolution in Early-Industrial England: The Halevy Thesis and Its Critics* (Lanham, MD: University Press of America, 1990), and the shrewd remarks of Rupp in *Religion in England 1688–1791*, 449ff.; e.g., "Some Methodists took Halevy's judgement as a compliment and laid themselves wide open to the retort that they had simply fostered an other-worldly pietism, diverting men from their true business—the amendment of the condition of the working class."

[57] For a well-rounded study of how Wesley's theology was oriented to social change, see Leon O. Hynson, *To Reform the Nation: Theological Foundations of Wesley's Ethics* (Grand Rapids: Francis Asbury, 1984).

personal influence against it wherever he could. His influential tract "Thoughts on Slavery" included a direct appeal to slaveholders, calling their attention to the cry of injustice that rose from their oppressive practices: "O, whatever it costs, put a stop to its cry before it be too late. . . . Thy hands, thy bed, thy furniture, thy house, thy lands, are at present stained with blood."[58] Wesley could sympathize with slaveholders in the sense that he fully understood how much financial loss they would suffer by rejecting slavery. But his advice was to suffer that loss as soon as possible, because it was the price of repentance from evil works: "Today resolve, God being your helper, to escape for your life. Regard not money! . . . Whatever you lose, lose not your soul; nothing can countervail that loss. Immediately quit the horrid trade."[59] Wesley's position on slavery was clear. He would stir up the hearts of Christians to bring the practice to an utter end, if possible.

In this context, it is striking that the final letter John Wesley ever wrote was on the subject of slavery and was written to William Wilberforce (1759–1833). Here, in its entirety, is the brief letter, dated February 24, 1791:

Dear Sir:

Unless the divine power has raised you up to be as *Athanasius contra mundum*, I see not how you can go through your glorious enterprise in opposing that execrable villainy which is the scandal of religion, of England, and of human nature. Unless God has raised you up for this very thing, you will be worn out by the opposition of men and devils. But if God be for you, who can be against you? Are all of them together stronger than God? O be not weary of well doing! Go on, in the name of God and in the power of his might, till even American slavery (the vilest that ever saw the sun) shall vanish away before it.

Reading this morning a tract wrote by a poor African, I was particularly struck by that circumstance that a man who has a black skin, being wronged or outraged by a white man, can have no redress; it being a "law" in our colonies that the oath of a black against a white goes for nothing. What villainy is this?

That he who has guided you from youth up may continue to strengthen you in this and all things, is the prayer of, dear sir,

---

[58] From Wesley's widely circulated 1774 pamphlet "Thoughts on Slavery." See Warren Thomas Smith, *John Wesley and Slavery* (Nashville: Abingdon, 1986), for a commentary on (90–103) and reprinting of (123–48) the original pamphlet.

[59] Cited in Rebekah L. Miles, "Happiness, Holiness, and the Moral Life in John Wesley," in Maddox and Vickers, *Cambridge Companion to John Wesley*, 216.

Your affectionate servant,
John Wesley[60]

This must have been a great encouragement to Wilberforce as he carried out his tireless campaign to abolish the slave trade in the coming years. The point is not just that one great man, John Wesley, had an influence on another great man, William Wilberforce. The point is that it is precisely in their agreement about the value of heart religion that they found common cause. It was heart religion that brought down slavery.

Six years after receiving the Wesley letter, Wilberforce published his great work *A Practical View of the Prevailing Religious System of Professed Christians, in the Higher and Middle Classes in This Country, Contrasted with Real Christianity.* Wilberforce's *Practical View* is especially eloquent about how real Christian faith moves the heart and motivates social action. He freely admits that what he calls "real Christian faith" is dangerously close to what the cultured in his time would call fanaticism or (in the eighteenth-century sense of the term) enthusiasm. Nevertheless, he is willing to run that risk because true religion is "the implantation of a vigorous and active principle; it is seated in the heart, where its authority is recognized as supreme, whence by degrees it expels whatever is opposed to it, and where it gradually brings all the affections and desires under its complete control and regulation." The definition would have warmed Wesley's heart, if Wesley's heart had not already been strangely warmed.

According to Wilberforce, slavery was permitted in England and America because this real Christianity had cooled; and real Christianity had cooled because essential Christian doctrines had been abandoned. If the nominal Christians of Britain were ignoring gross institutional wickedness like race-based chattel slavery, it was because their hearts were cold; and their hearts were cold because their heads were empty. What Dr. Wilberforce prescribes is a big dose of "the peculiar doctrines of Christianity": not morality or piety in general, but the core doctrines that we know only from special divine revelation in Scripture. Wilberforce's first major move in the book is to get a gigantic slab of Christianity's "peculiar doctrines" in front of his readers. Under the heading "scripture doctrines," he launches into a breathtaking survey of the big ideas of the Christian faith: the love of God, the humility of Christ, the atonement, the ascension of Christ, the

---

[60] Printed in *John Wesley*, ed. Albert Outler (New York: Oxford University Press, 1964), 86.

necessity of the indwelling Holy Spirit, and the resurrection of the dead. Wilberforce says that all of this is common Christian confession, and that even if the Anglican pulpiteers of his day are shy about the particulars, nevertheless the whole wonderful thing is faithfully preserved in "our excellent liturgy."

No wonder, he says, "the bulk of nominal Christians" show so little joy or trust in their Savior: they have no love for him. "The love of Christ is languid in them," so "joy and trust in him cannot be expected to be very vigorous." And if love for Christ has gone cold, "the doctrine of the sanctifying operations of the Holy Spirit appears to have met with still worse treatment." Even when they call these truths of the faith to mind, they lack the heart-felt response that is necessary for the arduous task of seeking justice in the world. This is where Wilberforce draws another very Wesleyan conclusion about heart religion. Emotional excitement has a crucial role in the life of service. We need "powerful stimulants" to get us moving.

> Mere knowledge is confessedly too weak. The affections alone remain to supply the deficiency. They precisely meet the occasion, and suit the purposes intended. Yet, when we propose to fit ourselves for our great undertaking, by calling them in to our help, we are to be told that we are acting contrary to reason. Is this reasonable, to strip us first of our armour of proof, and then to send us to the sharpest of encounters? To summon us to the severest labours, but first to rob us of the precious cordials which should brace our sinews and recruit our strength?

For Wilberforce, it all terminates in action. But you don't start into action with an empty head and a cold heart. And he puts his finger on the main problem, which is theological, focused on the gospel: "But the grand radical defect in the practical system of these nominal Christians, is their forgetfulness of all the peculiar doctrines of the Religion which they profess—the corruption of human nature—the atonement of the Saviour—and the sanctifying influence of the Holy Spirit." Following Wesley, Wilberforce knew that heart religion is the most practical and effective kind of religion.

The church in the twenty-first century faces a different situation than evangelicals like Wesley and Edwards faced in the eighteenth. In the intervening centuries there have been waves of romanticism in literature, expressionism in the arts, democratic egalitarianism in politics, and a general loosening of all kinds of formality in Western culture at large. If we champion heart religion in our time, we will have to find some new words for it, because many of the eighteenth-century terms have been worn out from abuse, overuse, and intentional neglect. In evangelical circles, the formalism of our day is just as likely to be an unbuttoned, low-church casualness as it is to be well-dressed, high-church stiffness. But today's objections to heart religion are the same as the ones Wesley and the evangelicals of the eighteenth century encountered, and none of them work. Christianity in its clearest form is heart religion. We do not need to be mawkish, precious, sentimental, manipulative, inward-focused, privatized, or weepy. We need to recover what Wesley argued for and acted out in the great revival of religion in the eighteenth century: heart religion.

CHAPTER 4

THE THEOLOGIAN
OF I JOHN

No Christian should ever have a *least* favorite book of the Bible. All Scripture is God-breathed, and the whole Bible in all its parts is good for teaching, training, and equipping us (2 Tim. 3:16). But it is perfectly permissible, and even desirable, to have a *favorite* book of the Bible. It could be the book that first reached us with the good news of salvation, or one through which God spoke to us in a difficult time. It might be the one book or passage that all the rest of Scripture seems to lead up to. As long as we resist the temptation to "play favorites" by letting the particular message of one book silence the distinctive message of another book, and as long as we recognize that the whole canon of Scripture belongs together, a good reader of the Bible can have a biblical book that is a spiritual home base.

John Wesley's favorite book was 1 John. As Robert Wall has recently argued, "although the entire Bible had authority for Wesley, one part of this biblical whole held extra special resonance for him—the first epistle of John."[1] Wesley's special regard for 1 John explains a lot about his approach to the Christian life. In fact, I believe John Wesley should be thought of as the theologian of 1 John.

---

[1] Robert W. Wall, "Wesley as Biblical Interpreter," in *The Cambridge Companion to John Wesley*, ed. Randy L. Maddox and Jason E. Vickers (Cambridge: Cambridge University Press, 2010), 117. Wall goes on to say, "This epistle was his canon within the canon." I will be using the phrase "canon within the canon" in a pejorative sense, warning against its dangers. For Wall, the phrase does not have these negative connotations. Wall's excellent chapter is the fullest presentation so far of the special influence of 1 John on Wesley, though he is not the first to have pointed it out.

No "Canon within the Canon"

I once heard a theologian muse that Lutherans tend to treat Galatians as the key book for interpreting the Bible. Galatians is stark, forceful, incisive, penetrating, confrontational. Is it merely coincidental that that list of adjectives sounds like a description of Martin Luther's personality? Luther expressed his fondness for the book by saying, "It is my wife." The Reformed, however, tend to gravitate to Ephesians, a book that presupposes the truth of Galatians ("by grace are ye saved through faith"), but sets it within a panoramic view of redemption traced back into God's eternal purposes, all rolling out of Paul's mind in very long sentences.

This Galatians-Ephesians contrast, of course, is relative. Protestants in general tend to agree in giving pride of place to Romans as the New Testament book that serves as the doctrinal capstone of the whole Bible, asking and answering all the right questions. Protestant systematic theology actually arose out of the habit of writing increasingly systematic Romans commentaries. "Every continental Reformer worth his salt wrote a commentary on Romans; it was almost a proficiency badge to show that he was a genuine Reformer."[2] Pentecostals, on the other hand, may read the whole Bible, but they tend to regard the book of Acts as the definitive and normative portrait of what the rest of the Bible must mean for our time.

Preferences like this can be a playful back and forth among believers of different types. For example, try assigning the four Gospels to the four core personality types or temperaments, and then see if you can find yourself in the Gospel that supposedly corresponds to your type. The same kind of insights and possibilities can arise from seeing how whole churches and traditions align with the distinctive message and tone of the various books of Scripture. This works as long as everybody involved earnestly seeks to embrace the whole canon. Favorite-book alignments can also, however, be markers of sectarianism: imagine a fellowship that agreed to regard Ecclesiastes as the key to the Bible, or a tradition that majored on the books of Zechariah and Revelation.

There is always a danger of a "canon within the canon" framework that privileges one or two books of the Bible over the rest. Any time a Christian promotes one book or author over the others and forms the habit of always

---

[2] T. H. L. Parker, *Calvin's Doctrine of the Knowledge of God* (Grand Rapids: Eerdmans, 1959), 31. Parker based another book on this observation: *Commentaries on the Epistle to the Romans, 1532–1542* (London: T&T Clark, 1986). He notes that in that decade alone, there were commentaries by Calvin, Melanchthon, Cajetan, Bullinger, Sadeleto, Bucer, and four others.

seeking answers in that section of the Bible while neglecting and losing familiarity with other sections, disaster awaits. The real Bible is replaced by an eclectic mini-Bible. The real canon is subordinated to a personal canon. Instead of hearing the Word of God, we begin to hear our own voices echoing back from our self-selected favorite verses. Settling for a canon within the canon is a terrible thing.[3] As fallible and sinful interpreters, we lapse into this error all too often, but when we do so, we should at least know we are erring and not pretend we are doing well. To play favorites with Bible books (in this sense) is to have a blind spot, not to have a privileged lens on the truth.

So we should be cautious in singling out any particular biblical book as a guide, or in describing it as the summit of biblical revelation. Above all, we had better be specific about how that book excels others, and we had better be right. We cannot call one biblical book better than another, but we can say what it is better at doing. Matthew is not better than Mark, but it is better at linking Jesus to the Old Testament. Ephesians, to look at the Reformed favorite mentioned earlier, is not better than Galatians, but it is better at sketching the big picture and relating salvation to God's glory. Galatians is not better than Ephesians, but it is better at refuting legalism. The traditional Protestant attachment to the theological categories of Romans is fully justified if Romans is in fact the most systematic presentation of the doctrine of salvation in the New Testament. To recognize what these books are uniquely accomplishing is not to use them to silence other books, but to respond to each by using each appropriately, setting it free to do its own work within the whole, perfect canon of Scripture.

First John as a Guide

Within the canon of Scripture, what is 1 John uniquely good at doing? And what was it that drew Wesley's attention to this one book of the Bible? The two questions have one answer, because what Wesley focused on was the central contribution of 1 John. What he found in the epistle was a portrayal of the Christian life as fellowship with God in the light. In his *Notes on the New Testament*, Wesley admits that the "scope and method" of 1 John are not immediately evident to readers. "But if we examine it with simplicity, these may

---

[3] D. A. Carson has repeatedly warned about the dangers of a canon within the canon. One of his best discussions of it is in "A Sketch of the Factors Determining Current Hermeneutical Debate in Cross-Cultural Contexts," in *Biblical Interpretation and the Church: Text and Context*, ed. D. A. Carson (Exeter: Paternoster, 1984), 11–29.

readily be discovered."[4] The aim of 1 John is "to confirm the happy and holy communion of the faithful with God and Christ, by describing the marks of that blessed state." Every word in Wesley's brief description is important, and the key noun is "communion." But by focusing for a moment on the idea of marks, or indicators, we can see to the core of what he learned from 1 John.

First John gives a kind of snapshot of fellowship in holiness. It shows a picture of light, and of a Christian standing in that light. There is a stunning simplicity to the picture: You are either in the light or out of it. It seems to be all or nothing. First John does not describe processes of moving in and out of the light, much less of being in any twilight zone of half-light in between the two states. The apostle John enforces a strict dualism: fellowship or no fellowship. He does not say things like "once you were not in the light, but now you are." Instead he gives his readers a set of signs or "marks of the blessed state," by which they can know with confidence that they are in this fellowship, so that their joy may be full.

The whole flow of this biblical book is important to understanding Wesley's passion for its message. The letter of 1 John (which Wesley describes as a tract rather than an epistle, believing that the apostle wrote it for those he was with rather than for those far away) has a loose structure, and compositionally it is repetitive, tending to circle back to the same few points. But it has an important flow of thought. It begins with the identity of Christ as "the one who was from the beginning," who was with the Father, who is the eternal life that has been revealed to us. Having motivated us to listen to such a speaker, John then announces that this Christ has brought a message. The message we have from this one who is the preexistent, divine word of life, is that "God is light." Considered in his character as light, God is awesomely unapproachable: "the light of wisdom, love, holiness, glory," notes Wesley. "What light is to the natural eye, that God is to the spiritual eye."[5] And when John goes on to say that "in him is no darkness at all," Wesley points out that God is all holiness, with "no contrary principle. He is pure, unmixed light"—high, holy, pure, and exalted. A modern commentator on 1 John clarifies that "the point is not so much that God did not create darkness but rather that living in the darkness is incompatible with fellowship with God."[6]

---

[4] Wesley, "Notes on the First Epistle of St. John," in *Explanatory Notes upon the New Testament* (London: Epworth, 1950), 902.
[5] Ibid., 904.
[6] I. Howard Marshall, *The Epistles of John* (Grand Rapids: Eerdmans, 1978), 109.

How then can we sinful creatures have fellowship with this God who is light? For any Christian who has looked from a pure God to an impure heart, this dilemma posed by the opening of 1 John is a pressing one. The answer shows up in a set of key words that feature prominently in the early verses of the book: *forgiveness* of our sins, a Son given as the *propitiation*, and an *advocate* with the Father. Only through the propitiation of the crucified Christ and the advocacy of the risen Christ can we have the forgiveness of sins. All of this is made possible by God's character as the one who is faithful and just to forgive us when we confess our sins (1:9). It might seem that a just God would surely punish, but Wesley says no: "for this very reason he will pardon. This may seem strange; but upon the evangelical principle of atonement and redemption it is undoubtedly true; because, when the debt is paid, or the purchase made, it is the part of equity to cancel the bond, and consign over the purchased possession."[7]

As Wesley's exposition shows, 1 John emphasizes the contrast between God's light and sin's darkness, and then gives the only possible solution to the problem. By drawing attention to this stark contrast, Wesley forces us back to reliance on free forgiveness through the atonement and advocacy of Christ. Only then can we turn the corner to the marks of the Christian life, which 1 John sets out in a famous series of "if" and "by this we know" passages. They are spread throughout the letter, but there is an especially intense cluster at the beginning of chapter 5:

> Everyone who believes that Jesus is the Christ has been born of God, and everyone who loves the Father loves whoever has been born of him. By this we know that we love the children of God, when we love God and obey his commandments. For this is the love of God, that we keep his commandments. And his commandments are not burdensome. For everyone who has been born of God overcomes the world. And this is the victory that has overcome the world—our faith. Who is it that overcomes the world except the one who believes that Jesus is the Son of God? (1 John 5:1–5, ESV)

Those "if" and "by this we know" passages specify orthodoxy, good works, and love as "marks of that blessed state" of "happy and holy communion." But these marks could not establish the fellowship itself; they can only manifest it. Great as they are, it is impossible that they could answer

---

[7] Wesley, *Explanatory Notes upon the New Testament*, 904.

the opening question of how we can have fellowship with the God who is light. Only the Son's atoning sacrifice can make that possible. In systematic theological categories, we could say the person and work of Christ constitute the only ground of fellowship with God and assurance of faith. But it is also valuable to examine the marks, which have a supportive role. The tests have introspective, retrospective, and prospective value. John offers these tests so that believers can gain confidence about their own status (introspective), so they can understand what happened to those who fell away (retrospective), and so they can be encouraged to persevere (prospective).[8]

Wesley is a good guide to reading 1 John because he understands how the message of the letter is supposed to work in a believer's life. The purpose of the letter is to increase the believer's confidence. It portrays the life of the Christian, showing the marks of communion with the Father and the Son (right doctrine, right conduct, right affections), so that the believer can be assured. But Wesley has preemptively eliminated any possibility that the "if" passages and the "by this we know" passages in 1 John might be brought forward as answers to the opening problem. It would be spiritually disastrous to think that our right beliefs, right conduct, and right affections are the ground of our fellowship with God. But it would also be disastrous to think that a life of fellowship with God is possible without showing these marks.

There is one last element of 1 John that captured Wesley's attention. In 2:12–14, the apostle gives a series of reasons for his writing, which he addresses to three subgroups of his audience: he is writing to little children, to fathers, and to young men. Twice he cycles through these two groups, commending the children (because their sins are forgiven for the sake of Christ's name), the fathers (because they "know him who is from the beginning"), and the young men (because they are strong, because the word of God abides in them, and they have overcome the Evil One). As far as I know, Wesley never offers any special, binding interpretation of the precise differences among these three groups, or among the three different ways the apostle characterizes them. What he notes, however, is the simple fact that according to the apostle John, there are gradations of maturity in the Christian life. This is a significant fact for Wesley, and it helps provide guidelines for interpreting the sharp dualism of 1 John, a dualism between

---

[8] For this way of describing 1 John's tests, see Christopher Bass, *That You May Know: Assurance of Salvation in 1 John* (Nashville: B&H Academic, 2008).

light and darkness that has misled other interpreters. The difference between walking in the darkness, on the one hand, and having fellowship in the light with the Father and the Son, on the other, is an absolute difference with no middle ground between. But on the side of those who walk in the light, there is such a thing as growth in maturity. There are gradations of experience and levels of understanding. Among believers, there are little children, young men, and fathers.

In his *Explanatory Notes upon the New Testament*, Wesley gives an outline of 1 John, which highlights the theme of communion with the Father and the Son in the Spirit. First John itself does not necessarily follow a Trinitarian structure, but Wesley's outline does. His goal is to make sure that the reader grasps the main idea of the most important book of the Bible, which he takes to be communion with the Trinity:

I. Father, Son, and Spirit Severally:
1. Of communion with the Father (1:5–10)
2. Of communion with the Son (2:1–12)
   with application to fathers, young men, and children (13–27)
   an exhortation to abide in him (2:28–3:24)
3. Of the confirmation and fruit of this abiding through the Spirit (4:1–21)

II. Father, Son, and Spirit Conjointly:
Of their testimony 5:1–12

As Wesley himself confessed, a great bulk of his *Explanatory Notes upon the New Testament* is material borrowed and condensed from various sources, chiefly the *Gnomon* of the Pietist commentator Johann Albrecht Bengel (1687–1752). But his notes on 1 John, according to Robert Wall, are more clearly his own original work and "reflect a depth of exegetical engagement much less dependent upon the prior work of others than the rest of the volume."[9] This is just one more sign of how invested he was in the letter.

"That Compendium of All the Holy Scriptures"

Wesley, then, is the theologian who allowed the epistle of 1 John to be his guide to the whole Christian message, leading to a theology of the Christian life that emphasized walking in the light and having fellowship with

---

[9] Wall, "Wesley as Biblical Interpreter," 118.

God, who is pure light, as well as a recognition that there is such a thing as progress in Christian maturity. We have already quoted Wall's observation that "although the entire Bible had authority for Wesley, one part of this biblical whole held extra special resonance for him—the first epistle of John."[10] Wesley scholars have long recognized the special place of 1 John in his thought. Franz Hildebrandt sketched the connections in 1959:

> Above all, 1 John, which holds him forever in its grip—here is the perfect love which casteth our fear; here are the comfortable words for those who confess their sins and the uncomfortable texts about the reborn who cannot sin; here is the twofold test for all "real Christians" through the Spirit that confesses the incarnate Christ and the love that serves Him in the brethren; here is the Wesleyan note of assurance in the repeated "hereby we know"; and here again, as in John's Gospel, the end of it all is "that your joy may be full."[11]

Nor is this priority of 1 John an invention of later scholars; Wesley was himself aware of how much he owed to 1 John's distinctive theological emphases. His journals record several outbursts of delight whenever he taught from 1 John. In 1763, for instance, he notes that he "began expounding a second time, after an interval of above twenty years, the first Epistle of St. John. How plain, how full, and how deep a compendium of genuine Christianity!"[12] And in 1765, taking it up again, he is struck by how the apostle's style could serve as a model for all preaching:

> I began expounding the deepest part of the holy Scripture, namely, the First Epistle of St. John, by which above all other, even inspired, writings, I advise every young preacher to form his style. Here are sublimity and simplicity together, the strongest sense and the plainest language! How can anyone that would "speak as the oracles of God," use harder words than are found here?[13]

There is some evidence that John Wesley had already taken his own advice here, since at his best he did "form his style" in a way that attained both "sublimity and simplicity." In the preface to his *Standard Sermons*, for

---

[10] Ibid., 117.
[11] Franz Hildebrandt, "Can the Distinctive Methodist Emphasis Be Said to Be Rooted in the New Testament?," *London Quarterly and Holborn Review* 184 (1959): 238.
[12] *The Journal of Reverend John Wesley* (New York: Carlston & Phillips, 1856), 158.
[13] Luke Tyerman, *The Life and Times of the Rev. John Wesley*, 3rd ed., 3 vols. (London: Hodder and Stoughton, 1876), 2:537.

example, he insists, "I labour to avoid all words which are not easy to be understood. . . . I design plain truth for plain people." In numerous ways John Wesley attempted to model his own life after that of the author of 1 John, and one foreign visitor did describe him as "a living representation of the loving Apostle John."[14] And whether he preached like the apostle John or not, Wesley certainly did preach from the apostle John a great deal. Randy Maddox has recently demonstrated that Wesley "favored the book in his own preaching," taking it as the basis "for his sermon text and alluding to it within sermons much more frequently (relative to the number of verses in the book) than any other biblical book."[15]

A few other factors contributed to Wesley's privileging of 1 John. For one thing, it is a general epistle without a specific audience, and Wesley counted this as one of the reasons its truths were stated so universally. "In this Epistle St. John speaks not to any particular Church, but to all the Christians of that age; although more especially to them among whom he then resided. And in them he speaks to the whole Christian Church in all succeeding ages."[16] For another thing, the apostle John's writing ministry stretched for decades after the resurrection of Christ, making John one of the final voices in the New Testament. Wesley indeed regarded John as the "last of the New Testament writers." Because of these two factors, 1 John has a comprehensiveness that presupposes and builds on the other New Testament authors. When Wesley taught 1 John in 1772, he noted in his journal that it is a "compendium of all the Holy Scriptures."[17] And in a late sermon, he sketched the way the apostle John fixes his attention directly on the goal that the other apostles approach more circuitously:

> In this letter, or rather tract, (for he was present with those to whom it was more immediately directed, probably being not able to preach to them any longer, because of his extreme old age) he does not treat directly of

---

[14] An anonymous Swedish visitor cited in Richard P. Heitzenrater, *The Elusive Mr. Wesley*, 2d ed. (Nashville: Abingdon, 2003), 280–81.

[15] Randy Maddox, "The Rule of Christian Faith, Practice, and Hope: John Wesley on the Bible," *Methodist Review* 3 (2011): 27. Maddox's proof is fascinating, but necessarily complex. Consulting the Scripture index of the online sermon register (http://divinity.duke.edu/initiatives-centers/cswt/research-resources/register) he summarizes, "We have records of Wesley preaching on a text from 1 John at least 503 times; since there are 105 verses in 1 John, this reflects use of the book at the rate of 4.8 times per verse. The comparative numbers for some other examples would be: Galatians (479 uses, 149 verses; 3.2 rate), Romans (924 uses, 433 verses; 2.15 rate), 1 Corinthians (835 uses, 437 verses; 1.9 rate), James (154 uses, 108 verses; 1.4 rate), Matthew (1460 uses, 1071 verses; 1.36 rate), Gospel of John (1044 uses, 879 verses; 1.18 rate)," etc.

[16] Sermon 77, "On Spiritual Worship," in *The Works of the Reverend John Wesley*, ed. John Emory, 7 vols. (New York: Emory and Waugh, 1831), 2:177.

[17] From Wesley's journal, November 9, 1772, cited in Wall, "Wesley as Biblical Interpreter," 117.

faith, which St. Paul had done; neither of inward and outward holiness, concerning which both St. Paul, St. James, and St. Peter, had spoken; but of the foundation of all,—the happy and holy communion which the faithful have with God the Father, Son, and Holy Ghost.[18]

Finally, Wesley believed that by the end of his life, the apostle John had reached a level of spiritual maturity unparalleled not only among the apostles, but perhaps also in the history of the human race. After citing a long series of "hereby we know" passages from the letter, Wesley says,

> It is highly probable, that never were any children of God from the beginning of the world unto this day, who were farther advanced in the grace of God, and the knowledge of our Lord Jesus Christ, than the apostle John at the time when he wrote these words, and the fathers in Christ to whom he wrote.[19]

Wesley's point is not that the apostle's exceptional spiritual maturity renders his words any more inerrant or infallible than any other words of Scripture; preservation from error is not what Christian perfection would accomplish anyway, according to Wesley's teaching (see chap. 8, below). In fact his point is the opposite, that even these believers so "advanced in the grace of God" had need of applying the 1 John tests (of doctrine, obedience, and love) to their own lives. But Wesley's observation does show the esteem in which he held John's authorship.

We should call one other witness to establish just how deep the influence of 1 John is on Wesleyan theology: the great nineteenth-century systematizer of Methodist theology, William Burt Pope. If it is a truism to say that John Wesley was not a systematic thinker, it is nevertheless the case that in William Burt Pope the movement produced a mind that was profoundly systematic and self-consistent. To understand the genius of Wesleyan theology, it is often most helpful to see what it developed into in Pope. In the matter of the primacy of 1 John, Pope understood well the importance of the letter to Methodist thought. In his *Compendium of Christian Theology*, Pope says that in the Bible, "the method of the Inspiring Spirit" is worth paying attention to. This method "was to complete the Christian revelation on the principle of a series of converging developments, the last

---

[18] Sermon 77, "On Spiritual Worship," 177.
[19] Sermon 10, "Witness of the Spirit," in *Wesley's 52 Standard Sermons*, ed. N. Burwash (Salem, OH: Schmul, 1988), 94.

and highest of which were committed to St. Paul and St. John."[20] In all of his theologizing, Pope attempts to name those "converging developments" and base his major doctrinal discussions around them. He has especially identified Paul's final writings and the epistles of John as the two decisive culminating points in biblical revelation. And between them, he opts for John as the last word on the last word. Doing his Wesleyan diligence and focusing on 1 John, in 1846 Pope published an English translation of Erich Haupt's German commentary on the book,[21] complete with a substantial preface.

In that preface, Pope calls 1 John "the closing doctrinal testimony of the last and greatest teacher of the Christian Church," adding further that we have in it "the final and finishing touches of the whole system of evangelical truth." Calling the letter "a general review of the whole sum of truth," he asserts that if you were to lose the whole New Testament except for one book, 1 John is the one that would give you the best chance of reconstructing the basic message of the whole apostolic witness! "It would, better than any other fragment of the New Testament, supply the place of the entire final revelation to such as might possess it alone."[22] Pope admits that 1 John is not "a general compendium of theology," since it has a scattered and episodic feel and was obviously written with the refutation of some specific errors in mind. "But we may say that it traverses, more than any other treatise, the whole field."[23]

Pope has his eye on three leading ideas in the New Testament, all indicating blessings of union with Christ: "righteousness, sonship, and sanctification." All three are consummately expressed in this epistle, with sonship receiving the highest praise. John weaves the three together inextricably:

> Let the reader begin with ch. 2:29, and go on to ch. 3:5, with this thought in his mind. He finds the three ideas of conformity to law or righteousness, perfection of the filial life in the image of the Son, and sanctification from all sin, distinct and yet blended inextricably. The order is there, righteousness, sonship, sanctification; but the three are one. The terms of the court, the household and the temple, confirm and illustrate each

---

[20] William Burt Pope, *A Compendium of Christian Theology*, 3 vols. (New York: Phillips & Hunt, 1881), 1:17.
[21] Erich Haupt, *The First Epistle of St. John: A Contribution to Biblical Theology* (Edinburgh: T&T Clark, 1879). Pope gave the same treatment to another large German commentary on 1 John, that of J. H. A. Ebrard, a translation of which he brought out in 1859.
[22] William Burt Pope, "Translator's Preface" to Haupt, *The First Epistle of St. John*, xxi.
[23] Ibid., xxxii.

other; and Jesus Christ—the Righteous, the Son of the Father, the Holy One—presides, in the glory of His holiness, over all and over each.[24]

Though he argues that John is the best guide in putting these three ideas together organically, Pope will not hear of any pitting John against the apostle Paul. The fact that John crowns the New Testament "may be perverted in its application," he warns. "It may be said that this final testimony of revelation has left behind and rendered obsolete much of St. Paul's forensic and judicial thought, and sublimated the Gospel into its higher and more simple character. But this is a mistake. This Epistle perfects all, but not by suppressing anything."[25] Here as usual Pope is a reliable guide to the innermost meaning of the theology of John Wesley, because Wesley was also eager to integrate Pauline thought into his Johannine theology.

Making Room for Paul

In fact, the formula "John plus Paul," or "John first, then Paul," may be the key to Wesley's theology. We have already seen that Protestant theologians tend to take their basic orientation from Paul, whether from the magisterial Romans or from one the "epistolary turrets" of the Reformation, Galatians and Ephesians.[26] The resulting theological emphasis is on faith, and the classic way of expressing it is with the Pauline contrasts between what believers were before and what they are after, experiencing justification and sanctification. Paul also habitually expresses his insights by moving from indicative statements ("we are accepted in the beloved") to imperative statements ("walk worthy of the calling"). But for John, the emphasis falls on love, and the classic expressions are not past versus present, or indicative followed by imperative. Rather, John describes the marks of communion, and his contrast is between light and darkness in themselves. The "theological grammar" of 1 John, as Robert Wall puts it, "differs from the Pauline witness," which guides "most Protestant communions."[27]

---

[24] Ibid., xxx–xxxi.

[25] Ibid., xxxi.

[26] See Gerald Bray, "Introduction to Galatians and Ephesians," in *The Reformation Commentary on Scripture*, vol. 10, *Galatians, Ephesians* (Downers Grove, IL: InterVarsity, 2011).

[27] Wall, "Wesley as Biblical Interpreter," 118. I have omitted Wall's reference to divergent "canons within the canon" to avoid confusion. As mentioned above, "canon within the canon" is a neutral or good term for Wall, whereas I am treating the phrase in a negative or cautionary sense.

Yet Wesley, as we will see shortly, was fully committed to Protestant theology, and he was even committed to sharply Pauline ways of talking. What he did in his theology was to start out from a base in 1 John and then make room for the works of Paul. Many Protestant theologians had moved in the opposite direction, starting out from Paul and then making room for John. A unified theology informed by all the prophets and apostles is, after all, mandatory for anyone who accepts the full canon as the Word of God. But John Wesley may be alone in having moved the opposite direction, starting out from John and then integrating Paul.

What difference did the direction make? It was revolutionary. First of all, consider how the sequence "John first, then Paul" mapped onto his own spiritual biography. Since 1725, Wesley had been committed to the "holiness of heart and life" school of Anglican spirituality that he found in authors like William Law and Jeremy Taylor. From this point on, his goal was set by the vision of holiness, obedience, and perfect love. In fact, he wore himself out and drove himself and others crazy in pursuit of this goal. When he came to Aldersgate in 1738, the voice of Luther drove the Pauline message of Romans home to him, leaving his heart "strangely warmed" with the conviction of salvation by faith alone. Paul, in other words, appeared on Wesley's horizon as the answer to the question posed by 1 John: How is it possible for sinners to live the holy life of fellowship with God, who is light?

By starting with John and then discovering Paul, Wesley relived the English Christian experience in a microcosm, experiencing his own Reformation two centuries after the fact. Just as England had been Christian before becoming Protestant, so Wesley had been committed to scriptural holiness before Aldersgate. That is why he came away from Aldersgate with a message that ignited such a fire of revival for his contemporaries. He sought holiness and found it by faith alone. He asked the Johannine question and found the Pauline answer. The resulting approach to the Christian life is what fueled the evangelical awakening and launched the Methodist movement. In an interview about the rise of Methodism, Wesley gave this telling account of the two major turning points:

> In 1729, two young men, reading the Bible, saw they could not be saved without holiness, followed after it, and incited others so to do. In 1737 they saw holiness comes by faith. They saw likewise that men are justi-

fied before they are sanctified; but still holiness was their point. God then thrust them out, utterly against their will, to raise a holy people.[28]

In the second place, the direction "John first, then Paul" helped Wesley show that faith and love are oriented to each other as a means to an end, that faith leads to love. Of course this is a lesson he could have learned directly from Paul alone, and in fact Wesley shows the relation of faith and love to each other in "The Law Established by Faith," sermon 36 in the *Standard Sermons*. The text is Romans 3:31, "Do we then make void the law through faith? God forbid: yea, we establish the law." How do believers, justified by faith, establish the law? "We establish the law," Wesley says, "when we so preach faith in Christ as not to supersede, but produce holiness; to produce all manner of holiness, negative and positive, of the heart and of the life." And that is because faith exists to serve love:

> We continually declare, (what should be frequently and deeply considered by all "who would not make void the law through faith,") that faith itself, even Christian faith, the faith of God's elect, the faith of the operation of God, still is only the handmaid of love. As glorious and honourable as it is, it is not the end of the commandment. God hath given this honour to love alone: Love is the end of all the commandments of God. Love is the end, the sole end, of every dispensation of God, from the beginning of the world to the consummation of all things.[29]

Wesley is not worried about any dangers from the genuine Pauline doctrine—he is preaching from Paul, after all. But he is worried about "those who magnify faith beyond all proportion, so as to swallow up all things else, and who so totally misapprehend the nature of it as to imagine it stands in the place of love." To them he points out that faith is temporary, but love is eternal: faith will be swallowed up in sight on the last day, but love "never faileth" (1 Cor. 13:8). Indeed, "all the glory of faith, before it is done away, arises hence, that it ministers to love: It is the great temporary means which God has ordained to promote that eternal end."[30]

Furthermore, Wesley argues, "as love will exist after faith, so it did exist long before it," because while faith is only as old as man's need to trust

[28] *Minutes of Several Conversations between The Rev. John Wesley and the Preachers in Connexion with Him* (London: Printed for George Whitefield, 1797), 9–10.
[29] Sermon 36, "The Law Established Through Faith," Burwash, 365.
[30] Ibid., 365.

the promises of God, love goes back into God's very being. "Love existed from eternity, in God, the great ocean of love." Love, therefore, is the goal which faith seeks to bring us to:

> Faith, then, was originally designed of God to re-establish the law of love. Therefore, in speaking thus, we are not undervaluing it, or robbing it of its due praise; but on the contrary showing its real worth, exalting it in its just proportion, and giving it that very place which the wisdom of God assigned it from the beginning. It is the grand means of restoring that holy love wherein man was originally created. It follows, that although faith is of no value in itself, (as neither is any other means whatsoever,) yet as it leads to that end, the establishing anew the law of love in our hearts; and as, in the present state of things, it is the only means under heaven for effecting it; it is on that account an unspeakable blessing to man, and of unspeakable value before God.[31]

The point could obviously be made, as it is here, using only Paul. Wesley's insight could be an insight into how Paul himself orders the virtues of faith, hope, and love. But Wesley experienced his Protestant breakthrough as a rediscovery of the radical message of Paul (mediated through Luther, no less) on a spiritual quest oriented toward 1 John. In Wesley's broad approach to the New Testament, Paul was the apostle of faith and John the apostle of love. This is no puppet show, but a helpfully personal way of handling vast doctrines of the New Testament. Of course John also teaches faith, and Paul also teaches love, and there is no contradiction or tension between them. It's not as if John is Catholic and Paul Protestant. But having his feet firmly planted in 1 John gave Wesley resources, and a way of thinking, that were uniquely suited to solve the problems of his own life and of his time.

Finally, the order "John first, then Paul" gave Wesley a way of ordering the doctrines that were most important to him. "Our main doctrines, which include all the rest, are three," he wrote in 1746: "that of repentance, of faith, and of holiness. The first of these we account, as it were, the porch of religion; the next, the door; the third is religion itself."[32] Again we see the ordering of means to end, expressed now in architectural metaphor.

---

[31] Ibid., 366.

[32] "Principles of a Methodist Farther Explained," section 6.4. Wesley was flexible in his terminology, but consistent in his basic approach. Elsewhere he listed his essentials as "1. original sin, 2. justification by faith alone, and 3. holiness of heart and life." Letter to George Downing, April 6, 1761, in *The Letters of John Wesley*, ed. John Telford, 8 vols. (London: Epworth, 1931), 4:146. See also the "Letter to Various Clergymen," April 19, 1764, in Telford, *Letters of John Wesley*, 4:237.

Holiness, or walking in the light in fellowship with God and Christ, is the building itself. Faith is the doorway into that building, and repentance is the porch leading to the door. First John, according to Robert Wall, "helped Wesley defend his sometimes awkward integration of his core belief about the gospel—salvation from sin by grace through faith—with its most distinctive experience—a life of practiced holiness that marks out who is 'not almost but altogether Christian.'"[33]

The preface to the *Standard Sermons* is perhaps Wesley's most insightful account of his own goals in preaching. There he says, "I have endeavored to describe the true, the scriptural, experimental religion, so as to omit nothing which is a real part thereof, and to add nothing thereto which is not."[34] He goes on to describe his two major spiritual opponents as formalism and antinomianism.

The first he saw as the major error afflicting an England that thought of itself as Christian simply because it had the outward trappings of Christianity. He preaches so as "to guard" his hearers "from formality, from mere outside religion, which has almost driven heart religion out of the world." To this end, the message of 1 John was especially suited, with its call to real fellowship with the God who is light, a fellowship marked by true belief and right actions, but also by right affections.

His second great opponent was antinomianism, especially the kind embraced by "those who know the religion of the heart, the faith which worketh by love," yet have learned the perverse habit of using gospel promises to overturn holy living. These, he said, managed to twist Paul's teaching and "make void the law through faith." Since antinomians tended to be well versed in a particular misreading of Paul, Wesley found his foundation in 1 John to be a powerful position from which to argue against them. "Wesley recognized clearly what few have before him or since: 1 John much better than Paul takes to task 'that grand pest of Christianity, a faith without works.'"[35]

"We love him, because he first loved us," says 1 John 4:19. In his *Notes on the New Testament*, Wesley calls this "the sum of all religion, the genuine model of Christianity." He goes on, "None can say more: why should anyone say less, or less intelligibly?" Randy Maddox recently argued that in calling this verse "the sum of the gospel," Wesley was pointing out

---

[33] Wall, "Wesley as Biblical Interpreter," 118.
[34] Wesley, preface to *Standard Sermons*, Burwash, xx.
[35] Wall, "Wesley as Biblical Interpreter," 119, quoting sermon 61, "The Mystery of Iniquity."

the deepest conviction that he gained in his own spiritual journey. He had always longed to love God fully, and had sought to do so with utmost seriousness. But it was only in the events surrounding 1738 that he finally and fully grasped the truth of 1 John 4:19, discovering that authentic and enduring love of God and others is a response to knowing God's pardoning love for us.[36]

And in a later controversy over his teaching on Christian perfection, Wesley would insist that what he taught was "in conformity therefore both to the doctrine of St. John, and to the whole tenor of the New Testament." Just by putting his claim in this order (John first, then "the whole tenor of the New Testament"), Wesley revealed that he "read Paul (and the rest of the Bible) through the lens of central convictions he found most clearly expressed in 1 John—not to discount Paul's message, but to highlight Paul's insistence on believers being set free from sin to be servants of righteousness (Rom. 6:18)."[37]

John versus Paul?

Wesley's fundamentally Johannine assimilation of Pauline theology was a dynamic new expression of biblical theology. Gordon Rupp is one of several scholars who have suggested that this might be the key to Wesley's impact. "For him, the Pauline doctrine of justification was closely linked with the Epistles of John and the doctrine of love. Was this perhaps the secret" of the Wesleyan revival?[38] We have seen how it recapitulates Wesley's own experience as a microcosm of the English Protestant experience and helps account for the explosive impact of his preaching after Aldersgate. Where most Protestants have spliced John into Paul, Wesley may be the only thinker to have attempted to splice a seriously Protestant reading of Paul into John. Only Wesley took an essentially Johannine stock and grafted in a vigorous Pauline branch, rather than vice versa.

But the formula "John first, then Paul" may also account for the intractable difficulties that some readers have had with Wesleyan soteriology ever since. Many people who read Wesley gradually become aware that on this issue he seems to be writing from two different frames of reference.

---

[36] Maddox, "The Rule of Christian Faith, Practice, and Hope," 28.
[37] Ibid.
[38] E. Gordon Rupp, *Principalities and Powers: Studies in the Christian Conflict in History* (London: Epworth, 1952), 82.

The frustration is typically expressed by noting the tension between, on the one hand, the obvious and insistent Protestant emphasis on justification by faith alone and, on the other hand, the pervasive suggestion that to walk out of fellowship with God in the light is to cease being a true Christian. The former suggests that everything has been settled; the latter suggests that something very important is still to be determined by our conduct. How can the two ideas go together?

Let us attempt to catch Wesley at his weakest in order to see the clearest contrast. In the 1760s, Wesley worked hard to sharpen his focus on the doctrine of justification. In an important tract and in at least one major sermon (number 20 in the *Standard Sermons*, to be discussed in chap. 5, below), he made his commitment to justification by faith crystal clear. He quoted Calvin on the subject with warm agreement and declared in a letter, "I think on justification just as Mr. Calvin does. In this respect I do not differ from him an hair's breadth."[39] But in the Methodist Conference of 1770, Wesley also agreed with the following resolution:

> Does not talking of a justified or a sanctified *state* tend to mislead men? Almost naturally leading them to trust in what was done in one moment? Whereas we are every hour and every moment pleasing or displeasing to God, "according to our works"; according to the whole of our inward tempers, and our outward behaviour.[40]

Taken by themselves, these words could indeed suggest a denial that there is any such thing as justification by faith, or that any Christian is in a state of having "been justified" (Rom. 5:1, ESV). The formula "we are . . . every moment pleasing or displeasing to God . . . according to . . . our inward tempers, and our outward behaviour" sounds like God accepts us on the basis of who we are and what we do. What could this mean but acceptance by works, or at least the maintenance of justification by works? And indeed the controversial 1770 minutes were taken by many to mean this. Especially among the Calvinistic evangelicals who had been growing less comfortable with Wesley, the words were treated as an alarm bell showing

---

[39] Letter to "a friend," May 14, 1765, in Telford, *Letters of John Wesley*, 4:298.
[40] These words are from the *Conference Minutes* of 1770; reprinted in *The Works of John Wesley* (London: Wesleyan-Methodist Bookroom, 1829–1831), 8:338. The most thorough discussion of this whole affair is in Allen Coppedge, *John Wesley in Theological Debate* (Wilmore, KY: Wesley Heritage, 1987), 191–265. For a briefer survey from a Reformed perspective, see Iain Murray, *Wesley and Men Who Followed* (Edinburgh: Banner of Truth, 2003), 217–31.

that Wesley had utterly repudiated justification by faith, or perhaps had never really believed it. One historian summarized the reaction:

> He was accused of denying the faith, of having apostatized, and become a work-monger—little better than an infidel. All this proceeded upon the assumption that, by making Christian obedience the condition of our continued acceptance before God, he was wickedly renouncing the grand Pauline and Lutheran doctrine of Justification by Faith alone.[41]

But taken in context of Wesley's life work from 1738 down to 1770, these disturbing words must surely have meant something else. What is their target? Though the words are poorly chosen, they are evidently intended as a criticism of the sort of spiritual life that is lived in perpetual retrospective, the sort that is always looking back to a moment of conversion and basing its confidence on what was felt and experienced at that time. If a person says, "I am in a justified state" or "I am in a sanctified state," and then offers as evidence only a story of what happened at the moment of conversion, he or she is in great danger of living in spiritual unreality. Such a person needs to shift attention from "what was done in a moment" to what is being done here and now. If this point is framed carefully, it is unobjectionable. Consider the way J. I. Packer says the same thing: "Only a life of present convertedness can justify confidence that a person was converted at some point in his or her past. . . . The only proof of past conversion is present convertedness."[42] Packer is probably a safe teacher of justification by faith.

In Wesley's context, the past event that nominal Christians would look back on as the anchor of their conversion was baptism, and infant baptism at that. Though Wesley as an Anglican believed in infant baptism, Wesley as an *evangelical* Anglican knew that it was not the same thing as salvation. When assaulting this stronghold, Wesley would use the strongest language:

> Say not then in your heart, "I *was once* baptized, therefore I *am now* a child of God." Alas, that consequence will by no means hold. How many are the baptized gluttons and drunkards, the baptized liars and common swearers, the baptized railers and evil-speakers, the baptized whoremongers,

---

[41] John Brown, *John Wesley's Theology: The Principle of Its Vitality, and Its Progressive Stages of Development* (London: Jackson, Walford, and Hodder, 1865), 24.

[42] J. I. Packer, *Keep in Step with the Spirit: Finding Fullness in Our Walk with God*, rev. ed. (Grand Rapids: Baker, 2005), 59–61.

thieves, extortioners? What think you? Are these now the children of God? Verily, I say unto you, unto whom any of the preceding characters belongs, "Ye are of your father the devil, and the works of your father ye do." . . . Lean no more on the staff of that broken reed, that ye *were* born again in baptism. Who denies that ye were then made children of God, and heirs of the kingdom of heaven? But notwithstanding this, ye are now children of the devil. Therefore ye must be born again.[43]

Remember that Wesley's two greatest opponents were formalism and antinomianism. A person who looked back to infant baptism as the evidence of his regeneration could be a potent mixture of both: Christian because he was English, he could do as he pleased and count on God's grace. This was the perfect target for Wesley's preaching. By 1770 he must have been applying his skills to a wider target, which perhaps had come to include also some adult converts who looked back to their conversion experiences in a way that paralleled the hapless appeal, "I was once baptized."

Wesley's target in the minutes of 1770 was the problem of people whose once-upon-a-time conversions were the prime evidence that they were Christians; but his mistake was to overanalyze the problem, thinking that people were misled by the very language of "a justified state." He thought this was what "almost naturally" led them "to trust in what was done in one moment." Surely he was right to warn people away from the tendency to rest our assurance of salvation on a particular experience in our past biography. But rejecting the language of "a justified state" is too drastic. He should have found a way to divert their attention from their conversion stories to the finished work of Christ, which does, after all, produce a justified state in believers. In the face of the inevitable controversy over his ill-chosen words, Wesley issued the following clarification the next year:

Whereas the doctrinal points in the Minutes of a Conference held in London, 7 August 1770, have been understood to favour justification by works, now we, the Rev. John Wesley, and others assembled in Conference, do declare that we had no such meaning, and that we abhor the doctrine of justification by works as a most perilous and abominable doctrine. . . . And though no one is a real Christian believer (and consequently cannot be saved) who doth not good works when there is time

---

[43] Sermon 18, "Marks of the New Birth," Burwash, 180.

and opportunity, yet our works have no part in meriting or purchasing our justification, from first to last, either in whole or in part.[44]

This clarification served to reassure most people, though some of Wesley's harsher critics (such as Augustus Toplady) continued to suspect him of being inadequately Protestant, and even to charge him with denying justification by faith.

But consider what happens when we apply the "John first, then Paul" framework to this famous controversy. Wesley was obviously provoked by a misreading of Paul's theology on this occasion. The kind of person who looks back to a conversion experience and claims on that basis alone to be in a state of justification or sanctification is misconstruing what Paul teaches about the great change that we experience when we trust Christ. There are grounds in Paul's own thought to refute them and to show that authentic faith is "faith working through love" (Gal. 5:6, ESV). In fact, that kind of Pauline argument is what Wesley wisely resorted to in his 1771 clarification. But that was not his first instinct. Faced with distorted Pauline teaching, Wesley punched back with an attempt to jar his opponents into thinking in Johannine terms: Are you walking in the light now, do you have communion with God now, do you have joy and confidence in God now? Instead of retracing the steps of the order of salvation (a Paul thing to do), Wesley's first instinct was to test the reality of the claims by appealing to the marks of the true Christian (a John thing to do). What Wesley cared about was spiritual reality and communion with God, and he preferred to safeguard it with the theology of 1 John. No wonder the layers of confusion began building up when other evangelicals began counterquestioning him with Pauline categories. Fortunately, though Wesley's native tongue was John, he was also fluent in Paul.

This has been a long and involved case study in the slippage between Johannine and Pauline frameworks, but it is worthwhile not only because the minutes controversy was an important turning point in evangelical history, but also because the principles involved are applicable to a great many other instances. One briefer case study may help cement the lesson. There were a couple of books that John Wesley had greatly admired since becoming serious about Christianity in 1725, books that typified for him

---

[44] Quoted in Iain Murray, *Wesley and Men Who Followed*, 222. Murray's treatment of Wesley in the entire chapter on justification (217–31) is a shining example of fair reporting and charitable interpretation even in the face of serious disagreements.

the school of Anglican thought most comfortable with a Johannine theology of holiness. The books were Bishop Jeremy Taylor's (1613–1667) famous *Holy Living* (1650) and *Holy Dying* (1651).

As Wesley came to understand after his discovery of Paul, Taylor's books need to be handled with care. *Holy Dying* has plenty of gospel in it, but like all of Taylor's writing, it specializes in applying the strictness of the law to the conduct of the Christian. It even features an extended application of the Ten Commandments to the scene of the deathbed, inviting dying people to consider carefully how they have kept the commandments. John Wesley said he knew a woman who

> would advise no one very young to read Dr. Taylor on Holy Living and Dying. She added, that he almost put her out of her senses when she was fifteen or sixteen year old; because he seemed to exclude all from being in a way of salvation who did not come up to his rules, some of which are altogether impracticable.[45]

One particular sentence of Taylor's drove Wesley himself to distraction. In *Holy Living*, Taylor wrote, "The true penitent must all the days of his life pray for pardon and never think the work completed till he dies. Whether God has forgiven us or no we know not, therefore still be sorrowful for ever having sinned."[46] Wesley agreed that a Christian should humbly ask for pardon on a daily basis, but recoiled vehemently against the idea that we cannot know "whether God has forgiven us or no." Even in the period between 1725 and 1738, Wesley knew something was wrong with this. He and his mother corresponded about the problems in Taylor's theology. But after Aldersgate, after taking Romans and Galatians on board his 1 John project, Wesley had the tools he needed to tame an Anglican holiness tradition that had been in constant danger of legalism and moralism.

A Protestant Doctrine of Holiness

As a theological thinker, John Wesley combined things that do not seem to belong together. One way interpreters have expressed this is by saying that Wesley seems to have combined a classically Protestant insistence

---

[45] Letter to his mother, January 18, 1725, in Emory, *The Works of the Reverend John Wesley*, 6:589.
[46] "The Rule and Exercise of Holy Living," in *The Whole Works of the Right Rev. Jeremy Taylor* (London: Frederick Westley and A. H. Davis, 1835), 495. Wesley's interaction with the quotation can be found in Tyerman, *The Life and Times of the Rev. John Wesley*, 1:34–35.

on justification by faith (wherein he professed to differ from Calvin not "an hair's breadth"), with an emphasis on a non-forensic holiness of heart and life ("without which no one shall see the Lord"—Heb. 12:14, ESV) that strikes many interpreters as either unintentionally Roman Catholic or (for the conspiracy-minded) sneakily crypto-Catholic. In sweeping summaries of Wesley's contribution, it was for some time commonplace to say that there was "a Protestant Wesley" and "a Catholic Wesley," or that Wesley combined the best of both worlds. George Croft Cell's influential 1935 book *The Rediscovery of John Wesley* put it this way: "The Wesleyan reconstruction of the Christian ethic of life is an original and unique synthesis of the Protestant ethic of grace with the Catholic ethic of holiness."[47] Statements like this are still easy to find, and it is equally easy to see what they are gesturing toward: Wesley teaches justification by faith, and he also teaches that the pursuit of holiness really matters. "Indeed," says Kenneth Collins, "the intricate theological synthesis that Wesley painstakingly crafted held together the grand project of much of his theological career, namely, the task of articulating 'faith alone' and 'holy living.'"[48]

But why call this combination Protestant and Catholic respectively? Gordon Rupp called the cliché into question some time ago: "The statement that Methodism combines a Protestant doctrine of Justification with a Catholic doctrine of holiness is one that is so much over-simplified as to be dangerously misleading, and I would not accept it without grave qualification." What Rupp wisely goes on to suggest in its place is what we have already explored in some detail: "But we might suggest that Wesley combines in a marvelous way the Pauline and Johannine elements in the Christian testimony when, within the safe orbit of sovereign grace and pardoning love, he insists on the power and good pleasure of the Father to fulfil in us his perfect will."[49] Once again, coming to understand Wesley as the theologian of 1 John enables us to get our bearings. As Rupp argues elsewhere,

---

[47] Cell, quoted in Kenneth Collins, *The Theology of John Wesley: Holy Love and the Shape of Grace* (Nashville: Abingdon, 2007), 16. Collins does not fully endorse Cell's judgment, and goes on to provide one of the most balanced discussions of this subject. He does, however, juxtapose the two themes: "A nearly exclusive Protestant reading of Wesley's theology would be no more accurate than a Catholic one. Rather it is the conjunction, the tension, of both a Protestant and Catholic reading that is most descriptive of his theology" (see *The Theology of John Wesley*, 334).

[48] Ibid., 4.

[49] Gordon Rupp, "The Future of the Methodist Tradition," *The London Quarterly and Holborn Review* 184 (1959): 269.

it is worth questioning the motives and interests of those who resort to the Protestant-Catholic distinction in describing Wesley:

> The Methodist gospel has a shape and a coherence. Evangelical Armin-ianism stood for a certain combination of Christian truths as expounded by John and Charles Wesley in their sermons and their hymns. It has sometimes been explained by saying that John Wesley combined the Prot-estant teaching of justification by faith with the Catholic conception of holiness. I do not find this an enlightening statement at all. In England it is almost always made by people slightly ashamed of their Protestantism, and I do not think it bears close inspection. John Wesley perhaps was not a subtle theologian, but he was not a muddleheaded one. What he had to say about holiness was bound together with what he believed about justification by faith: it was not an afterthought, but the original starting point of his search for Christian perfection.[50]

The main problem with describing Wesley's theology as a mix of Prot-estant and Roman Catholic themes is that Wesley did not describe it that way. It is a description that can help some hearers grasp the basic drift of Wesley's thought: "Imagine Wesley as a real Protestant who refuses to let go of what's good in the Roman Catholic doctrine of salvation." But the kind of person who would find that description most helpful is either someone "slightly ashamed of [his] Protestantism," as Rupp says, or at best someone for whom the word "Catholic" suggests the great tradition, an expansive sort of original Christianity that has flowed down through the ages. The word *catholic* with a small *c* might have suggested that for Wesley, but when combined with *Roman* it made Wesley think the opposite. For Wesley—a convinced Anglican who had read the classic Anglican sources of the Ref-ormation—the term *Roman Catholic* suggested something limited, sectar-ian, recent in vintage, and abusive of power. Protestant, on the other hand, meant for him a restoration of the great ancient church's doctrine of salva-tion and holiness.

Though it is far better to picture Wesley as intentionally combining Johannine and Pauline themes of Scripture, there is yet one grain of truth in picturing him as straddling Protestant and Catholic traditions. He did find himself drawing from Protestant and Roman Catholic books increas-

---

[50] Rupp, *Principalities and Powers*, 82. This is the passage where Rupp goes on immediately to make the observation with which we started this chapter: "For him the Pauline doctrine of justification was closely linked with the Epistles of John and the doctrine of love. Was this perhaps the secret?"

ingly as he elaborated his "John first, then Paul" perspective. At one point in a sermon about the rise of Methodism he says:

> Many who have spoken and written admirably well concerning justifica-
> tion, had no clear conception, nay, were totally ignorant, of the doctrine
> of sanctification. Who has wrote more ably than Martin Luther on jus-
> tification by faith alone? And who was more ignorant of the doctrine of
> sanctification, or more confused in his conceptions of it? In order to be
> thoroughly convinced of this, of his total ignorance with regard to sancti-
> fication, there needs no more than to read over, without prejudice, his cel-
> ebrated comment on the Epistle to the Galatians. On the other hand, how
> many writers of the Romish Church (as Francis Sales and Juan de Cas-
> taniza, in particular) have wrote strongly and scripturally on sanctifica-
> tion, who, nevertheless, were entirely unacquainted with the nature of
> justification! Insomuch that the whole body of their Divines at the Coun-
> cil of Trent, in their *Catechismus ad Parochos*, (the catechism which every
> parish Priest is to teach his people) totally confound sanctification and
> justification together. But it has pleased God to give the Methodists a full
> and clear knowledge of each, and the wide difference between them.[51]

He goes on to say that it is "a great blessing given to this people," the Methodists, "that as they do not think or speak of justification so as to supersede sanctification, so neither do they think or speak of sanctification so
as to supersede justification." The Methodists following Wesley have drawn
from both streams of teaching, and above all what they have learned is how
to combine them fruitfully:

> They take care to keep each in its own place, laying equal stress on one
> and the other. They know God has joined these together, and it is not
> for man to put them asunder: Therefore they maintain, with equal zeal
> and diligence, the doctrine of free, full, present justification, on the one
> hand, and of entire sanctification both of heart and life, on the other;
> being as tenacious of inward holiness as any Mystic, and of outward, as
> any Pharisee.[52]

But priority, for Wesley, goes to the Protestant side, for only on that
side is there any possibility of distinguishing justification from sanctifi-

---

[51] Sermon 107, "On God's Vineyard"; reprinted in *John Wesley*, ed. Albert Outler (New York: Oxford University Press, 1964), 107–8.
[52] Ibid., 109.

cation so as to combine them in one unified quest for holiness by faith. The whole point, for Wesley, was to push the Protestant church of England to see that salvation by faith entailed, demanded, required, the holiness without which no man shall see the Lord. Evangelical Protestantism didn't need to go out and find a theologically alien influence in order to pursue holiness. It could cultivate its own resources in cultivating holiness.

This understanding of John and Paul finally brings us back around to the spiritual jolt that Martin Luther provided for John Wesley. It was a public reading of Luther's *Preface to Romans* that shocked Wesley to life. Specifically, it was Luther's description of "the change which God works in the heart through faith in Christ." Not just any listener would have picked out that thread of Luther's argument. Other ears might have registered Luther's description of the law as a death-dealing enemy to be overcome; out of context, plenty of Luther's contrasts between grace and law can sound antinomian. But Wesley was already well on his way to making room for Paul in his theology of 1 John, and he already knew what he was listening for. Characteristically, Wesley's heart was not warmed by the element of Lutheran teaching that sounds nearly antinomian. Though it may sound paradoxical to anyone who has an oversimplified Luther and a cartoony Wesley in their minds, Wesley is one of the great interpreters of Luther. For Luther had much to say about the personal holiness that necessarily followed on the imputed righteousness of Christ,[53] and was not interested in presenting justification as some sort of forensic declaration that left the sinner unchanged. "To anyone who has had a whiff of Luther's writings," wrote G. C. Berkouwer, "this conception is incredible. Even a scanty initiation is enough to be convinced that justification for Luther meant much more than an external event with no importance for the inner man."[54] Wesley heard what Luther said: "It is impossible to separate works from faith, as impossible as to separate heat and light from fire."[55]

Thus it was a Lutheran historian (H. J. Holmquist) who once, somewhat quirkily, described Methodism as "the Anglican translation of the Evangelical-Lutheran doctrine of salvation," in a line quoted by Method-

---

[53] See for example the important early sermon from 1519, "Two Kinds of Righteousness," in *Martin Luther's Basic Theological Writings*, 2nd ed., ed. Timothy F. Lull (Minneapolis: Fortress, 2005), 134–40.
[54] G. C. Berkouwer, *Studies in Dogmatics: Faith and Sanctification*, quoted in Michael Horton, *The Christian Faith* (Grand Rapids: Zondervan, 2011), 648. This is the first page of Horton's twentieth chapter, "The Way Forward in Grace: Sanctification and Perseverance." Horton's treatment of the relationship between justification and sanctification is excellent, even Wesleyan in spite of itself.
[55] Quoted in Philip S. Watson, *The Message of the Wesleys: A Reader of Instruction and Devotion* (Grand Rapids: Francis Asbury, 1984), 9.

ist theologian Philip S. Watson at the beginning of a book about Luther.[56] Certainly the Lutheran fingerprints are all over the Wesley story: John's arguments with Spangenberg in Georgia, his help from Boehler in Oxford, Luther on Romans at Aldersgate in May 1738, John's translations of the Moravian Lutheran hymns, his use of *Gnomon* by the Lutheran Pietist Bengel for his *Notes on the New Testament*, and so on. Furthermore, "anyone who is but familiar with Charles Wesley's hymns has already a fair acquaintance with Luther's theology, albeit in its Anglican translation." There are of course plenty of differences between Luther and Wesley on salvation and the Christian life. "Yet deeper than all the differences," says Watson,

> is the essential spirit, in which the Wesleys are more nearly akin to Luther than to any other great exponent of the Christian faith and life. There is an extraordinary similarity between the spiritual evolution of the sixteenth-century monk into the Reformer and that of the eighteenth-century Oxford Anglicans into leaders of the Evangelical Revival; and the Revival itself is aptly named, for it was fundamentally a renewal and extension of the work of Luther's Reformation.[57]

Wesley would no doubt add that his goal was not to be Lutheran, but to be biblical (though that is itself a rather Lutheran point to make). He was attempting to take the basic point of view given to him by 1 John, and fill it out with the categories of Paul the apostle. The result was a dynamic tension between the claims of perfect justification by faith (the Paul moment) and the quest for holiness that would result in fellowship with God and Christ in the light (the John moment).

---

[56] Philip S. Watson, *Let God Be God: An Interpretation of the Theology of Martin Luther* (Philadelphia: Muhlenberg, 1950), 3.
[57] Ibid.

CHAPTER 5

THE LORD OUR RIGHTEOUSNESS

Wesley agreed wholeheartedly with the eleventh of the Thirty-Nine Articles, which affirms: "We are accounted righteous before God, only for the merit of our Lord and Saviour Jesus Christ by Faith, and not for our own works or deservings. Wherefore, that we are justified by Faith only, is a most wholesome Doctrine, and very full of comfort." He may have been confused about justification before 1738, but once he came to understand it, he clung to it tenaciously and taught it gladly. Much of what Wesley taught on the doctrine of justification throughout his life was plain old Protestant Christianity, taught with passion and precision. But he also came to approach the doctrine in a unique way, one that complemented his emphasis on the heart renewed in love. Above all, he was determined to make sure the doctrine was guarded against antinomian misunderstanding. He wanted to make sure the doctrine remained not only "very full of comfort" in assuring believers that God had accepted them in Christ, but also "most wholesome" in catalyzing fuller fellowship with God, underwriting holiness as well as trust in God's promises.

The Place to Start

When Wesley edited and appointed the *Standard Sermons* as the doctrinal norm for his followers, he guaranteed that the doctrine of justification by faith would always have pride of place in Methodist thought. Sermons 5 and 6, both on justification, have a prominent place near the beginning of the collection. In sermon 5, "Justification by Faith," Wesley starts the presentation on justification by tracing the thought all the way back in God's purposes in creation: "In the image of God man was made, holy as he that created him is holy; merciful as the Author of all is merciful; perfect as his Father in heaven is perfect."[1] Man's original goal was this kind of moral perfection, and since the fall, God has necessarily provided a new way to reach that goal. The only way forward for the fallen is free justification, which, as we have already seen,

> is not the being made actually just and righteous. This is sanctification; which is, indeed, in some degree the immediate fruit of justification; but nevertheless, is a distinct gift of God, and of a totally different nature. The one implies, what God "does for us" through his Son; the other, what he "works in us" by his Spirit.[2]

But while justification is a forensic act that involves God's accounting us righteous on the merits of another, it does not imply "that God is deceived in those whom he justifies." God is well aware that sinners are sinners; in fact, "the plain scriptural notion of justification is pardon, the forgiveness of sins." And God does not clean up sinners before forgiving them, but forgives them as they are: "For it is not a saint but a sinner that is forgiven, and under the notion of a sinner. God justifieth not the godly, but the ungodly."[3] No sanctification precedes justification, and the sinner brings nothing to the bargaining table. "Whatever good he hath or doth from that hour, when he first believes in God through Christ, faith does not find, but bring. This is the fruit of faith. First the tree is good, and then the fruit is good also."[4] Beneath this sovereign mercy of God, all we can do is receive and be grateful. "It does not become poor, guilty, sinful worms, who receive whatsoever blessings they enjoy (from the least drop of water that cools our tongue, to the immense riches of glory in eternity,) of grace, of mere favour, and not of debt, to ask of God the reasons of his conduct."[5]

Wesley's preaching on justification is among his most immediate and most powerful. Justification is not just another doctrine for him, but the

---

[1] Sermon 5, "Justification by Faith," in *Wesley's 52 Standard Sermons*, ed. N. Burwash (Salem, OH: Schmul, 1988), 43.

[2] Ibid., 45.

[3] Ibid., 46.

[4] Ibid., 48.

[5] Ibid., 49.

word of salvation, the very thing that must be presented to his audience. He seems aware that this message of justification is the word that can spark immediate response, and he preaches it with fervor that speaks to us across the generations. Here is how he concludes his greatest sermon on justification:

> Thou ungodly one, who hearest or readest these words, thou vile, helpless, miserable sinner, I charge thee before God, the Judge of all, go straight unto him, with all thy ungodliness. Take heed thou destroy not thy own soul by pleading thy righteousness more or less. Go as altogether ungodly, guilty, lost, destroyed, deserving and dropping into hell; and thou shalt then find favour in his sight, and know that he justifieth the ungodly. As such thou shalt be brought unto the blood of sprinkling, as an undone, helpless, damned sinner. Thus look unto Jesus! There is the Lamb of God, who taketh away thy sins! Plead thou no works, no righteousness of thine own! No humility, contrition, sincerity! In no wise. That were, in very deed, to deny the Lord that bought thee. No; plead thou, singly, the blood of the covenant, the ransom paid for thy proud, stubborn, sinful soul. Who art thou, that now seest and feelest both thine inward and outward ungodliness? Thou art the man! I want thee for my Lord! I challenge thee for a child of God by faith! The Lord hath need of thee. Thou who feelest thou art just fit for hell, art just fit to advance his glory; the glory of his free grace, justifying the ungodly and him that worketh not. Oh come quickly! Believe in the Lord Jesus; and thou, even thou, art reconciled to God.[6]

The law says, "Do this and live," but the message of the gospel is based on a better covenant, and says, "Believe and live, and thou shalt be saved; now saved, both from the guilt and power of sin, and, of consequence, from the wages of it."[7] Some will not pay heed to this call; they "vehemently refuse to submit themselves unto the righteousness of God." But this is "the folly of trusting in the righteousness of the law," and stands in opposition to "the wisdom of submitting to that which is of faith." To stand before God, a perfect righteousness is needed, and that means we must have the righteousness of another, of "the Lord our righteousness." "Thou art sin! God is love! Thou by sin art fallen short of the glory of God; yet there is mercy with him. Bring then all thy sins to the pardoning God, and they shall vanish away as a cloud."[8]

---

[6] Ibid., 50.
[7] Sermon 6, "The Righteousness of Faith," Burwash, 52–53.
[8] Ibid., 56.

Wesley's teaching on justification, in other words, was a matter of great and passionate emphasis. It was an electrifying doctrine for him, never one to be taken for granted. But Wesley's teaching on justification underwent one significant shift during his lifetime, a shift brought about when he came into conflict with a Calvinistic Methodist named James Hervey. The issue was the imputation of Christ's active obedience, and the net result of the conflict was that Wesley came to affirm this doctrine more clearly and more precisely than he had before. The story is somewhat complex, but deserves close study because it marks a turning point in John Wesley's teaching about the Christian life. The most important publication that came from the conflict was Wesley's sermon "The Lord Our Righteousness," enshrined as number 20 in the *Standard Sermons*. Some scholars recognize the publication of this sermon as a shift from "the early Wesley" to "the later Wesley."[9] To understand what happened, we will have to meet James Hervey and understand what was at stake for him.

James Hervey's *Theron and Aspasio*

James Hervey (1714–1758) was one of Wesley's collaborators since the days of the early Oxford Methodists, that small group of earnest young men who worked with both John and Charles Wesley in the Holy Club before the evangelical revival broke out. Hervey was ordained in 1737, served as curate for several years, and then settled as the rector of Weston-Favell in Northamptonshire. He labored under weak health all his life and suffered from symptoms that would normally have been treated with opium during the eighteenth century (still a time of medicinal bloodletting as well). Since the drug did not agree with him, Hervey lived with the considerable pain for most of his adult life and died on Christmas day, 1758, at the age of forty-four.

Hervey's most popular works were a series of pious meditations on the natural world. His books, with titles like *Meditations among the Tombs*, *Reflections on a Flower Garden*, *A Descant upon Creation*, and *Contemplations of the Starry Heavens*, went through many editions and sold thousands of copies.[10] They are characterized by effusive appreciation of natural beauty

---

[9] Kenneth Collins reports this as Albert Outler's view. See Collins, "Wesley's Life and Ministry," in *The Cambridge Companion to John Wesley*, ed. Randy L. Maddox and Jason E. Vickers (Cambridge: Cambridge University Press, 2010), 54.

[10] Flora McLaughlin Kearney, *James Hervey and Eighteenth-Century Taste* (Muncie, IN: Ball State University, 1969).

and the intricacy of creation, they make minute use of scientific observations just being published by contemporary writers, and they are didactic to the core.

In 1755 Hervey published his longest work and his masterpiece, *Theron and Aspasio; or, A Series of Dialogues and Letters on the Most Important Subjects.*[11] The book is written in the form of a dialogue between two friends. In the eighteenth century, the dialogue format was a conventional genre that authors used to make their messages more enjoyable. Generally in these dialogues, one particular character more or less speaks for the author. The other characters serve as foils, cautionary examples, straw men, or representative presences of readers who are destined to become converted to the author/spokesman's point of view. Among the other conventions understood to be part of the eighteenth-century dialogue genre are the dignified air of the leisurely conversation partners and their cultured surroundings. Both of these conventions are heightened by the author's setting the dialogue on a country estate with neoclassical features and giving the participants names that conjure Greek antiquity. In Hervey's book, the Greek names of the title characters are significant: Theron means "hunter," and Aspasio means "welcome."

The narrative thread of *Theron and Aspasio* is minimal: two friends have a series of long conversations, broken in the middle by an interval of separation during which they exchange letters (which allow them to state their points of view in a more extended fashion). The setting is Aspasio's country estate with an art gallery, gardens, and library, and the surrounding countryside. The plot revolves around whether Theron will find what he is seeking and be converted to Aspasio's view of salvation by the imputation of Christ's righteousness. Theron is a wealthy, educated man who (far from self-consciously "hunting" for something) is satisfied in his own abilities and his scientific understanding of the world. Aspasio is a scholarly Christian who, though not ordained, plays a priestly role among his circle of friends. The general pattern of exposition that Hervey follows is to begin a chapter with observations and descriptions of some neutral subject matter such as science, anatomy, gardening, or painting. These subjects are then moralized and become the subject of edifying discourse, to the mutual satisfaction of all hearers. Then Aspasio turns the conversation to

---

[11] *Theron and Aspasio* was originally published in three volumes. I will be using the edition printed in *The Whole Works of the Rev. James Hervey* (Edinburgh: Peter Brown and Thomas Nelson, 1834), 141–621.

explicitly theological themes, usually the righteousness of Christ or a related subject. Thus emerges what is obviously the main theme of the book:
the imputed righteousness of Christ.

Hervey has already announced in the preface that although he will
treat subjects such as the beauty of Scripture, the fall of humanity, and the
atonement, his main goal is to "vindicate, illustrate, and apply" the doctrine of Christ's imputed righteousness, "an article which, though eminent
for its importance, seems to be little understood, and less regarded; if not
much mistaken and almost forgotten."[12] This main subject arises when
Aspasio, spontaneously praising God for the beauties of creation, makes
a sudden transition to thanking God for imputing the righteousness of
Christ to those who believe. Theron chides him, asking for a retraction of
this "puritanical nostrum." On his way to defending the doctrine, Aspasio
discovers that Theron is in the bad habit of using arguments that he has
picked up from skeptics, liberals, and Socinians. Thus much of the book is
devoted to convincing Theron of basic Christian doctrines under attack by
eighteenth-century freethinkers.

Theron, it turns out, is quite the rationalist under the thin veneer of the
Christian gentleman, and has to be talked into a belief in atonement first of
all, which he finds repugnant to reason. After that, he makes it clear that to
the modern mind, any vicarious or substitutionary or imputational ideas
are unacceptable. Then, finally, he sketches his plan of salvation, which
consists mainly in a kind of softened legalism that has learned nothing
from the New Testament except that rational people can count on God to
be reasonable in his demands. Theron will do his best, with sincerity, and
the God who published the gospel will surely cut him whatever slack is
necessary in the standards of the law. Aspasio remarks that he would find
this plan of salvation eminently reasonable if he had never read the Bible.
He goes on to say, "If the light of nature was to publish a gospel, I believe it
would be formed upon your plan."[13]

Aspasio's main concern is classically Protestant: Theron's scheme is
yet another instance of salvation by works, and the problem with all such
schemes is that they "invert the order of the gospel." Practical godliness
and holy living can never be the foundation of a right relation with God,
but only a more or less satisfactory edifice built upon the only possible

---

[12] Hervey, *Theron and Aspasio*, 141.
[13] Ibid., 219.

foundation, Christ.[14] Aspasio talks Theron out of his confidence in salvation by sincere obedience and hope in God's clemency, mainly by comparing the divine law to a pack of hunting dogs that chase a wild stag through the woods until it collapses dead from exhaustion and harassment. "Thus the strictness of the law pursues the soul."[15] When this task is discharged, Aspasio can turn to his, and Hervey's, favorite subject: the imputation of the active obedience of Christ.

"Justification," says Aspasio, "is an act of God Almighty's grace; whereby he acquits his people from guilt, and accounts them righteous, for the sake of Christ's righteousness, which was wrought out for them, and is imputed to them." "By Christ's righteousness," he goes on, "I understand the whole of his active and passive obedience; springing from the perfect holiness of his heart, continued through the whole progress of his life, and extending to the very last pang of his death."[16]

"The punishment which we deserved, he endures: The obedience which we owed, he fulfils." Having established this parallelism between our sins going to Christ and his righteousness coming to us, Hervey rings the double chime again and again, formulating over and over sentences that combine the obedient life and the atoning death: "The doctrine of a Redeemer obeying and dying in our stead, is the very hinge and center of all evangelical revelations, is the very life and soul of all evangelical blessings."[17] Christ lived our life and died our death, obeyed for us and paid for us, earned our title to heaven and blocked our road to hell, started our new life of obedience and finished our old life of disobedience, satisfied the preceptive and the punitive demands of the law.

As the parallels mount and the life of Christ emerges as a theme equal with his death, Theron voices an objection: Does not the Scripture ascribe the whole of our salvation to the death of Christ? Aspasio replies: "This part of our Lord's meritorious humiliation is, by a very usual figure, put for the whole. The death of Christ includes, not only his sufferings, but his obedience. The shedding of his precious blood was at once the grand instance of his suffering, and the finishing act of his obedience."[18] Theron goes on to object that the twofold imputation seems to be redundant, and he accuses Aspasio of inventing a distinction without a difference. Saying

---

[14] Ibid., 230.
[15] Ibid., 249.
[16] Ibid., 158.
[17] Ibid., 198.
[18] Ibid., 254.

that we need our unrighteousness removed and righteousness restored is to multiply expressions about the same thing. Theron points out that this is like saying that crookedness may be removed from an object, yet the object is not straight until straightness is added to it. "No, Theron," replies Aspasio. "According to my account, it is impossible that the active and passive obedience of our Redeemer should be disjoined. . . . As Christ in suffering obeyed, and in obeying, suffered, so, whoever receives Christ as an atonement, receives him also as a righteousness."[19]

Theron is eventually persuaded that he stands in need of a better righteousness than his own, and he has only one final major question before adopting Aspasio's view. Will this doctrine deliver holy living? Will the claims of morality be answered? Early on, he had objected, "The followers of your opinion, I have observed, are perpetually dwelling upon this one favourite topic, to the exclusion of that grand and truly essential part of Christianity—sanctification."[20] Aspasio warms to his subject: "When this faith is wrought in your heart, nothing will be so powerful to produce holy love, and willing obedience, to exalt your desires and enable you to overcome the world."[21]

Marshall's *Gospel Mystery of Sanctification*

In the preface to *Theron and Aspasio*, Hervey, speaking in his own voice, had entertained the idea that he should have written a book railing against vices or exhorting to morality. But he reminds his readers that "morality never makes such vigorous shoots, never produces such generous fruit, as when ingrafted on evangelical principles."[22] In one of his countless flower metaphors, Hervey says that books of exhortation and moral instruction are like a bouquet gathered from a garden, whereas his goal is to plant the whole flower garden and provide a constant supply of life and beauty.

This declaration of intent, and Hervey's claim to be undertaking his work with a view toward making holy living possible, reveals his indebtedness to a seventeenth-century work by Walter Marshall (1628–1680) entitled *The Gospel Mystery of Sanctification Opened: In Sundry Practical Directions, Suited Especially to the Case of Those Who Labor under the Guilt and Power of Indwelling Sin*. This may be the greatest book on sanctification ever

---

[19] Ibid.
[20] Ibid., 159.
[21] Ibid., 316.
[22] Ibid., 143.

written, though it is little read today. It is claimed alike by the Reformed, by holiness traditions and Keswick teachers, and even by a few Wesleyans (though Wesley himself did not like it much). The argument of Marshall's *Gospel Mystery* is that the way to keep the law is to go to the gospel. Marshall takes an interesting position: he begins by heightening our awareness of the absolute demand to keep the law, the whole law, and to keep it spiritually as well as externally. He then demonstrates the impossibility of doing this without availing ourselves of the means that God has provided to enable us to keep the law. Finally, he names that means: justification by faith, as the Holy Spirit unites us to Christ and his benefits.

Marshall admits that half his book sounds legalistic while the other half sounds antinomian, but he hopes that the resulting tension will help his readers learn that Christians work *from* life, not *for* life. We do not have to do guesswork or elaborate historical reconstruction to link Hervey to Marshall: *The Gospel Mystery of Sanctification* was Hervey's favorite book, and he never tired of recommending it. He bought copies and gave them away, he oversaw the republication of it with an enthusiastic introduction by himself, and in general he talked it about it so often that it became a sort of joke among his friends. "In spite of the sarcastical reflections you say are thrown upon me, I must recommend to every one *Marshall on Sanctification*, and Jenks' *Submission to the Righteousness of God*. These are with me the two fundamental books; these teach vital religion."[23]

We could say that Hervey's goal as a theological writer, especially in *Theron and Aspasio*, was to make Marshall readable and get his vision of the Christian life before the public eye again. And the main thing in Marshall is that Christians work from life, not for life. Hervey advanced this argument in his own way, especially availing himself of the more scholastic teaching about the imputation of Christ's active obedience, which he drew from other sources than Marshall (perhaps Owen or Witsius). Had he lived longer, Hervey would have written a sequel to *Theron and Aspasio*, devoted to sanctification, with deathbed scenes of the Christian (Aspasio) that would have given Jeremy Taylor's *Holy Dying* a run for its money. Hervey insisted in *Theron and Aspasio* that "sanctification is equally necessary, both to our present peace and to our final felicity."[24] Had he lived beyond age forty-four, he would have expanded on this.

---

[23] Ibid., 921.
[24] Ibid., 160.

Wesley versus Hervey

Theron and Aspasio was very popular with a large general public, and it caused some theological controversy. It was attacked by anonymous critics, by the Scottish Congregationalist Robert Sandeman, and most famously by John Wesley. At the time of his death, Hervey was preparing a polemical response to Wesley's attack. The fragment of this response was published posthumously, against Hervey's request. Wesley and Hervey had been friends since their Oxford days, when Wesley tutored Hervey in Hebrew. Hervey was passionately committed to the evangelical awakening and is rightly numbered among the Oxford Methodists who launched the movement. He and Wesley trusted each other and cooperated in any work they could. Wesley sent a draft of his *Notes on the New Testament* to Hervey, asking for his comments, which Hervey provided. And Hervey sent a draft of *Theron and Aspasio* to Wesley, seeking improvements. Wesley responded with a few minor notes and suggestions. But Hervey was not satisfied, and he earnestly asked Wesley to tell him what he really thought.

So Wesley sent a more severe critique, and, as it turned out, he had been restraining himself from voicing some real doctrinal and exegetical disagreements: In a 1756 letter to Hervey, Wesley genuinely praised the book, sometimes lavishly, for its many merits. But he begged Hervey to reconsider a couple of points: "do not dispute for that particular phrase, 'the imputed righteousness of Christ.' It is not scriptural; it is not necessary . . . it has done immense hurt."[25] He goes on to pick his way through each chapter, interacting with objectionable passages. In dialogue 2, Aspasio says: "To ascribe pardon to Christ's passive, eternal life to his active, righteousness, is fanciful rather than judicious. His universal obedience from his birth to his death is the one foundation of my hope." Wesley comments: "This is unquestionably right. But if it be, there is no manner of need to make the imputation of his active righteousness a separate and laboured head of discourse. O that you had been content with this plain scriptural account, and spared some of the dialogues and letters that follow!"[26] In other words, Wesley is troubled in part by Hervey's emphasis on imputed righteousness, but also in part by the very act of making the distinction between passive and active righteousness.

Another line of argument Wesley advances is that Hervey's distinc-

---

[25] Reprinted in "Preface to a Treatise on Justification," in *Works*, 10:318.
[26] Ibid., 318.

tion between active and passive obedience distracts our attention from the place where the New Testament would have it focused: the cross. In dialogue 13, Aspasio says, "'The obedience of one' is Christ's actual performance of the whole law." Wesley comments: "So here his passion is fairly left out!"[27] When Aspasio says, "My faith fixes on both the meritorious life and atoning death of Christ," Wesley replies, "Here we clearly agree. Hold then to this, and never talk of the former without the latter."[28] In the tenth letter, Aspasio praises "Those treasures which spring from the imputation of Christ's righteousness," and Wesley interjects,

> Not a word of his atoning blood! Why do so many men love to speak of his righteousness, rather than his atonement? I fear, because it affords a fairer excuse for their own unrighteousness. To cut off this, is it not better to mention both together? At least, never to name the former without the latter?[29]

Another objection Wesley raises is that Hervey is claiming as central to the gospel a doctrinal distinction that most people have never thought of, a construction that most Protestants have done perfectly well without. Aspasio says, "Faith is a persuasion that Christ has shed his blood for me, and fulfilled all righteousness in my stead." Wesley responds, "I can by no means subscribe to this definition! There are hundreds, yea, thousands of true believers, who never once thought one way or the other of Christ's fulfilling all righteousness in their stead."[30] If this doctrine is central, if it is part of the very definition of saving faith, why is it so little known? Hervey could of course respond that he was doing everything in his power to ensure that it is published as widely as possible. But Wesley's question is more rhetorical, his point being that this doctrine should not in fact be considered central to the gospel or part of the definition of saving faith.

We have already observed Wesley's most passionate objection to the doctrine: that it leads to antinomianism. When Aspasio says that "the righ-

---

[27] Ibid., 331.
[28] Ibid.
[29] Ibid., 332.
[30] Ibid., 333. These are perennial charges. Mark R. Talbot's blurb advertising John Piper's fine book *Counted Righteous in Christ: Should We Abandon the Imputation of Christ's Righteousness?* (Wheaton, IL: Crossway, 2002) is enlightening in regard to the vitality and also the sense of novelty raised by the doctrine: "Although I have been a Christian for a long time, I became aware of the doctrine of the imputation of Christ's active righteousness only fairly recently. Yet in the years since I have become aware of the 'Blessed Exchange'—my sin for Christ's righteousness—I doubt that a day has gone by without my feasting on this core truth of biblical faith."

teousness which justifies us, is already wrought out," Wesley explodes: "A crude unscriptural expression!" "'The goodness of God leadeth to repentance.' This is unquestionably true. But the nice, metaphysical doctrine of imputed righteousness, leads not to repentance, but to licentiousness."[31] He goes on:

> This is the grand, palpable objection to that whole scheme. It directly makes void the law. It makes thousands content to live and die transgressors of the law, because Christ fulfilled it for them. Therefore, though I believe he hath lived and died for me, yet I would speak very tenderly and sparingly of the former, and never separately from the latter, even as sparing as do the Scriptures, for fear of this dreadful consequence.[32]

In his response, Hervey is nonplussed. To begin with, Wesley at the end of his letter crossed a line of civility by alleging that it was Hervey's Calvinism that had got the best of him. But Hervey, while admittedly Reformed and one who routinely fed his soul on the most Calvinistic of the Puritan devotional writings, was actually rather soft on the most difficult Calvinist doctrines. For instance, when Wesley published a pamphlet against predestination, Hervey wrote to a mutual friend in 1752 that he had not even read it, since it was devoted to controversy, and specifically to Calvinist controversy.

> I can't say, I am fond of that controversy. The doctrine of the perseverance of Christ's servants, Christ's children, Christ's spouse, and Christ's members, I am thoroughly persuaded of. Predestination and reprobation I think of with fear and trembling. And, if I should attempt to study them, I would study them on my knees.[33]

Hervey, in other words, was a lover rather than a fighter.

> I would beg leave to decline all controversy. I can very freely converse or correspond with persons who either adopt or discard Predestination; provided, they will not drag in the litigated proposition, and force me to engage in disputation. . . . I readily confess, that I am not master of the subject.[34]

---

[31] Quoted in Hervey, *Theron and Aspasio*, 473.
[32] Ibid., 478.
[33] Quoted in Luke Tyerman, *The Oxford Methodists: Memoirs of the Rev. Messrs. Clayton, Ingham, Gambold, Hervey, and Broughton* (New York: Harper & Brothers, 1873), 270.
[34] Ibid., 306.

He seems to have adopted a strategy of refusing to be aggressively Calvinistic. He wanted to be Anglican, and he believed the Thirty-Nine Articles to be sufficiently Reformed for the taste of any churchman. Thus when Wesley, because of other pressures, emerged as rather aggressively anti-Calvinistic, Hervey could not help but see it as a case of Wesley agitating for his favorite doctrinal scheme in a way that compromised pan-evangelical unity in the midst of the revival.

Second, Hervey actually seems to have believed that the doctrine of imputed active obedience was the common property of all Protestants, and not just of the Calvinists. He had some good reason for thinking that Wesley, at least, had affirmed it all along. He quotes to John the words of a Charles Wesley hymn:

> Join earth and heaven to bless
> The Lord our righteousness.
> The mystery of redemption this.
> This the Saviour's strange design;
> Man's offence was counted his,
> Ours his righteousness divine.
>
> In him complete we shine,
> His death, his life is mine.
> Fully am I justified;
> Free from sin, and more than free;
> Guiltless, since for me he died,
> Righteous, since he lived for me.

It may seem like fighting dirty to throw Charles's hymns in John's face, but it was actually a strategy that might have borne fruit eventually. If anybody could make the exchange of imputation seem less dry and more a matter apprehended by the heart and by vital Christian experience, it would be Charles Wesley. Tragically, communication between Hervey and Wesley broke down shortly after this volley, for a number of reasons. William Cudworth, an avowed and bitter foe of Wesley, caught Hervey's ear and seems to have agitated against Wesley. Earlier commentators have noted the sad spectacle of two servants of God, committed to a common work, falling out so completely just before the death of Hervey ended all hope of reconciliation on earth.

The Lord Our Righteousness

But in 1765, ten years after the publication of *Theron and Aspasio* and seven years after Hervey's death, Wesley preached a remarkable sermon entitled "The Lord Our Righteousness." It is number 20 in the *Standard Sermons*, indicating that it has a strategic place in the structure of Wesley's overall gospel message. In this sermon, Wesley clearly has as one of his concerns to make peace across the divides that had formed in the work that grew out of the awakening. He begins the sermon with general reflections on the disaster of allowing disagreements to lead to fighting and divisions in the church. He then turns to his subject, the way in which Christ can be said to be our righteousness.

Wesley begins his answer by arguing that Christ lived a perfect life, and that this righteousness consists especially in obedience: "In the whole course of his life he did the will of God on earth . . . all he acted and spoke was exactly right in every circumstance. The whole and every part of his obedience was complete. He fulfilled all righteousness."[35] Wesley then goes on to make the distinction between active and passive obedience: "His obedience . . . implied not only doing, but suffering; suffering the whole will of God, from the time he came into the world, till 'he bore our sins in his own body upon the tree.'" No sooner does Wesley distinguish them than he unites them: "But as the active and passive righteousness of Christ were never in fact separated from each other, so we never need separate them at all, either in speaking or even in thinking. And it is with regard to both these conjointly that Jesus is called 'The Lord our righteousness.'"[36] This exact move, distinguishing active and passive obedience in order to unite them, is surely something Wesley learned from Hervey, though it is not altogether clear whether Wesley believed that he had learned it by example or by cautionary tale.

At any rate, we have Christ's righteousness clearly defined, and in the next movement of the sermon we find it imputed by faith. Given Wesley's previous admonitions to Hervey, this affirmation raises several questions, which Wesley answers explicitly: To whom is it imputed? "To all believers the righteousness of Christ is imputed; to unbelievers it is not." When is it imputed to them? When they believe. "There is no true faith, that is, justifying faith, which hath not the righteousness of Christ for its object." Well, then, who denies this doctrine? Not I, answers Wesley, but only "in-

---

[35] Sermon 20, "The Lord Our Righteousness," Burwash, 194.
[36] Ibid.

fidels, baptized or unbaptized."[37] And who would those be, those baptized infidels who deny salvation by the imputation of Christ's righteousness? The list is short:

1. All who deny the Godhead of our Lord (since denying Christ's deity would entail that he had to earn salvation for himself first);
2. Roman Catholics, insofar as they follow their church's official teaching;
3. Those Protestants who are mystics, like William Law, or Quaker Robert Barclay who dares to say "Imputed righteousness! Imputed nonsense!"
4. Most members of the church of England, plus a large number of Anabaptists, Presbyterians and Independents who have recently been reading dangerous books like Jeremy Taylor's *Aphorisms on Justification.*[38]

This is the old feisty Wesley, on the warpath and naming names of those who are beyond the pale. But by now he has decided that his true opponents are all those who have gone soft on the doctrine of justification, and he seems to have decided that imputed righteousness, twofold obedience and all, is a solid safeguard. "Blessed be God, we are not among those who are so dark in their conceptions and expressions."[39] The imputation of the active obedience of Christ has become part of Wesley's armament for defending his core doctrine of justification by faith.

On the other hand, Wesley continues to urge restraint when it comes to making these terms mandatory, and in arguing for this restraint, he cites James Hervey himself:

> I cannot express this better than in Mr. Hervey's words, worthy to be wrote in letters of gold. "We are not solicitous as to any particular set of phrases. Only let men be humbled as repenting criminals at Christ's feet, let them rely as devoted pensioners on his merits, and they are undoubtedly in the way to a blessed immortality."[40]

"Who denies this?" exclaims Wesley. "Do not we all meet on this ground? What then shall we wrangle about? A man of peace here [Hervey] proposes terms of accommodation to all the contending parties. We desire no better: we accept of the terms; we subscribe to them with heart and hand."

What became of Wesley's primary practical concern over this concep-

---

[37] Ibid.
[38] Ibid., 198.
[39] Ibid.
[40] Ibid.

tion, the fear that it would lead to antinomianism? Only at the end of the sermon, after he has settled all the accounts, does he mention the danger of abusing this doctrine: he warns his hearers to beware of those who use the phrase to cover personal unrighteousness, an abuse that he believes happens far too often. A Christian drunkard, when reproached, may reply, "I pretend to no righteousness of my own; Christ is my righteousness."[41] Wesley's old foe, that "grand pest of Christianity," antinomianism, comes in for direct attack here. "Thus, though a man be as far from the practice as from the tempers of a Christian; though he neither has the mind which was in Christ, nor in any respect walks as he walked; yet he has armour of proof against all conviction, in what he calls the righteousness of Christ."[42]

Wesley is acutely conscious of having gone a great distance to meet his opponents, so in closing, he asks them to return the favor. He allows the phrase to be used now, and only asks that he in turn be allowed *not* to use it, or at least not often.

> Be not angry with me if I cannot judge it proper to use any one express every two minutes. You may, if you please; but do not condemn me because I do not. Do not, for this, represent me as a Papist, or "an enemy to the righteousness of Christ." . . . Do not make tragical outcries, as though I were "subverting the very foundations of Christianity."[43]

Wesley concludes with the appeal for unity in the essential points of the Protestant doctrine of justification by faith: "As we have 'One Lord, one faith, one hope of our calling,' let us all strengthen each other's hands in God, and with one heart and one mouth declare to all mankind, The Lord Our Righteousness."[44]

We could read this sermon as a disingenuous attempt to say the right words in order to end evangelical in-fighting and solidify a coalition. But that would be overly suspicious, and the fact that Wesley included the sermon among the *Standard Sermons* argues for a higher view. He intended "The Lord Our Righteousness" to guide Wesleyan doctrine from that point on. It is far better to take the public, published sermon as normative and then to look back on Wesley's letter to Hervey as a minor objection, however strongly stated. Indeed, Wesley had initially written his objections, and subsequently

---

[41] Ibid., 199.
[42] Ibid.
[43] Ibid., 200.
[44] Ibid.

published them, in order "to preserve those to whom I had frequently and strongly recommended Mr. Hervey's *Dialogues*, from what I disapproved of therein. . . . I wished to preserve from everything wrong, while they profited by what was admirably right, in his Dialogues." Therefore he recommends that his remarks should be read as emendations rather than condemnations, which explains why they "have rather the air of a caveat than a confutation."[45] This could have been interpreted to mean that Wesley agreed with everything in *Theron and Aspasio* except for the teaching on the imputation of Christ's active obedience. However, in light of the strong statements in "The Lord Our Righteousness," it seems preferable to see his earlier remarks to Hervey as minor objections to the tone and phraseology, or to the frequency of repetition of the terms, but not a rejection of the doctrine itself.

Consider the situation: Hervey was so drawn to the formula "imputed righteousness" that he made it the centerpiece and main focus of his book and of his spiritual program. Perhaps Hervey could be charged with using the phrase "every two minutes" and persuading others to do likewise. Wesley was disappointed by this, not because he did not believe in the doctrine or understand its value in defending the critical Protestant doctrine of justification, but because he saw this as a squandered opportunity to publish simple gospel teaching to the large audience that read the popular *Theron and Aspasio*. His objections still stand: the language is not scriptural, it is not necessary, and it has done immense harm. But Wesley never said it was untrue.

Wesley on Justification and Imputation

James Hervey was a minor figure within a major movement. He played his limited role ably and humbly, but is now largely forgotten and is hardly ever read. John Wesley was a titan and a one-man social force in his own lifetime, who belongs on the short list of major figures in the history of the Christian church. Nevertheless, when these two came into conflict, Hervey won. John Wesley altered the way he taught one of his leading doctrines.

Before his collision with Hervey, Wesley was standoffish about the doctrine of imputation. He had an undeveloped intuition, a sneaking suspicion, that the doctrine was useful to antinomians as a way of shielding themselves from the demands of the law of Christ. In Hervey he met an evangelical brother who was so passionate about the doctrine of imputa-

---

[45] "Preface to a Treatise on Justification," 336.

tion that Wesley could no longer leave it unexamined. When he looked closely at the doctrine, he eventually came to see that it was something he could affirm. In fact, he found the doctrine of imputation to be a way of saying what he had always said about justification by faith, but saying it more elaborately and, if possible, even more sharply. As Kenneth Collins argues, for Wesley "imputation is a testament to the sheer grace and utter favor of God in forgiving sinners."[46]

Wesley finally became comfortable in using the doctrine as Hervey had done, to underline the fact that nothing in the life of the sinner could provide grounds for acceptance with God. After a bit of a false start, Wesley took up Hervey's challenge to think through the doctrine of imputation more thoroughly. Having done so, Wesley was back in business doing what he did best: distinguishing God's work *for* us (justification, now elaborated as the imputation of Christ's obedience) from God's work *in* us (sanctification), and insisting that these distinct things belong together. All the well-practiced Wesley tricks can come back into play now: "He breaks the power of cancelled sin"—that is, God freely cancels the guilt of sin by justification, and at the same moment begins to push back the power of that cancelled sin through regeneration and sanctification.

Perhaps only someone like James Hervey could have convinced Wesley that he could embrace imputation and still oppose antinomianism. Hervey had credibility in this regard. Wesley and Hervey already trusted each other quite a bit because of their work together in the Oxford Methodist group. And Hervey is a classic example of a Calvinist who did not give up on the call to holy living. For someone who started out with the revival movement before it split into Calvinistic and Wesleyan streams, it would have been easy to let the Arminian Methodists sweep the field and corner the market on themes of sanctification. Hervey did not do so. He devoted himself to winning a hearing for Walter Marshall's *Gospel Mystery of Sanctification*, and stands as an important witness to a variety of Reformed spirituality that does not lag behind the Wesleyans one bit in terms of its commitment to evangelical holiness. In fact, Hervey delivers a minor jab at anybody who backs down from affirming the imputation of Christ's righteousness:

> As for making holiness go slack, Do they who deny faith, and extol their good works, distinguish them by the practice of them? I will be bold to

---

[46] Kenneth Collins, *The Theology of John Wesley: Holy Love and the Shape of Grace* (Nashville: Abingdon, 2007), 175.

say, that, on an impartial examination, the majority will be found on the side of those who embrace the doctrine of the imputation of Christ's righteousness, and who expect salvation by him alone.[47]

Hervey obviously has much in common with the kind of holiness tradition that makes a strategic commitment that it is better to run the risk of antinomianism than the risk of legalism. That tradition proceeds in the confidence that the life of a Christian will bear more fruit if we are unquestionably rooted in justification by faith and hold resolutely to the insight that Christians do not work *for* life, but *from* life. Yet he is vigilant against "making holiness go slack," even to the point of being willing to engage in a friendly competition to see which tradition has produced more saints ("the majority will be found on the side of those who embrace the doctrine of the imputation of Christ's righteousness").

Kenneth Collins has referred to Wesley's "fencing of the doctrine of imputation to keep it from flowing into the doctrine of sanctification."[48] He also points out that the fence Wesley constructed enabled him to distinguish Christ's alien righteousness (imputed to us all at once) from our inherent righteousness (worked in us by the Spirit over time). The fence that kept imputed righteousness from obliterating the need for sanctification also kept inherent righteousness from playing any role in justification. Wesley affirmed that believers walk increasingly in an inherent righteousness, but "in its proper place; not as the ground of our acceptance with God, but as the fruit of it; not in the place of imputed righteousness, but as consequent upon it." And he goes on to underline the dual act of God that constitutes full salvation: "That is, I believe God implants righteousness in every one to whom he has imputed it."[49] Elsewhere he distinguished between the two somewhat differently, with eschatology in mind: "The righteousness of Christ is necessary to entitle us to heaven, personal holiness to qualify us for it. Without the former we could have no claim to glory; without the latter we could have not fitness for it."[50] Thus the result of Wesley's deep pondering of the doctrine of imputation is that he was able to present justification by faith, in the terms of the Thirty-Nine Articles, as "a most wholesome Doctrine," as well as one "very full of comfort."

[47] Hervey, *Whole Works of the Rev. James Hervey*, xiii.
[48] Collins, *The Theology of John Wesley*, 175.
[49] Sermon 20, "The Lord Our Righteousness," Burwash, 197.
[50] Sermon 123, "On the Wedding Garment," quoted in John T. Waaddy, "Wesley as an Aphorist," in *Wesley Studies* (London: Charles Kelly, 1903), 205.

CHAPTER 6

GRACE FIRST, THEN LAW

Even if all you read from Wesley's *Standard Sermons* is the table of contents, you can see the basic shape of the Christian life. There are two major blocks of material in the *Sermons*, just as there are two major factors in the Christian life. The collection begins with a loud and clear trumpet blast of free grace. Wesley starts with the epochal sermon 1, "Salvation by Faith," and continues through "The Almost Christian," "Awake, Thou That Sleepest," and "Scriptural Christianity," and then on to the great trilogy of salvation sermons (5–7): "Justification by Faith," "The Righteousness of Faith," and "The Way to the Kingdom." Wesley could not be more emphatic: he begins with the gospel of grace, the atonement, faith, justification, and free forgiveness.

But around the middle of the collection, Wesley turns a corner and (just after sermon 20, "The Lord Our Righteousness") launches into an exposition of the sermons about the law, in the form of a commentary on Matthew 5–7. This series of discourses "upon our Lord's Sermon on the Mount" extends from *Standard Sermons* 21 to 33. It is by far the longest series of sermons in the collection. It is followed by a few other sermons on the law, such as the programmatic sermon 34, "The Original, Nature, Properties, and Use of the Law," and the two-part "The Law Established through Faith" (35 and 36). Taken together, this is a block of sermons devoted to the law that is the equally imposing counterpart to the opening sermons on grace. "One way and another," comments Rupp, "within this definition, one-third of the standard sermons of John Wesley are concerned with the preaching of the law to believers."[1]

The Law to Believers

"The law to believers." First they must be believers; they must believe in salvation by grace. Then they begin hearing and applying the law to their lives. This is the inescapable order of Wesleyan spirituality. Some theologians talk as if grace and law are mutually contradictory and can never mix. Law may come first to condemn and drive you to Christ, but it has no place in the Christian life itself according to such theologians. In contrast, Wesley insisted on preaching the law to Christians because the law is God's means of crafting a holy people. But Wesley knew the perils of the law as well as any Lutheran ever did. He was well aware that the preaching of the law brings with it certain dangers: legalism, condemnation, and pharisaic judgmentalism. So he placed his preaching of the law in the context of free grace. Grace first, then law. The result of this combination, in this order, is the dynamo that drives Wesleyan spirituality.

When Wesley gave close attention to describing the law, he tended to describe it in terms so exalted as to be shocking. Consider, for instance, the passage in "The Original, Nature, Properties, and Use of the Law." There Wesley says things about God's law that we might normally think of reserving for Jesus Christ himself:

> Now this law is an incorruptible picture of the high and holy One that inhabiteth eternity. It is he whom, in his essence, no man hath seen or can see, made visible to men and angels. It is the face of God unveiled; God manifested to his creatures as they are able to bear it; manifested to give, and not to destroy life,—that they may see God and live. It is the heart of God disclosed to man.[2]

In fact, Wesley does not hide from the christological echoes in his language about the law. He goes on, "Yea, in some sense, we may apply to this law, what the apostle says of his Son, it is *apaugasma tes doxes, kai character tes hupostaseos autou,*—the streaming forth (or out-beaming) of his glory,

---

[1] E. Gordon Rupp, *Principalities and Powers: Studies in the Christian Conflict in History* (London: Epworth, 1952), 84.
[2] Sermon 34, "The Original, Nature, Properties, and Use of the Law," in *Wesley's 52 Standard Sermons*, ed. N. Burwash (Salem, OH: Schmul, 1988), 345.

the express image of his person."[3] Wesley is serious about this. He has not accidentally promoted the law to being the second person of the Trinity. The law is not the Son, nor vice versa. But insofar as the law is an expression of God's will, it must be thought of as part of God's essential Word, and must be considered in its necessary and vital connection to his Son. The law is not an external work that God undertakes, but is an expression of who he is, of his own moral character. It reveals more about God's character than creation itself does; it is more inherent to God than creation is. This high view of the law is not a doctrine unique to Wesley; it could be illustrated from numerous Protestant theologians before him, especially in the Puritan stream. Ernest Kevan has gathered a few of the testimonies:

> The evidence for this high view of the Law is abundant in the Puritan writings. The moral Law in man is a copy of the Divine nature, and what God wills in the moral Law is so "consonant to that eternall justice and goodness in himself," that any supposed abrogation of that Law would mean that God would "deny his own justice and goodnesse." "To find fault with the Law, were to find fault with God," for "the original draft is in God himself." It is "the express idea, or representation of God's own image, even a beam of his own holiness."[4]

This high view of the law continued to be the common property of many of the evangelicals after Wesley, including those who were not especially influenced by him. Charles Simeon (1759–1836), for example, said that God's law "is as immutable as he himself is: it is a perfect transcript of his mind and will."[5] This is the kind of thing theologians are driven to say when they think about the nature of God's law in its broadest sense.

Wesley also follows a major Protestant tradition of recognizing three uses of the law. First, the law convicts the entire world of sin and provides a basis for civil society; second, it brings people to recognize their need for Christ ("It drives us by force, rather than draws us by love"); and third, it serves believers "to keep us alive," or guide us in how to live a Christian life that pleases God.[6] This third use of the law is not an afterthought, but is in

---

[3] Ibid.; see Heb. 1:3.

[4] Ernest F. Kevan, *The Grace of Law: A Study in Puritan Theology* (Grand Rapids: Baker, 1965), 63, with footnotes there pointing to Anthony Burgess, Ralph Venning, and Thomas Manton. See also J. I. Packer's claim that "Jesus Christ himself is, so to speak, the law incarnate and is also the Christian's Lawgiver." *Keep in Step with the Spirit: Finding Fullness in Our Walk with God*, rev. ed. (Grand Rapids: Baker, 2005), 135.

[5] Simeon, *Horae Homileticae*, vol. 17 (London: Holdsworth and Ball, 1833), 99. This is Simeon's sermon on Gal. 3:19, "Wherefore then serveth the law?"

[6] Sermon 34, "The Original, Nature, Properties, and Use of the Law," Burwash, 348–51.

fact the most important use of the law. Though it comes third chronologi-
cally, it is primary in the sense that it comes first in God's intention. What
God really wants is to be the God of a holy people. So when Wesley preached
the law, he certainly presented it as a sharp demand that would drive its
hearers to Christ (think of the pack of hounds in Hervey's *Theron and Aspasio*). But his overwhelming concern was with the third use of the law,
the main use: to preach it as the guideline for the Christian life. "I cannot
spare the law one moment, no more than I can spare Christ," he declared.

> I now want it as much, to keep me to Christ, as I ever wanted it to bring
> me to him. Otherwise, this "evil heart of unbelief" would immediately
> "depart from the living God." Indeed each is continually sending me to
> the other—the law to Christ, and Christ to the law. On the one hand, the
> height and depth of the law constrain me to fly to the love of God in Christ;
> on the other, the love of God in Christ endears the law to me "above gold
> or precious stones"; seeing I know every part of it is a gracious promise,
> which my Lord will fulfil in its season.[7]

The more you love Jesus, the more you will love the law of God, according to
Wesley. This stance marks Wesley as the kind of Protestant who is, to coin
a term, *nomophilic*: law loving. He sees the law not as an obstacle to grace,
but as an image of the very righteousness that grace is intended to bring us
into. "His concern was to uphold the truth that where the work of salvation
is real there will always be the ethical, moral dimension."[8]

For Wesley, the priority of grace over law is crucially important. It is
built into every sermon; in fact, it is built into the structure of the *Standard Sermons*. You can also find the same point, and the same order, put
into seven words by Charles Wesley, in the hymn that comes first in any
decent Methodist Hymn Book, "O For a Thousand Tongues to Sing." There
he says of Christ, "He breaks the power of cancelled sin." Note again the
order: first the sin is cancelled, then its power is broken. God's order is
to justify the sinner freely and then go on to liberate the forgiven sinner
from the power of sin. If we reversed the order, God would first break the
power of sin in our lives, and only then cancel its guilt. But that would be
a scheme of self-salvation, even if it were grace-empowered self-salvation.
The Wesleys would have recognized it as a Roman Catholic ordering. Their

---

[7] Ibid., 350.
[8] Iain H. Murray, *Wesley and Men Who Followed* (Edinburgh: Banner of Truth), 66.

whole evangelical breakthrough was to understand that God forgives and then empowers. We may even say that God forgives specifically so that he can go on to empower; that he cancels sin so that he can go on to break its power; that he says to the soul, "Be of good cheer, thy sins are forgiven: So forgiven, that they shall no more rule over thee."[9]

Wesley and Nomophilic Protestantism

Nomophilic Protestantism is not a negligible or marginal tradition. Lovers of the law are everywhere among the evangelicals; they are arguably the mainstream of Protestant evangelicalism. The classic book on the subject is Kevan's work *The Grace of Law: A Study in Puritan Theology*, in which "it is shown that Puritanism stands for a view of Christian liberty which is consistent with the continued right of God to command the believer."[10] There have been dissenting voices, of course. Some evangelicals have preferred to talk about the Christian walk as a way of life that, while not quite lawless, is somehow lived above the law, or at least without reference to the law. These teachers would insist that a heart that has been renewed in love will naturally break forth in spontaneous obedience to God, with no need of law. J. I. Packer argues against that point of view, claiming instead that the law is a necessary part of the Christian life. "Holiness means law keeping as one's way of love." Packer says, "The Wesleyan voiced this most vigorously," but Packer's point is that it is a doctrine much broader than Wesleyanism. "No evangelical Christian can ever have been wholly unaware that the heart of holiness is love." But then he puts the crucial question: "How then is love to God and men to find expression?" and he gives the answer that the nomophilic stream of evangelical Protestantism is united in giving:

> The answer is by keeping God's commands and holding to his revealed ideals for human life—in other words, by keeping his law, as interpreted for Christians in the New Testament. Law keeping out of love is the true path of holiness. . . . But this is something biblical Christians have not always managed to grasp well. There have always been those on the one hand who have claimed that if the Spirit indwells you and the motive of love is strong within you, you do not need to study God's law in Scripture

---

[9] Sermon 1, "Salvation by Faith," Burwash, 9.
[10] Kevan, *The Grace of Law*, 44.

in order to learn his will, for you will always be made immediately aware in every situation what it is that he wants.[11]

It's one thing to say that we should love God and our neighbor. It's another thing to have a concrete and specific answer about how that love is to be shown. As Packer summarizes, "The way to show that you love God and men is to keep God's law."[12]

To reject the law of God outright is to be antinomian, and we know that antinomianism is the great disease ("that grand pest") Wesley was set to confront in the Christian church. Evangelicals who stand outside the nomophilic tradition are not always antinomians; perhaps a better word for them would be *nomophobic*. They prefer to say that the law may chase an unbeliever across the border of conversion to Christ, but that it has no rights inside the territory of the gospel. As nomophiles are quick to point out, the only way to maintain this position is to ignore the fact that the New Testament contains so many commands, directions, and principles of conduct. These legal ways of speaking are on the same pages as the clearest gospel statements. Bishop J. C. Ryle made this point strikingly:

> I would say it with all reverence, but say it I must, I sometimes fear if Christ were on earth now, there are not a few who would think His preaching legal, and if Paul were writing his Epistles, there are those who would think he had better not write the latter part of most of them as he did. But let us remember that the Lord Jesus did speak the sermon on the mount, and that the Epistle to the Ephesians contains six chapters and not four. I grieve to feel obliged to speak in this way, but I am sure there is a cause.[13]

There are many reasons to love God's law. Wesley (as we will see further below) saw the closest possible relationship between gospel and law, and loved the law for the gospel's sake. This was his fundamental orientation, and it explains in part the vehemence of his reaction against antinomianism. Having established justification by faith, fenced and guarded it with the necessary distinctions (between justification and sanctification), and elaborated it in detail (extending it to the imputation of the active obedience of Christ to the believer), Wesley was confident that he held the theological high ground on this doctrine. As a result, he pushed back

---

[11] Packer, *Keep in Step with the Spirit*, 135.
[12] Ibid., 135.
[13] J. C. Ryle, *Holiness: Its Nature, Hindrances, Difficulties, and Roots* (Darlington: Evangelical Press, 1979), 46.

hard against anyone who drew the false, antinomian conclusion from the doctrine.

When he argued that Christians should obey the law, Wesley knew that antinomians would object, "But are we not justified by faith, without the works of the law?" Certainly, he replied, "without the works either of the ceremonial or the moral law. . . . This is the cornerstone of the whole Christian building." But the right conclusion to draw from justification by faith is that wherever genuine faith is, a desire to obey God's law will also be. Faith works by love, and love takes the shape marked out by the law. Wesley connects the dots:

> We are, doubtless, justified by faith. This is the corner-stone of the whole Christian building. We are justified without the works of the law, as any previous condition of justification; but they are an immediate fruit of that faith whereby we are justified. So that if good works do not follow our faith, even all inward and outward holiness, it is plain our faith is nothing worth; we are yet in our sins. Therefore, that we are justified by faith, even by our faith without works, is no ground for making void the law through faith; or for imagining that faith is a dispensation from any kind or degree of holiness.[14]

He puts works in their place, completely locked out of justification, but constitutive of the response that the justified will make to grace.

As a result, Wesley preached the law to gatherings of believers, and he trained his followers to do likewise ("I advise every preacher continually to preach the Law"[15]), applying commands and warnings as directly as possible to the congregation as an instrument of sanctification. He was always on guard against a certain kind of evangelical preacher who never preached anything but free forgiveness, and who never brought the word of the law to his hearers. Such preachers boasted that they were the true "gospel preachers" preaching "gospel sermons," but Wesley warned that if the gospel were being presented in abstraction from the law, it was losing its true character. When preachers with no love for the law prided themselves on being more gospel-centered than others, Wesley complained that "the term [*gospel*] has become a mere cant word. I wish none of our Society would use it. It has no determinate meaning." He feared that key words

---

[14] Sermon 35, "The Law Established by Faith," Burwash, 359.
[15] Quoted in John Brown, *John Wesley's Theology: The Principle of Its Vitality, and Its Progressive Stages of Development* (London: Jackson, Walford, and Hodder, 1865), 47.

like *gospel* and *grace* were being used as a cover for antinomianism or as a place to hide from the bracing wind of spiritual reality. "Let but a pert, self-sufficient animal, that has neither sense nor grace, bawl out something about Christ and his blood or justification by faith, and his hearers cry out, 'What a fine gospel sermon!'"[16]

Preaching the gospel without the law, Wesley believed, had disastrous effects on the hearers. He compared it to eating a steady diet of sweets and traced the effect it would have on the spiritual digestive system.

> The gospel preachers, so called, corrupt their hearers; they vitiate their taste, so that they cannot relish sound doctrine; and spoil their appetite, so that they cannot turn it into nourishment; they as it were, feed them with sweetmeats, till the genuine wine of the kingdom seems quite insipid to them. They give them cordial upon cordial, make them all life and spirit for the present; but meantime, their appetite is destroyed, so that they can neither retain nor digest the pure milk of the word. Hence it is, that . . . preachers of this kind (though quite the contrary appears at first) spread death, not life, among their hearers.[17]

By contrast, Wesley advised believers to seek out serious preaching of the law. "Love the strictest preaching best, that which most searches the heart, and shows you wherein you are unlike Christ."[18] And he took for his role model in this regard the preaching of Jesus Christ.

Our Lord's Sermon on the Mount

The series of sermons dedicated to expounding Jesus's Sermon on the Mount (Matthew 5–7) is the longest series of continuous discourses in the *Standard Sermons*. We can now see some of Wesley's reasoning behind devoting so much space to these three chapters of Matthew. Wesley wants to provide an example of the kind of searching, penetrating preaching of the law that he commends. He settles on the Sermon on the Mount as the best text for expounding the law because, though the law was classically presented in the Old Testament, it was explained more fully by Christ himself. The law was "never so fully explained, nor so thoroughly under-

---

[16] Letter to Mary Bishop, October 18, 1778, in *The Letters of John Wesley*, ed. John Telford, 8 vols. (London: Epworth, 1931), 6:326–27.

[17] "Letter to an Evangelical Layman," December 20, 1751, in *Works*, 26:487–88.

[18] "A Blow at the Root," in *The Works of the Reverend John Wesley*, ed. John Emory, 7 vols. (New York: Emory and Waugh, 1831), 6:140.

stood, till the great author of it himself condescended to give mankind the authentic comment on all the essential branches of it; at the same time declaring it should never be changed, but remain in force to the end of the world."[19] So the sermon series "Our Lord's Sermon on the Mount" gave Wesley the opportunity to present the central meaning of the law by expounding the words of Christ. It is a way of reaffirming the Old Testament on the ground of the New Testament; maintaining the connection with God's intent in the law, but acknowledging that the gospel has come in the meantime.

There are Protestant precedents for this kind of move. The Heidelberg Catechism, for example, does something like this when it introduces the law with the question, "What does the law of God require of us?" (question 4), and then goes directly to the words of Jesus for its initial answer:

> Christ teaches us that briefly, Matt. 22:37–40, "Thou shalt love the Lord thy God with all thy heart, with all thy soul, and with all thy mind, and with all thy strength. This is the first and the great commandment; and the second is like unto it, Thou shalt love thy neighbour as thyself. On these two commandments hang all the law and the prophets."

It is a consummately Christian maneuver to receive the Old Testament law from Jesus, and the nomophilic Heidelberg Catechism sends an important signal with this early move. But the catechism postpones its full treatment of the law until much later (questions 91 and following), when it asks, "What is the law of God?" and then answers with the Ten Commandments, which it then proceeds to work through, one at a time. The Ten Commandments, in fact, are a set piece within any Protestant catechism; you can't have a decent catechism without exposition of the Ten Commandments. The Heidelberg Catechism therefore signals the fact that it intends to teach the law in a Christian manner ("Christ teaches us that briefly . . .") before setting in to expounding the words of the Old Testament.

But Wesley, preaching rather than catechizing, has more space and more options. He takes advantage of this freedom to frame his entire exposition of the law as a commentary on the words of Christ. Wesley confronts his hearers (or readers) with the whole law of God, at some length, in the words and from the mouth of Jesus Christ.

---

[19] Sermon 25, "Upon Our Lord's Sermon on the Mount, Discourse V," Burwash, 252.

In his *Explanatory Notes upon the New Testament*, Wesley offers an ingenious outline of the Sermon on the Mount. He describes the large middle section (Matt. 5:17– 7:12) as "a description of true Christian holiness," noting that Jesus proceeds through this section with a series of "you have heard . . . but I say" contrasts. In each of these contrasts, Jesus focuses on some aspect of the law of God, intensifying it and applying it to the heart of the hearer. That is the main point of the sermon, according to Wesley: true holiness in Christ, distinguished from merely external religion. The beatitudes (5:3–12) he calls "a sweet invitation to true holiness and happiness, and the sayings about Christ's followers being salt and light (5:13–16) he calls "a persuasive to impart" that true holiness and happiness "to others." Christ concludes the sermon (7:13–27) with a series of stark alternatives (the two paths, the two trees, and the two foundations), which Wesley says provide "a sure mark of the true way."[20] The key text in the Sermon on the Mount, then, is Jesus's statement in 5:17 that he came "not . . . to destroy the law, or the prophets . . . , but to fulfil [them]." True Christian holiness is placed in contrast to mere outward religion, but never in contrast to God's law.

It is when Wesley comes to this key text (in sermon 25, the fifth in this sermon series) that he explains how true Christian holiness coheres with law keeping. When Jesus says, "Think not that I am come to destroy the law, or the prophets: I am not come to destroy, but to fulfil," he does not primarily mean "I am come to fulfil this by my entire and perfect obedience to it." Jesus is not, in this context, teaching about justification by faith, the imputation of righteousness, or even the atonement. "It cannot be doubted," says Wesley, that Jesus "did, in this sense, fulfil every part" of the law. But here in the key text of the Sermon on the Mount, Jesus explains his fulfillment of the law in a different sense. Wesley gives an extended paraphrase of Jesus's statement about the law:

> I am come to establish it in its fullness, in spite of all the glosses of men: I am come to place in a full and clear view whatsoever was dark or obscure therein: I am come to declare the true and full import of every part of it; to show the length and breadth, the entire extent, of every commandment contained therein, and the height and depth, the inconceivable purity and spirituality of it in all its branches.[21]

---

[20] Wesley, *Explanatory Notes upon the New Testament* (London: Epworth, 1950), at Matt. 5:3, p. 28.
[21] Sermon 25, "Upon Our Lord's Sermon on the Mount, Discourse V," Burwash, 252.

How does the law, thus internalized and clarified, cohere with the gospel of grace? According to Wesley, "There is no contrariety at all between the law and the gospel." In fact, the gospel does not even supersede the law, according to Wesley, nor (of course) the law the gospel. "Indeed neither of them supersedes the other, but they are perfectly well together."

Command and Promise

The Sermon on the Mount is both law and gospel in the mouth of Jesus not because it is a unique section of Scripture, but because no passage in Scripture is pure law or pure gospel, as if it did not presuppose and even contain the other part of the Christian message. Law and gospel are not sections that can be set one beside another; they occur in the same exact teachings:

> Yea, the very same words, considered in different respects, are parts both of the law and of the gospel: if they are considered as commandments, they are parts of the law; if as promises, of the gospel. Thus, "Thou shalt love the Lord thy God with all thy heart," when considered as a commandment, is a branch of the law; when regarded as a promise, is an essential part of the gospel;—the gospel being no other than the commands of the law, proposed by way of promise.[22]

According to Wesley, when God commands, "Thou shalt not lie," it means both "I command you not to lie" (the law) and "I will bring it about that you become one who does not lie" (the gospel). The gospel is to be understood as "the commands of the law, proposed by way of promise." This transformation is easiest to see in the broadest of the commands, such as the covenant formula "I will be your God and you will be my people." On Wesley's terms, this is both a command ("be my people!") and a promise ("I will make you my people"). But since the law, properly preached, searches out even the smallest aspect of our lives, it applies also to the minutest moral command. "Every command of holy writ is only a covered promise," says Wesley. "Does he command us then to 'pray without ceasing'? to 'rejoice evermore'? to be 'holy as he is holy'? It is enough; he will work in us this very thing; it shall be unto us according to his word."[23]

"There is, therefore," says Wesley, "the closest connection that can be conceived, between the law and the gospel. On the one hand, the law con-

---

[22] Ibid., 253.
[23] Ibid.

tinually makes way for, and points us to, the gospel; on the other, the gospel continually leads us to a more exact fulfilling of the law."[24] When making this constant journey from law to gospel and back again, we do not flip from page to page or passage to passage. We hear the same God speaking to us in the voice of promise and command, of gift and task. Law and gospel are not identical, because command is not promise. But they are unified because the God who commands is the God who, in the very same words, promises.

"Every command in Holy Writ is only a covered promise." Wesley's way of apprehending the unity of law and gospel is especially sharp, but it is not new. It is in fact Augustinian, though with an evangelical accent. It was Augustine who, in the fifth century, prayed to God, "Give what you command, and command what you will."[25] This was the very line from the *Confessions* that bothered the British monk Pelagius so much, because it presupposed too much reliance on God's grace. But Augustine, and Wesley following his lead, believed that whatever God's commands required, God would enable his children to attain. Of course it only works if God shows up in at least two distinct ways: first to forgive, and then to empower. First he cancels the penalty of sin; then he breaks its power. First he imputes righteousness, and then he imparts righteousness.[26] The result is a comprehensive concept of grace that includes both pardon and power. Packer calls the Wesleyan teaching "Augustinianism augmented rather than abandoned," a teaching better seen as "reorchestrating elements in the Augustinian tradition than as breaking with it."[27]

If there is anything novel in Wesley's way of teaching about the gospel and the law, it comes from the fact (which we have explored in his biography) that he learned the Protestant lesson so thoroughly. He was jealous to keep the gospel of free forgiveness from being juggled away into some system of salvation by good works or merit seeking. Even if those good works and merits are made possible by the power of God (as in the theology of Thomas Aquinas), Wesley knew that the preacher must be absolutely clear about justification by faith. "It is impossible," he said, "to have too high an esteem for 'the faith of God's elect.' And we must all declare, 'By grace ye are saved through faith; not of works, lest any man should boast.'"[28] In offering

---

[24] Ibid.
[25] Augustine, *Confessions* 10.29.
[26] "God implants righteousness in every one to whom he has imputed it." Sermon 20, "The Lord Our Righteousness," Burwash, 197.
[27] Packer, *Keep in Step with the Spirit*, 111.
[28] Sermon 25, "Upon Our Lord's Sermon on the Mount, Discourse V," Burwash, 256.

salvation, "we must cry aloud to every penitent sinner, 'Believe in the Lord Jesus Christ, and thou shalt be saved.'" Wesley insisted on this and did not add to it. He did, however, characteristically guard the gospel against an antinomian misinterpretation:

> But at the same time we must take care to let all men know we esteem no faith but that "which worketh by love"; and that we are not "saved by faith" unless so far as we are delivered from the power as well as the guilt of sin. And when we say, "Believe, and thou shalt be saved," we do not mean, "Believe, and thou shalt step from sin to heaven, without any holiness coming between, faith supplying the place of holiness"; but, believe and thou shalt be holy; believe in the Lord Jesus, and thou shalt have peace and power together. Thou shalt have power from him in whom thou believest to trample sin under thy feet; power to love the Lord thy God with all thy heart, and to serve him with all thy strength. Thou shalt have power "by patient continuance in well-doing to seek for glory and honour and immortality." Thou shalt both "do and teach" all the commandments of God, from the least even to the greatest. Thou shalt teach them by thy life as well as thy words, and so "be called great in the kingdom of heaven."[29]

It is typical of Wesley that he strove to hold together things that often fall apart. He refused to back down from the Protestant breakthrough to salvation by faith alone, but he equally refused to recognize any faith that was not "working through love" (Gal. 5:6, ESV).

There is no need for these things to be separated, because God has joined them together. Justification and regeneration are given together, and regeneration is all about a new nature, created in holiness and geared toward the restoration of the full image of God. When Wesley found the law and the gospel together in the words of Jesus, he recognized that this unity is the key to the doctrine of grace, and the reason that the Christian faith is really good news: it brings both forgiveness and renewal. Forgiveness without renewal would be antinomian; renewal without forgiveness would be legalism. Any message that proclaims both is good news indeed. Commenting on Matthew 4:23, the narrative passage just before the Sermon on the Mount, Wesley noted that what Jesus went through Galilee preaching was "the gospel of the kingdom." "The gospel," Wesley pointed out, means "the joyous message," which is "the proper name of our religion; as will be

---

[29] Ibid.

amply verified in all who earnestly and perseveringly embrace it."[30] Wesley preached the Christian message as joyous, containing everything necessary for life and godliness. It is the message in which we hear the voice of Jesus say, "Be of good cheer, thy sins are forgiven: So forgiven, that they shall no more rule over thee."[31]

Wesley also admonished others to preach similarly, properly combining gospel and law. In a classic letter to a layman in 1751, Wesley surveyed the two errors of "preaching the law only" and "preaching the gospel only." What Wesley recommended was "neither one nor the other, but duly mixing both, in every place if not in every sermon."[32] There is never a time when the law ceases to be a fit subject of Christian proclamation. It is preached in one way to awaken consciences, in another way to strengthen believers, and in another way to those who are growing in their faith. Wesley especially recommended that when one begins to preach in a new place, "the right method of preaching" is first to make "a general declaration of the love of God to sinners and His willingness that they should be saved," and then to "preach the law in the strongest, the closest, the most searching manner possible, only intermixing the gospel here and there and showing it, as it were, afar off." When the law has done its work of convicting, the offer of the gospel can be made credibly.

But even when preaching to converted people, Wesley claimed that

> a wise builder would preach the law to them again, only taking particular care to place every part of it in a gospel light as not only a command but a privilege also, as a branch of the glorious liberty of the sons of God. He would take equal care to remind them that this is not the cause but the fruit of their acceptance with God; that other cause, "other foundation, can no man lay than that which is laid, even Jesus Christ"; that we are still forgiven and accepted only for the sake of what He has done and suffered for us; and that all true obedience springs from love to Him, grounded on His first loving us. He would labour, therefore, in preaching any part of the law, to keep the love of Christ continually before their eyes, that thence they might draw fresh life, vigour, and strength to run the way of His commandments. [33]

---

[30] Matt. 4:23 in Wesley, *Explanatory Notes upon the New Testament*, 27.
[31] Sermon 1, "Salvation by Faith," Burwash, 9.
[32] Letter to Ebenezer Blackwell, December 20, 1751, in Telford, *Letters of John Wesley*, 3:79ff. I am quoting it from Timothy L. Smith, *Whitefield and Wesley on the New Birth* (Grand Rapids: Francis Asbury, 1986), 159–63. Smith's brief introduction is very helpful.
[33] Smith, *Whitefield and Wesley on the New Birth*, 161.

Some preachers might preach the demands of the law in order only to make their listeners hungry for the gospel, but Wesley considered the law itself to be wholesome and nourishing, because it is found in the same oracles of God as the gospel. "Thus light and strength are given by the same means and frequently in the same moment." Using the first person, he described how it works:

> For instance, I hear the command, "Let your communication be always in grace, meet to minister grace to the hearers." God gives me more light into this command. I see the exceeding height and depth of it. At the same time I see (by the same light from above) how far I have fallen short. I am ashamed; I am humbled before God. I earnestly desire to keep it better; I pray to Him that has loved me for more strength, and I have the petition I ask of him. Thus the law not only convicts the unbeliever and enlightens the believing soul, but also conveys food to a believer, sustains and increases his spiritual life and strength.[34]

There is never a need to choose between preaching law or preaching gospel. "Undoubtedly both should be preached in their turns; yes, both at once, or both in one." And so his concluding advice:

> According to this model, I should advise every preacher continually to preach the law—the law grafted upon, tempered by, and animated with the spirit of the gospel. I advise him to declare, explain, and enforce every command of God. But meantime to declare in every sermon (and the more explicitly the better) that the first and great command to a Christian is, "Believe in the Lord Jesus Christ"; that Christ is all in all . . . that all life, love, and strength are from Him alone, and all freely given to us through faith. And it will ever be found that the law thus preached both enlightens and strengthens the soul, that it both nourishes and teaches, that it is the guide, "food, medicine, and stay" of the believing soul.[35]

The message that Wesley preached was a comprehensive one, built on the full counsel of the Word of God. Grace comes first, but law is not to be omitted. Wesley built his preaching about the Christian life on a solid foundation, as well: a doctrine of grace that included both forgiveness and empowerment.

---

[34] Ibid., 162.
[35] Ibid., 163.

All Our Works, O God, Are Wrought in Thee

We have already described Wesley's holistic doctrine of grace in several ways. We have described it as "first grace, then law," and come to understand the unity of these two. We have seen the outline of Wesley's nomophilic doctrine of grace in the table of contents of the *Standard Sermons*, in the lines of Charles's hymns ("He breaks the power of cancelled sin"), and in the principles John derived from his exposition of the Sermon on the Mount. But the doctrine is everywhere, deeply engrained in all Wesley's writings and woven into every sermon. More than any of the distinctive traits he may be famous for, his doctrine of grace is what is most characteristic of him. To show how deep the doctrine runs in his way of thinking, we turn our attention to a classic specimen of his preaching: the first paragraph of sermon 1. We have already examined the context of this historic sermon (see above, chap. 2) that Wesley preached soon after Aldersgate. But now we are in a position to see further into it.

The paragraph, though rarely treated with the kind of attention it deserves, is classic.[36] Only 140 words long, it was written to be read aloud and to be understood immediately by listeners. Its prose is clear and accessible, "plain truth for plain people," as Wesley said in the introduction to the *Standard Sermons*. But for all its accessibility, it is a carefully crafted product of a well-trained mind that was steeped in Scripture and the great Christian tradition. It repays close study. Here is the paragraph itself:

> All the blessings which God hath bestowed upon man are of his mere grace, bounty, or favour; his free, undeserved favour; favour altogether undeserved; man having no claim to the least of his mercies. It was free grace that "formed man of the dust of the ground, and breathed into him a living soul," and stamped on that soul the image of God, and "put all things under his feet." The same free grace continues to us, at this day, life, and breath, and all things. For there is nothing we are, or have, or do, which can deserve the least thing at God's hand. "All our works, Thou, O God, hast wrought in us." These, therefore, are so many more instances of free mercy: and whatever righteousness may be found in man, this is also the gift of God.[37]

---

[36] Close readings of Wesley's sermons are rare, but it is evident that he crafted some of his writings with such diligence that they repay intense scrutiny. One of the best explorations of Wesley's powers of composition is George Lawton, *John Wesley's English: A Study of His Literary Style* (London: George Allen & Unwin, 1962).

[37] Sermon 1, "Salvation by Faith," Burwash, 3.

This is Wesley praising God, but you can hear a lot of doctrine in the doxology: the classic Protestant teaching on grace rings out in these lines, and behind it the Christian confession of our radical dependence on God, both as creatures and sinners. The leading idea is obviously the gratuity of grace, which Wesley underlines with a fourfold repetition: "his mere grace, bounty, or favour" (here Wesley is multiplying synonyms); "his free, undeserved favour" (here Wesley is expanding the main noun with two adjectives); "favour altogether undeserved" (here Wesley is intensifying the main noun with an absolute adverb); "man having no claim to the least of his mercies" (here Wesley paraphrases the main idea, bringing in new words and concepts).

He makes his point: grace is free! What Wesley presents here is the classic Reformation description of grace as God's unmerited favor. In sermon 1, Wesley is going to talk about salvation by faith, so he begins with the Protestant statement about grace. But his next move is to leap back to the doctrine of creation *ex nihilo*, to make a point about how freely God created: "It was free grace that 'formed man of the dust of the ground, and breathed into him a living soul,' and stamped on that soul the image of God, and 'put all things under his feet.'" It is impressive how many Bible passages about creation come together in this short section (Gen. 1:26; 2:7; Ps. 8:6).

What Wesley is going to tell his audience is that they are saved by sheer grace, but he knows that these lukewarm Anglicans of the eighteenth century might be inclined to disagree. The eighteenth century was quite impressed with human achievements and the potential for progress. So he secures their agreement with a less controversial point: none of us did anything to deserve to be created. When we were nothing, God not only brought us into being, but made us bodies with souls, in God's own image, and in dominion over the rest of creation.

The grammar of the next sentence needs some updating for our times: When Wesley says, "The same free grace continues to us, at this day, life, and breath, and all things," he is using "continue" as a transitive verb, meaning "to cause something to endure or extend." To us, the word sounds more intransitive, so we want to read "grace continues" as "grace keeps coming." But with a transitive verb, the sentence means "grace makes these things reach all the way down to us: life, breath, and all things." The blessings of creation-by-grace are not in some primeval past, but reach all the way down to us, giving us "life, and breath, and all things."

That little catalog is an allusion to Acts 17:25, a passage from Paul's speech on Mars Hill. The immediate context is Paul's point that God does not need to receive anything from humanity, least of all religious duties like temple building and temple service. On the contrary, God gives what humanity needs. When John Wesley quotes six words from another part of Scripture, he might just be decorating his sentence with the beauty of Bible language. Sometimes he does that. But surprisingly often, his borrowing of a few words is in fact a pointer to real, extended overlap between his current topic and the entire passage he takes the words from. This is one of those cases.

In fact, the reason Wesley's mind reaches out to grab the specific words "life, and breath, and all things," is that he is proclaiming a doctrine taught there in Paul's speech in Acts. First, he thinks of the doctrine, then his mind gravitates toward the key passage, and then his mind returns from Acts carrying a half-dozen words that he uses for their poetic force. But he covers his tracks as he returns: he doesn't cite chapter and verse; he doesn't signal the theology of the Areopagus speech in any other way. The members of his audience who are fluent in Scripture will know where the words are from, and their minds will be flooded with the associations from Acts. In terms used by Richard Hays to describe hearing echoes in Scripture, the "canonical memories" of the audience will be activated by the allusion.[38] The listeners with less developed canonical memories will miss out on the power of the allusion, but they will still feel the force of the words themselves: "life, and breath, and all things" is a great little triadic phrase made of one-syllable words. It just packs a punch, with or without the echoes.

It also sets Wesley up for the most important move in the paragraph, the hinge on which his opening argument turns. He jumps from one triad of monosyllables to another, from "life, and breath, and all things," to all that "we are, or have, or do." With the poetic beauty and the momentum of these linked triads, Wesley moves his audience forward from our existence (what we are) through our possessions (what we have) to the main point of a sermon about salvation by faith: our actions (what we do). Under the banner of grace, Wesley brings us to the point of agreeing that just as our

---

[38] Richard B. Hays, *Echoes of Scripture in the Letters of Paul* (New Haven, CT: Yale University Press, 1993), 51.

existence is by God's favor, and our possessions are gifts from him, any good actions we perform are also from him. The question to be decided in a discussion about salvation by faith is a question about our works, and Wesley has placed that question before his readers in a very artful and effective way.

That is why, having turned the decisive corner of his introduction, he immediately quotes (without citation) a version of Isaiah 26:12: "All our works, Thou, O God, hast wrought in us." This is a passage that has been popular in the Christian mystical tradition for a long time, because it gives a glimpse of some mysterious presence of God's own work in our human works. When quoted by a mystic like Meister Eckhart (d. 1327), this concurrence of divine and human works can become all a matter of mingling, blurring distinctions that ought to be kept clear. But sober souls like the Protestant martyr Nicholas Ridley (d. 1555) were also fond of using these words from Isaiah to point to the mystery of our good works proceeding from God. In his commentary on Philippians, expounding the statement that "he who began a good work in you will be faithful to complete it," Ridley thinks very carefully about the way God's *operatio* precedes and makes possible our *co-operatio*. Whomever Wesley was reading (and he read too widely for us to be certain of his influences in many cases), his use of Isaiah 26:12, "All our works, Thou, O God, hast wrought in us," aligned with Bishop Ridley's gospel-centered Anglicanism.[39] In Wesley's explanatory notes on the Bible, his comment on Isaiah 26:12 is, "All the good works done by us, are the effects of thy grace."

To conclude his opening paragraph, Wesley says that all good works are therefore "so many more instances of free mercy," and he summarizes that "whatever righteousness may be found in man, this is also the gift of God." This paragraph reflects a comprehensive view of grace. Grace is the basis of man's physical creation, soulish image bearing, ongoing preservation, moral action, and righteousness. Grace is both favor and power. We receive it both passively (inoperatively, when we are created from nothing) and actively (cooperatively, when God works in us). In both cases, what draws Wesley's attention is its gratuity, its freedom. All of it is "free, underserved favour" "altogether undeserved," "free grace," "free mercy," "gift." His opening paragraph drives toward a conclusion about human action: it is as much

---

[39] Ridley's Philippians commentary can be found in *Fathers of the English Church*, vol. 2, *Ridley and Latimer* (London: John Hatchard, 1808), 191.

a gift from God as our existence and our possessions. Wesley begins with our creation, in which we had no part, as the clearest instance of "mere grace," and locates moral action ("our works") and uprightness ("whatever righteousness") inside of that framework.

Thus he approaches the teaching about salvation. Wesley's approach helped launch the great evangelical awakening of the eighteenth century. This awakening was, in fact, a work that God wrought through him.

Grace means free forgiveness, in which we receive from God the favor that we do not deserve and are guilty of having violated. But grace also means God's empowering us and drawing us to become more Christlike, freely giving us the help and power we also do not deserve and are also guilty of having violated. Wesley knows that both of these free gifts are grace, and that even in reading the New Testament, we need to have both meanings in mind. In the pages of Scripture, grace sometimes means free love, unmerited mercy. But sometimes it means the power of God the Holy Ghost. Wesley distinguishes the two as clearly as possible, precisely so he can argue that they belong together in reality. He says elsewhere in the *Standard Sermons*: "As soon as ever the grace of God in the former sense, his pardoning love, is manifested to our souls, the grace of God in the latter sense, the power of his Spirit, takes place therein. And now we can perform, through God, what to man was impossible. Now we can order our conversation aright."[40]

The key to Wesley's teaching on grace is to see that it includes, rather than excludes, the power of God for transformation. When the preacher moves from grace to law, he is in fact only moving around inside the comprehensive doctrine of a grace that is always bigger than, but never the opposite of, law. God's goal is to be the holy God of a holy people, and to that end he gives grace in every sense: free forgiveness in the Son that sets the stage for the work of the Spirit in the Christian life.

Much more could be said about John Wesley's notion of grace, because it is the central theme of his message. To it he connects everything he has to say about conversion, the Christian life, and the church. All God's ways with man pass through grace, and the theme grew more expansive as Wesley continued to preach on it. Albert Outler once summed up Wesley's theology of the Christian life as an elaboration of the theme of grace:

---

[40] Sermon 12, "The Witness of Our Own Spirit," Burwash, 114. "Conversation" here means behavior, not speech. The word has shifted since the eighteenth century.

The Christian life, in Wesley's view, is empowered by the energy of grace: prevenient, saving, sanctifying, sacramental. Grace is always interpreted as something more than forensic pardon. Rather, it is experienced as actual influence—God's love, imminent and active in human life. Its prior initiative makes every human action a reaction; hence "pre-venting." It is a function of God's mercy that is over all his works; hence it is universal. It can be "resisted," hence it is co-operant rather than irresistible. And since it is always mediated in and through various outward and visible signs, grace is typically sacramental. But, since it is always God's grace, it is never at man's disposal.[41]

With Outler's final note, on the mediation of grace through the sacraments of the church, we are ready to explore Wesley's teaching on the means of grace.

---

[41] Albert Outler, ed., *John Wesley* (New York: Oxford University Press, 1964), 33.

CHAPTER 7

THE MEANS OF GRACE

Salvation is the gift of God, a miracle of divine initiative that works an invisible and inward change in a person's heart. "God so works upon the soul by His immediate influence, and by a strong, though inexplicable, operation, that the stormy wind and troubled waves subside, and there is a sweet calm—the heart resting as in the arms of Jesus."[1] Call that pietistic, or experientialist, or emotional, or whatever else you may want to call it, but at least Wesley was clear about the goal of his ministry: to bring the soul into personal contact with the gracious God. But just because the contact is direct and personal doesn't mean that it is arbitrary or formless. God has ordained particular channels through which he normally brings people into contact with himself. In other words, God has appointed means of grace.

Making Too Little of the Means

As early as 1740, Wesley came into conflict with certain evangelical believers (the Moravians again) who shared his two great presuppositions: that we need to encounter God directly, and that our encounter with God is totally dependent on God's initiative. But the conflict arose when these evangelicals drew erroneous conclusions from these true premises. Since the encounter is up to God, they argued that all we can do is wait for it passively and quietly. The practical result was to stop attending church services, to abandon prayer and Bible study, and to avoid the Lord's Supper.

---

[1] Sermon 11, "Witness of the Spirit," in *Wesley's 52 Standard Sermons*, ed. N. Burwash (Salem, OH: Schmul, 1988), 101.

"The Moravian Philip Henry Molther contended that until persons had full assurance of faith (also understood as 'conversion' or the reception of the Holy Spirit) they ought to abstain from any means of grace and be 'quiet' or wait upon the Lord until such assurance was perceived."[2] The particular eighteenth-century details of Moravian "meanslessness" may not seem familiar, but the mistake they made is a perennial one for evangelicals. The idea is that we should simply wait for God to reach down and touch us. We should, by doing nothing, let grace be grace.

Wesley confronted this error in many ways, but his most important statement on the subject is sermon 16, "The Means of Grace." His text is Malachi 3:7: "Ye are gone away from mine ordinances, and have not kept them." He begins his exposition of it by asking whether God's stated requirement that we come to his ordinances and keep them is something that passed away with the coming of the new covenant. "But are there any ordinances now, since life and immortality were brought to light by the gospel? Are there, under the Christian dispensation, any means ordained of God, as the usual channels of his grace?"[3] Wesley answers that there certainly are, and that they are so self-evident that the question could not even have been posed in the earliest church, until "in the process of time . . . the love of many waxed cold." God has made it clear what thing we are to do to receive from him, which is why the early Christians "continued steadfastly in the apostles' doctrine and fellowship, and in breaking of bread, and in prayers" (Acts 2:42).

Wesley defines the means of grace as "outward signs or words, or actions ordained of God, and appointed for this end, to be the ordinary channels whereby he might convey to men, preventing, justifying or sanctifying grace."[4] He says there are many of them, and he never undertakes to make a comprehensive list. But in sermon 16 he lists as "the chief of these means" prayer, Bible study, and the Lord's Supper. Since God has ordained these things as his ordinary channels of grace, we know this is where grace is to be expected and awaited.

Wesley's argument that we should make great and regular use of the means of grace is a kind of appeal to common sense. He begins with what evangelical Christians agree on: grace is a spiritual reality that only God

---

[2] Karen B. Westerfield Tucker, "Wesley's Emphases on Worship and the Means of Grace," in *The Cambridge Companion to John Wesley*, ed. Randy L. Maddox and Jason E. Vickers (New York: Cambridge University Press, 2010), 229.
[3] Sermon 16, "Means of Grace," Burwash, 150.
[4] Ibid., 152.

can give. He even agrees that our posture as believers is one of waiting on God's initiative to do for us what we can never do for ourselves. But the live question that Wesley presses is: *where* should we wait? Should we wait for God's action inside the means of grace, or outside of them? Inside, obviously, answers Wesley. We should count on God to show up in the places, practices, and ordinances where he has promised to show up, and we should camp out in the ordained means.

Wesley did not invent the term *means of grace*. It is a piece of traditional terminology that he picked up from general Anglican usage. He uses the term simply "because I know none better; and because it has been generally used in the Christian church for many ages—in particular by our own church."[5] His teaching about the means of grace was neither unique nor unusual. But his championing of the means of grace in the new situation created by the evangelical awakening was crucially important for evangelical Christianity. It helped anchor the revival movement to traditional forms of Christianity, and preserved it from drifting into sectarian aloofness from the great forms of traditional Christianity. Wesley was uniquely positioned to say the right thing about the means of grace because he was such an advocate of the interior heart religion. He knew the difference between outward forms and inward reality, and he constantly preached on the need for inward, spiritual experience. But wherever evangelicals made false dichotomies between inward reality and outward forms, Wesley was there to demand that God had joined the two together, and no man should separate them.

Anyone who teaches that God intends to come into direct contact with the human soul is likely to be accused at some point of indulging in mysticism. And Wesley certainly had some affinities with mysticism; he was at least utterly unafraid of using much of the language of intimacy and communion that the mystical traditions within Christianity have made use of through the centuries.[6] His brother Charles's poetry and hymns, saturated with vivid and expressive imagery, also contributed to the sense that the Wesleyan message was, as one commentator said, "within a hair's breadth of mysticism." And in a letter to his older brother Samuel, John confessed, "I think the rock on which I had the nearest made shipwreck of the faith

---

[5] Ibid.

[6] See the careful discussion in Robert G. Tuttle Jr., *Mysticism in the Wesleyan Tradition* (Grand Rapids: Francis Asbury, 1989). After discussing early mystic influences, Tuttle goes on to document Wesley's "initial acceptance" of mystic spirituality, followed by his "reluctant rejection" of it.

was the writings of the Mystics; under which term I comprehend all, and only those, who slight any of the means of grace."[7]

But ultimately, *mysticism* is a bad word according to Wesley, and he used it pejoratively throughout most of his work. The reason lies in how he defined the famously vague word, which he parsed with considerable precision. As in the letter to Samuel, John consistently defines *mystic* as "those who slight any of the means of grace," or those who seek immediate encounter with God outside of those ordinary channels ordained by God. Notice that Wesley agrees with the mystics that we need to encounter God personally and inwardly; he draws the line, however, in any abandoning or neglecting of the means of grace. Broadly speaking, he tends to affirm what the mystics affirm (closeness with God), but draws a sharp line at what they deny (the necessity of the means of grace).

The definition that Wesley offers is highly useful. Mysticism is a slippery subject, and Christians with the temperament for mysticism tend to indulge in vague and obscure statements, but with a passion and sometimes a depth that can be alarming. How are they to be evaluated? Wesley's answer is not exhaustive, but it is a powerful tool for making firm decisions about when somebody has gone too far. A mystic has gone too far when he imagines he has passed beyond the need for the means of grace. Whether the mystic is a super-spiritual visionary who claims to need no fellowship with lesser Christians, a warmhearted evangelical who believes that his personal relationship with Jesus makes the Lord's Supper irrelevant, or an antinomian who takes justification by faith to mean that it would be an insult to God's grace to practice spiritual disciplines, Wesley's definition of mysticism enables us to recognize that each of these has crossed into the mystic error. The problem is not with having, or even cultivating, a strong sense of God's presence. The problem is with using that sense to eliminate the ordinances of God.

Making Too Much of the Means

As a revivalist, as a promoter of heart religion, Wesley had to exert considerable energy reminding his fellow evangelicals that they could not neglect the means of grace. Such neglect was the immediate danger among the newly awakened, as he learned early in the course of the revival. Yet

---

[7] Quoted in Ole E. Borgen, *John Wesley's View of the Sacraments: A Critical Response to John Wesley on the Sacraments: A Theological Study* (Grand Rapids: Francis Asbury, 1985), 99. Bishop Borgen is the commentator who said Wesley came "within a hair's breadth of mysticism."

Wesley was well aware of the danger posed by the opposite error, the error of making too much of the means of grace. In fact, that error is worse. It seems to have come first and to have provoked some to react by neglecting the means. The larger problem of the church in the 1700s, after all, was the coldhearted religiosity that resided only in outward forms. The major problem of the age was churchgoers who thought churchgoing was the whole point of Christianity. They mistook the means (going to church) for the end (meeting with God) and came to be satisfied with the means. They made the channels of grace serve as replacements for the grace itself.

Remember that Wesley lamented in the preface of the *Standard Sermons* that "mere outside religion . . . has almost driven heart religion out of the world." Wesley had a full supply of his strongest warning language against this error. "Above all," he warned, if the means "are used as a kind of commutation for the religion they were designed to subserve, it is not easy to find words for the enormous folly and wickedness of thus turning God's arms against himself; of keeping Christianity out of the heart by those very means which were ordained for the bringing it in."[8] It was against this cold and external form of religion that the evangelicals reacted, and they sometimes were in danger of overreacting. If the churches made too much of outward forms, they would make nothing of them.

Both errors—of excess and of defect, of making too much of the means and of making too little—lead to self-righteousness. A Christian who considers himself above the means of grace has far too high and unrealistic a view of his own inward spirituality, having become more spiritual than Jesus and the apostles. And a Christian who considers the outward forms to be the thing itself is in the grip of the delusion that God values the outward forms for their own sake. The danger is in engaging in the means of grace while suspecting that "there was something in them wherewith God was well pleased, something that would still make them acceptable in his sight, though they were not exact in the weightier matters of the law, in justice, mercy, and the love of God."[9] Here is the root of all hypocrisy and pharisaism.

Wesley called the overestimation of the means of grace "resting in the means." By "rest," he meant the error of relying on them as sufficient in themselves. If we think of his teaching as a call for balance between the

---

[8] Sermon 16, "The Means of Grace," Burwash, 151.
[9] Ibid.

extremes, we could say that one extreme is to *wait outside of the means*, and the opposite extreme is to *rest in the means*. But the balance between them is to *wait in the means of grace*. It is not a matter of how long you dwell there, because waiting in the means implies being there a long time. But to rest, in this sense, is to cease to wait. For this reason Wesley also called this error abusing the means of grace, that is, using them wrongly (as opposed to the opposite error, which is not so much abusing them as not using them at all). God gave the means for us to use; we disobey when we fail to use them, and we also disobey when we misuse them by trusting them instead of God.

The worst problem with resting in the means is that it leaves God out of the picture, replacing him with his gifts or his institutions. Wesley argued that we must "retain a lively sense that God is above all means." God has ordained certain ordinary channels, and it is unfaithful of us to be found waiting anywhere else for him but where he has promised to meet us. But God himself is not bound:

> He doeth whatsoever and whensoever it pleaseth him. He can convey his grace, either in or out of any of the means which he hath appointed. Perhaps he will. "Who hath known the mind of the Lord? Or who hath been his counsellor?" Look then every moment for his appearing! Be it at the hour you are employed in his ordinances; or before, or after that hour; or when you are hindered therefrom: He is not hindered. He is always ready, always able, always willing to save. "It is the Lord: Let him do what seemeth him good!"[10]

For all his insistence on the means of grace, Wesley was clear that God could work anywhere he wanted, means or no means.

Though Wesley loved the sacraments and held an Anglican view of baptism and the Lord's Supper, he recognized that of all the means of grace, the two official sacraments had been twisted to become a substitute for grace itself. But the sacraments, of course, do not save. God has not rigged them up as an apparatus to administer grace in his absence. The sacraments are not self-sufficient mechanisms that channel some fungible quantity of supernatural power to us if we use them rightly. The giving of grace through the ordinary means is nothing less than God himself choosing to act in our lives; sovereignly, personally, and repeatedly. Even when grace reaches us through unexceptional, appointed, scheduled, repeatable, official means, it

---

[10] Ibid., 161.

is nonetheless God himself who is acting in these sacraments.[11] As Wesley said of baptism in particular, it is "the ordinary means he hath appointed" for salvation, a means, "to which God hath tied us, though he may not have tied himself."[12] We are bound, not God.

In the long story of the history of the church, "the number of those who abused the ordinances of God was far greater than of those who despised them." Indeed, the point of the revival was to wake up nominal Christians from the state of resting in the means of grace. The theme is central to Wesley's preaching:

> External worship is lost labour, without a heart devoted to God . . . the outward ordinances of God then profit much, when they advance inward holiness, but, when they advance it not, are unprofitable and void, are lighter than vanity; yea, that when they are used, as it were, *in the place of* this, they are an utter abomination to the Lord.[13]

So Wesley battled against the main problem of the age, the abuse of the means of grace, which propped up the system of mere outward religion. But closer to home, he kept a watchful eye out for the overreaction of men who "in their fervent zeal for the glory of God, and the recovery of souls from that fatal delusion" went on to the opposite error and "spake as if outward religion were absolutely nothing, as if it had no place in the religion of Christ."[14] It was against these latter that he announced the prophetic warning from God, "Ye are gone away from mine ordinances, and have not kept them."

Charles Wesley on the Means of Grace

John Wesley preached the classic sermon on the means of grace, but his brother Charles decided that this was a doctrine that could be sung. So he wrote a very didactic hymn on the subject, "The Means of Grace," published as hymn number 83 in *Hymns and Sacred Poems* (1740). Every line of thought in John's sermon finds poetic expression somewhere in Charles's twenty-three-stanza hymn. He puts it in the first person, making it his own personal testimony of experience, and also enabling anyone who reads it or sings it to take it up as their own confession about meeting God in the means of grace.

---

[11] See Borgen, *John Wesley's View of the Sacraments*, 128.
[12] "On Baptism," in *John Wesley*, ed. Albert Outler (New York: Oxford University Press, 1964), 324.
[13] Sermon 16, "The Means of Grace," Burwash, 151.
[14] Ibid.

Charles begins with a description of the lifestyle of the unawakened Anglican formalist:

> Long have I seem'd to serve Thee, Lord,
> With unavailing pain;
> Fasted, and pray'd and read Thy word,
> And heard it preach'd, in vain.
>
> Oft did I with th' assembly join,
> And near Thine altar drew;
> A form of godliness was mine,
> The power I never knew.

But a reflection on the spiritual and inward nature of the law of God shakes him loose from this fruitless round of religious duties, and he now writes these lines with a knowledge that God seeks the heart:

> To please Thee thus (at last I see)
> In vain I hoped and strove:
> For what are outward things to Thee,
> Unless they spring from love?
>
> I see the perfect law requires
> Truth in the inward parts,
> Our full consent, our whole desires,
> Our undivided hearts.

Charles diagnoses the dangers of outward religion in exactly the same language that John used in his sermon. It was "resting in" the externals, which amounts to both boasting and idolatry.

> But I of means have made my boast,
> Of means an idol made;
> The spirit in the letter lost,
> The substance in the shade.
>
> I rested in the outward law,
> Nor knew its deep design;
> The length and breadth I never saw,
> The height of love Divine.

Charles confesses that he was dealing with the externals and was cut off from the "deep design" of the law, which, rightly understood from the inside, is to communicate the love of God. He must have direct divine intervention, because only God can save him from this plight.

> Where am I now, or what my hope?
> What can my weakness do?
> JESU, to Thee my soul looks up,
> 'Tis Thou must make it new.

Thus far, Charles is perfectly reciting the central Wesleyan message of salvation by grace and applying it in a way calculated to awaken the sleeping formalist from his churchly slumbers. Here, however, he turns the same corner John turned, and asks the question: If we are to wait for salvation, where shall we wait? In the ordinances, or out of them? The question is quickly raised and answered:

> Thine is the work, and Thine alone—
> But shall I idly stand?
> Shall I the written Rule disown,
> And slight my God's command?
>
> Wildly shall I from Thine turn back,
> A better path to find;
> Thy holy ordinance forsake,
> And cast Thy words behind?
>
> Forbid it, gracious Lord, that I
> Should ever learn Thee so!
> No—let me with Thy word comply,
> If I thy love would know.

The Wesleyan answer is that God has commanded the ordinances, and that is the end of the question. God was in earnest in giving the law and establishing the means of grace.

> Suffice for me, that Thou, my Lord,
> Hast bid me fast and pray:
> Thy will be done, Thy name adored;
> 'Tis only mine t'obey.

> Thou bidd'st me search the Sacred Leaves,
> And taste the hallow'd Bread:
> The kind commands my soul receives,
> And longs on Thee to feed.

Charles's poetic finesse may hide the fact that this is a list of the chief means: fasting, prayer, Bible study ("search the Sacred Leaves"), and the Lord's Supper. The resulting state is no longer resting in the means as if they were sufficient, but waiting in the means for God to move sovereignly and give his grace anew. The specific point is that the speaker waits in the appointed place:

> Still for Thy loving kindness, Lord,
> I in Thy temple wait;
> I look to find Thee in Thy word,
> Or at Thy table meet.
>
> Here, in Thine own appointed ways,
> I wait to learn Thy will:
> Silent I stand before Thy face,
> And hear Thee say, "Be still!"

The command "Be still!" is one that Charles knows he must handle with care. The problem the Wesleys confronted with the Moravians was a kind of quietism, a "being still" that required neglect of the means. It was an erroneous way of "letting go and letting God" that ignored the commands God had given. So Charles unpacks the notion of stillness, explaining, with considerable precision for a poem, the senses in which he is waiting, and the senses in which he is working:

> "Be still—and know that I am God!"
> 'Tis all I live to know;
> To feel the virtue of Thy blood,
> And spread its praise below.
>
> I wait my vigour to renew,
> Thine image to retrieve,
> The veil of outward things pass through,
> And gasp in Thee to live.

I work, and own the labour vain;
And thus from works I cease:
I strive, and see my fruitless pain,
Till God create my peace.

Fruitless, till Thou Thyself impart,
Must all my efforts prove:
They cannot change a sinful heart,
They cannot purchase love.

I do the Thing Thy laws enjoin,
And then the strife gives o'er:
To Thee I then the whole resign:
I trust in means no more.

The proper sense of waiting and being still is not about inactivity, for that would set God's commands against each other. As John argued in his sermon, when God commanded his people, "Stand still and see the salvation of God," he also commanded Moses, "Speak unto the children of Israel that they go forward." That is, as John aggressively paraphrases the passage from Exodus 14, "This was the *salvation of God*, which they *stood still* to see, by *marching forward* with all their might!"[15]

Waiting does not mean passivity; it means faith. It means trusting Christ to save and to provide the power for Christian life. Charles even puts the means of grace in their subordinate place by calling Jesus the true means of grace, or (stretching the language a bit) the "great eternal Mean":

I trust in Him who stands between
The Father's wrath and me:
JESU! Thou great eternal Mean,
I look for all from Thee.

Thy mercy pleads, Thy truth requires,
Thy promise call Thee down!
Not for the sake of my desires—
But, O! regard Thine own!

---

[15] Ibid., 159.

I seek no motive out of Thee:
Thine own desires fulfill;
If now Thy bowels yearn on me,
On me perform Thy will.

Doom, if Thou canst, to endless pains,
And drive me from Thy face:
But if Thy stronger love constrains,
Let me be saved by grace.

It is a long and didactic poem (I doubt any congregation has ever sung it), but it begins with an awakening from formalism to real Christianity and ends with the affirmation of salvation by grace. That is where the Wesleyan teaching on the means of grace fits.

Sacraments or Spiritual Disciplines?

Thinking in terms of means of grace is a key for coming to terms with the Christian life. The dynamic tension that we have just explored, with its balance between two opposite errors and its orientation toward a personal relationship with God, is practical Wesleyan spirituality in a nutshell. With that dynamic tension in mind, we can fill in some more detail about what counts as a means of grace.

When Wesley lists prayer, Bible study, and the Lord's Supper as the three chief means of grace, he lumps together two things we would normally put in the category of "spiritual disciplines" (prayer and Bible study) and one thing we would put in the category of "sacrament" or "church ordinance" (the Lord's Supper). As is so often the case with reading Wesley, what might initially seem like sloppiness or theological confusion turns out to be profound theological intuition. The category "means of grace" is wider than either spiritual discipline or sacrament and includes them both. By thinking in these terms, Wesley is able to make a more wide-ranging theological point. The wider category offers a fruitful way of thinking about a whole range of things, from disciplines to sacraments to general revelation. Wesley's theological genius is to get a solid grip on grace and then to ask about the means by which God ordinarily channels it to us.

A danger of including spiritual disciplines and sacraments together under one larger category might be that we could drag the sacraments down from their special place to the level of other spiritual disciplines. The

Lord's Supper is especially worth considering here. We need not discuss water baptism, because though it is a means of grace, Wesley does not list it prominently in his discussions of the means. The reason is that Wesley is usually intent on talking about practices that are repeated throughout the Christian life, and water baptism is a one-time event at the beginning of the Christian life.[16] But the Lord's Supper is something believers partake of regularly, and Wesley takes care not to demote it to the same status of personal spiritual devotions. For one thing, the doctrine of the Lord's Supper that Wesley always presupposes is the Reformation Anglican doctrine, so it is a "higher" view of the sacrament than mere memorialism. For Wesley, more happens at the sacrament of the Lord's Supper than happens in prayer, if only because the supper is public, corporate, and instituted by Jesus. The bread and wine of Communion are not the vehicles of Christ's physical presence, either by transubstantiation or in any other way. But they are also not merely visual aids. Jesus, who is present among his people, is present to the one who takes the sacrament by faith.

Wesley recognizes that there is something special about the Lord's Supper, and he tends to describe it in terms of Christ and the believer meeting for an especially important ceremony that celebrates the covenant they have between them. One commentator says that for Wesley, taking Communion is "a collision of the two time frames occupied by the believing participant (the present) and the crucified Christ (the historical past)." Christ died at a time and place remote from my current time and place, but that distance is collapsed or telescoped in the event of Communion. The believer is present at the cross, and the cross is present in the life of the believer. What happens is a "two way suspension of time and place: Christ is crucified now and here; and my sins drive the nails through his hands on Calvary, then and there."[17] More than an imaginative exercise, Communion is a spiritual form of remembrance that activates a real encounter with the death of Christ, which happened long ago. It is interesting that Wesley captures so much of what a strong doctrine of memorialism strives after. As an Anglican, he has other eucharistic motifs to draw on, and he and Charles

---

[16] Baptistic readers should always bear in mind that Wesley unwaveringly affirmed infant baptism throughout his life. His emphasis on personal, adult conversion may sometimes produce tension for this traditional Anglican belief, but Wesley took the usual evangelical Anglican paths for reconciling infant baptism with adult regeneration; he did not seek a believer's baptism theological option. He certainly did notify his fellow Anglicans that their infant baptisms could not save them! See sermon 45, "The New Birth," Burwash, 458.

[17] Borgen, *John Wesley's View of the Sacraments*, 92.

utilize the full range of Protestant options. But with such a strong emphasis on the death of Jesus then and there, it is the act of remembrance that gives the Wesleyan Lord's Supper its most prominent character.

The language of mysticism, as mentioned above, is clearly present in Wesley's theology, and there is something mystical in this presentation of the supper. But using Wesley's definition of mysticism as neglect of the means of grace, "eucharistic mysticism" would be a contradiction in terms. To Wesley's mind, mysticism (in the pejorative sense) is centrifugal; it flings people out of church. Wesley's intensity about the supper was centripetal; it drew worshipers into church, to the altar. In fact, all the most rapturous expressions, all the most explosive doxologies and references to immediate apprehension of Christ and all his benefits, stem from and center on the ordinary means of grace. It is almost shocking to read the passionate descriptions of communion with God and then realize that the Wesleys are describing ordinary sacramental observances at church. Charles Wesley sings,

'Tis done, the Lord sets to his Seal,
The Prayer is heard, the Grace is given,
With Joy unspeakable we feel
The Holy Ghost sent down from Heaven,
The Altar streams with sacred Blood,
And all the Temple flames with GOD![18]

When we read those vivid words, it is difficult to keep in mind that he is describing an ordinary Communion service. But he is. Clearly, for John Wesley the Lord's Supper as a sacrament stands in a special position among the other means of grace. Charles sings its praises, ranking it higher than fasting, hearing the Word, and praying:

Glory to him who freely spent
His blood, that we might live,
And through this choicest instrument
Doth all his blessings give.

Fasting he doth, and hearing bless,
And prayer can much avail,

---

[18] From Charles Wesley's 1745 *Hymns on the Lord's Supper*. Westerfield Tucker points out that these hymns were based on Brevant's 1673 book *The Christian Sacrament and Sacrifice*. See her "Wesley's Emphases on Worship and the Means of Grace," 230.

Good vessels all to draw the grace
Out of salvation's well.

But none, like this mysterious rite
Which dying mercy gave,
Can draw forth all his promised might
And all his will to save.[19]

But even though "this mysterious rite" stands out as the "choicest instrument" among all the means of grace, it is nevertheless a means. The distinctively evangelical note is sounded precisely here: the supper is not grace itself, but the channel of grace. That rules out not only Roman Catholicism, but also any Anglo-Catholic view that would permit worshipers to adore the consecrated host.

Now that we have seen how a sacrament can be described as a means of grace, there is one other means of grace that seems at first to be too large to fit comfortably within the category: prayer. In a 1760 letter, John Wesley called prayer "certainly the grand means of drawing near to God; and all others are helpful to us only so far as they are mixed with or prepare us for this."[20] It makes sense to call prayer "the grand means" of communion with God, but if Wesley has already defined means of grace as being "outward signs, words or actions" that convey grace, then it is not clear how prayer is outward. It seems to be already internal, already a matter of the heart. But the words of prayer are indeed outward in one sense. Words, spoken or unspoken, solitary or congregational, are outward in the sense of things distinct from us. So they are subject to the same manipulation and externalization as the other means:

> We know that there is no inherent power in the words that are spoken in prayer, in the letter of Scripture read, the sound thereof heard, or the bread and wine received in the Lord's supper, but that it is God alone who is the giver of every good gift, the author of all grace; that the whole power is of him, whereby, through any of these, there is any blessing conveyed to our souls.[21]

---

[19] Quoted in *John and Charles Wesley: Selected Prayers, Hymns, Journal Notes, Sermons, Letters and Treatises*, ed. Frank Whaling (New York: Paulist, 1981), 257.

[20] Letter to "a member of the society," March 29, 1760, in *The Letters of John Wesley*, ed. John Telford, 8 vols. (London: Epworth, 1931), 4:90.

[21] Sermon 16, "The Means of Grace," Burwash, 154.

The same dynamic that applies to any means of grace applies to the words of prayer as well.

No Exhaustive Catalog Is Possible

Important as the teaching of the means of grace is to Wesley, it is instructive that he never attempts to produce an exhaustive list of the means. His tendency is to list the three most important ones: prayer, searching the Scriptures, and the Lord's Supper. But elsewhere he lists others, and he can describe all manner of things as means of grace. In the "Large Minutes," which became part of the Discipline of American Methodism, Wesley explains the ways in which pastors should hold each other accountable for their spiritual lives. In particular, he inquires into the way seasoned ministers should give guidance to their helpers. He launches a series of searching questions, climaxing with a question about the means of grace:

> We might consider those that are with us as our pupils; into whose behavior and studies we should inquire every day. Should we not frequently ask, Do you walk closely with God? Have you now fellowship with the Father and the Son? At what hour do you rise? Do you punctually observe the morning and evening hour of retirement? Do you spend the day in the manner which we advise? Do you converse seriously, usefully, and closely? To be more particular: Do you use all the means of grace yourself, and enforce the use of them on all other persons?

Immediately afterward, Wesley spells out the chief means of grace, and this time it is a list of five. The standard three are there (prayer, searching the Scriptures, and the Lord's Supper), but he adds two more: meditating and Christian conference. He gives illustrations of each, along with instructions about what a helper ought to ask concerning them:

> 1.) Prayer. Private, family, public; consisting of deprecation, petition, intercession, and thanksgiving. Do you use each of these? Do you use private prayer every morning and evening? If you can, at five in the evening; and the hour before or after morning preaching ? Do you forecast daily, wherever you are, how to secure these hours? Do you avow it every where? Do you ask every where, "Have you family prayer?" Do you retire at five o'clock?

2.) Searching the Scriptures by

(i.) Reading: Constantly, some part of every day; regularly, all the Bible in order; carefully, with the Notes; seriously, with prayer before and after; fruitfully, immediately practicing what you learn there?

(ii.) Meditating: At set times ? by any rule?

(iii.) Hearing: Every morning? carefully; with prayer before, at, after; immediately putting in practice? Have you a New Testament always about you?

3.) The Lord's Supper: Do you use this at every opportunity? with solemn prayer before; with earnest and deliberate self devotion?

4.) Fasting: How do you fast every Friday?

5.) Christian conference: Are you convinced how important and how difficult it is to "order your conversation right"? Is it always in grace? seasoned with salt? meet to minister grace to the hearers? Do not you converse too long at a time? Is not an hour commonly enough? Would it not be well always to have a determinate end in view; and to pray before and after it?

Clearly Wesley is prepared to descend into particulars. A question about fasting, for instance, becomes a question about fasting "every Friday." And he has practical wisdom, based on principle and on long pastoral experience, to offer in each area ("Do not you converse too long at a time?"). But Wesley shows no urgency about fine-tuning his technique in any of these areas. Especially when training helpers, he trusts that it will be enough to sketch in the big picture and allow prudent people to be led by the Spirit into the right practical decisions. As long as they recall the spiritual dynamic that animates the means of grace, the rest is technical detail. And while every detail is worth attending to for a man whose movement is nicknamed Methodism, Wesley knows that the life is not in the details of the means of grace, but in the encounter of a soul with God. For the same reason, Wesley shows no urgency about making an exhaustive list of every means of grace, or every spiritual discipline. God will meet us in the appointed ("instituted") places and times, through appropriate ("prudential") tools and methods. All that matters is that we wait for him, and use the means.

CHAPTER 8

SAVED TO THE UTTERMOST

"Let patience have her perfect work, that ye may be perfect and entire, wanting nothing," says James 1:4. In his *Explanatory Notes upon the New Testament*, Wesley offered these brief comments on the passage: "Give it full scope, under whatever trials befall you." As for being "perfect and entire," Wesley paraphrased that as "adorned with every Christian grace," and his only remark about "lacking nothing" is that this completeness is the very thing "which God requires in you."[1]

These are not just random remarks on James 1:4; they are consistent with Wesley's teaching throughout his ministry. This is how he always talked. Wesley believed that Scripture promises to believers a renewal of the heart in love, opening up a range of Christian experience in which the prevailing attitude is not simply struggling against sin, but actively taking delight in doing God's will from the heart. He anchored this belief not in optimism about human nature, but in confidence that Jesus is a competent and comprehensive Savior, and that he will deliver his people from sin altogether—from its guilt and condemnation (by justification), as well as from its power and dominion (by sanctification)—before setting them free from the very existence of sin (by glorification). Jesus, Wesley taught, "saves to the uttermost," and intends to "reign in our hearts alone, and subdue all things to himself."[2] Wesley called this blessing by various names, but he especially favored these three: entire sanctification, Christian perfection, and perfect love.

---

[1] Wesley, *Explanatory Notes upon the New Testament* (London: Epworth, 1950), 856.
[2] "A Plain Account of Christian Perfection," in *John and Charles Wesley: Selected Prayers, Hymns, Journal Notes, Sermons, Letters and Treatises*, ed. Frank Whaling (New York: Paulist, 1981), 306.

What Is Sanctification, and Can It Be Complete?

Three facets of salvation are traditionally put together to describe the entire course of the Christian life: justification, sanctification, and glorification. In contemporary evangelical usage, they mean something like being forgiven (justification), growing in Christlikeness (sanctification), and going to heaven (glorification). Wesley certainly thought in these traditional terms, broadly speaking. "We allow," he wrote, that "it is the work of God alone to justify, to sanctify, and to glorify; which three comprehend the whole of salvation."[3] We have seen how passionately he taught justification by faith, and how he defended it as a complete work accomplished in Christ and applied by the Spirit. He also proclaimed glorification, the hope of heaven, with its complete deliverance from the presence of evil and sin. But the distinctiveness of Wesleyan theology is most prominent in the way he thought about that middle factor, sanctification. He considered it not as a catch-all for everything that happens between conversion and death, but more concretely, as a specific blessing given by God.

The best way to clarify the nature of sanctification is to contrast it with justification. Justification is a change in a person's status and does not imply anything about a person's actual condition. A sinner who becomes justified does not have more virtues or fewer vices as a result of being justified. But sanctification names the actual transformation of the person's character and conduct. The crucial distinction is between what is purely relational (justification) and what is real (sanctification). Wesley put it this way:

> Justification implies only a relative, the new birth a real, change. God, in justifying us, does something for us; in begetting us again, he does the work in us. The former changes our outward relation to God, so that of enemies we become children; by the latter our inmost souls are changed, so that of sinners we become saints. The one restores us to the favour, the other to the image, of God. The one is the taking away of the guilt, the other the taking away of the power, of sin.[4]

This way of distinguishing the two gifts is not unique to Wesley; aside from being biblical, it is also standard Protestant soteriology. As early as

---

[3] "Predestination Calmly Considered," in *Works*, 4:42.
[4] Sermon 19, "The Great Privilege of Those That Are Born of God," in *Wesley's 52 Standard Sermons*, ed. N. Burwash (Salem, OH: Schmul, 1988), 183.

1519, Martin Luther preached about the "two kinds of Christian righteousness" described by Scripture. The first kind is Christ's own proper righteousness, which is utterly alien to us and must be imputed to us. "This is an infinite righteousness, and one that swallows up all sins in a moment, for it is impossible that sin should exist in Christ. On the contrary, he who trusts in Christ exists in Christ; he is one with Christ, having the same righteousness as he."[5]

But the other kind of Christian righteousness is "our proper righteousness," which consists in "that manner of life spent profitably in good works," in love toward neighbors, and in meekness toward God. Anyone who knows Luther knows that he emphasized the first kind of righteousness, the justifying righteousness of Christ that is ours by imputation. "This righteousness is primary," he insisted, but he did not stop there. "It is the basis, the cause, the source of all our own actual righteousness." Our own proper righteousness is called our own, of course, not "because we alone work it, but because we work with that first and alien righteousness."[6] Both are brought about by God, but in different ways. In Wesley's terms, the first kind of righteousness comes to us from outside, from the finished work of Christ; the second is formed within us by the indwelling Spirit. Justification "is not being made actually just and righteous," says Wesley: "This is sanctification; which is, indeed, in some degree the immediate fruit of justification; but nevertheless, is a distinct gift of God, and of a totally different nature. The one implies, what God 'does for us' through his Son; the other, what he 'works in us' by his Spirit."[7]

As we saw above (in chap. 3, on regeneration), the two gifts always go together. As constituent parts of the one saving act of God, they even imply one another. God forgives us just as we are so that he can make us stop being just as we are and instead become just as Christ is. For example, a habitual liar who repents and believes in Jesus is forgiven, but still has the character, instincts, and habits of one who lies. The same God who forgave him also empowers him to stop lying. The relative change (justification) clears the way for the real change (sanctification). The voice of Christ says, "Be of good cheer; thy sins are forgiven thee," as well as, "Go and sin no more."[8]

---

[5] Martin Luther, "Two Kinds of Righteousness," in *Martin Luther's Basic Theological Writings*, 2d ed., ed. Timothy F. Lull (Minneapolis: Fortress, 2005), 135.

[6] Ibid., 136.

[7] Sermon 5, "Justification by Faith," Burwash, 45.

[8] Sermon 45, "The New Birth," Burwash, 462 (Wesley is combining Jesus's words from Matt. 9:2 and John 8:11).

It is this real moral change in the life of a justified sinner that Wesley believed could be completed. He taught that sanctification can reach its ful-fillment before glorification. All three aspects of salvation have their own integrity as elements of the one great salvation: justification is a complete act, and glorification is a complete act. For Wesley, sanctification is not just a hallway between these two acts, but a distinct aspect of salvation that can be complete in its own right. It is one phase of God's work to deliver us from sin. God totally delivers us from the guilt and condemnation of sin by justi-fication, totally delivers us from its power and dominion by sanctification, and totally delivers us from its very presence and existence by glorification.

But there is one other matter to clear up if we want a sharp understand-ing of Wesley's teaching on entire sanctification. Alongside the traditional triad of justification, sanctification, and glorification, there has also been a recognition among Protestant theologians that the word *sanctification* is often used in the New Testament to point not to the real change we have been talking about, but to the same relative change that we call justifica-tion. This fact has led theologians to recognize a reality called positional sanctification or definitive sanctification. In the best recent treatment of this view, David Peterson summarizes it this way:

> Several texts point to the fact that God sanctifies his people once and for all, through the work of Christ on the cross. Other texts link sanctification with conversion or baptism into Christ, highlighting the work of the Holy Spirit through the gospel, consecrating believers to God as his holy people under the New Covenant.[9]

In other words, God sanctifies definitively when he designates some-body as holy by setting that person apart. This is the main way the Bible tends to talk about sanctification: God's definitive action whereby he de-clares a person to be holy before him and places that person in a position of holiness (hence "positional sanctification"). For example, Paul says that Christ gave himself for the church "that he might sanctify and cleanse it" (Eph. 5:26). The Corinthian Christians are told "you were washed, you were sanctified" (1 Cor. 6:11, ESV). Hebrews affirms that Jesus suffered "that he

---

[9] David Peterson, *Possessed by God: A New Testament Theology of Sanctification and Holiness* (Grand Rapids: Eerdmans, 1995), 13. Peterson's book is indispensable for the way it uses New Testament categories to discipline the widespread, loose speech about sanctification. Though Peterson's correctives push hard against Wesleyan teaching, he has the excellent taste to give Charles Wesley the last word, ending his book with a stanza of "Love Divine, All Loves Excelling." See also John Murray's article "Definitive Sanc-tification," *Calvin Theological Journal* 2, no. 1 (April 1967): 5–21.

might sanctify the people with his own blood" (Heb. 13:12). In these and many other cases, the Bible is using the word "sanctify" to point to a definitive past act. [10] The New Testament certainly goes on to talk about a process of growth and gradual transformation over the course of the Christian life. But that progressive sanctification is subsequent to the definitive sanctification. Believers are positionally holy in Christ, and therefore they are supposed to go on and become experientially holy in Christ.

If we are thinking of sanctification in this definitive or positional sense, then the question "Can sanctification be complete?" requires an obvious answer of yes. In fact, on a Protestant view, it would be impossible for it ever to be anything but complete, since in this case "sanctification" is the same thing as "justification." It uses temple imagery rather than legal imagery, but the point is the same. Both are definitive, instantaneous, and based on unilateral divine action.

John Wesley understood and affirmed all of this. Thomas Oden has described Wesley's sanctification teaching as "a complex constellation of ideas and exegetical applications," adding that

> in most ways it is close to what some Reformed writers have called positional sanctification. There is a profound doctrine of sanctification in the Calvinist teaching of our sharing in the righteousness of Christ, assuming that our sanctification is already embedded in this juridical act. This idea of sanctification Wesley strongly affirmed, yet with the recurring alarm that it might drift toward antinomian license. The only way he was refashioning it was by speaking steadily of the possibility and necessity of a full and unreserved consecration of the whole of one's redeemed powers for the remainder of one's life. [11]

In other words, the only adjustments Wesley made to the standard Protestant teaching on *positional* sanctification were parallel to the adjustments he made to the doctrine of justification: he hedged it against antinomianism in any way possible. In the case of holiness and sanctification teaching, he was especially jealous to make sure Christians did not try to use

---

[10] The New Testament use of *sanctify* in the definitive or positional sense is not a surprise to Wesley scholars. The three biblical examples cited here are taken from John R. Tyson, *Charles Wesley on Sanctification: A Biographical and Theological Study* (Grand Rapids: Francis Asbury, 1986), 174. Tyson's summary of the biblical material is excellent, setting the stage for his account of Charles Wesley's flexible use of sanctification language throughout his hymns.

[11] Thomas Oden, *John Wesley's Scriptural Christianity: A Plain Exposition of His Teaching on Christian Doctrine* (Grand Rapids: Zondervan, 1994), 313.

imputed holiness as an excuse for avoiding imparted holiness. But sanctification, in the positional or definitive sense, is something that can and must be complete.

The Principle of Real Change

However, if we turn our attention from definitive sanctification to the experience of progressive sanctification during the course of a Christian's life, we have a different set of issues altogether. Can progressive sanctification ever be said to be complete? Can a Christian look forward to the possibility of experiencing entire sanctification? Justification must be perfect and complete; glorification will surely be perfect and complete; but what about the process of sanctification during the Christian life? Can it reach its goal?

Wesley said yes, and meant it. He believed that at regeneration, God implanted a principle of new life in the forgiven sinner. That principle of holiness would progressively work its way out in character and behavior, and would finally do what is in its nature to do: destroy the dominion of sin in the human heart. Wesley spent a great deal of his ministry on this doctrine of entire sanctification: promoting it, defending it, and clarifying it.

But saying "Wesley taught entire sanctification" is already a bit too abstract and tidy to do justice to his work. He talked about this doctrine in many ways, most of them involving directly biblical language and sometimes long conglomerations of scriptural terms. In popular evangelical language, we may have a tendency to use the word *sanctification* as shorthand to signify the process of Christian growth; when we use the term that way, we are not so much using the Bible's own language (according to which, as we saw above, *sanctification* more often refers to a definitive event) as using a conventional and traditional theological term. Wesley's instincts led him to quote the words of Scripture as much as possible, and as a result he often talked about what we call progressive sanctification without ever using those terms.

His most frequent term for this reality was "growth in grace," or "growing in grace and in the knowledge of our Lord Jesus Christ." This language is from the final verse of 2 Peter, and in his *Explanatory Notes upon the New Testament*, at 2 Peter 3:18 Wesley has an unusually long and full comment. As is typical of his *Notes*, he is not really offering an exegesis of the passage; he presupposes the exegesis and moves on to indicate what should be preached from the passage. He glosses the phrase "grow in grace" as meaning "in every Christian temper" and then explores the meaning of growth: "There may be, for a time, grace without growth; as there may be natural life without growth. But such sickly life, of soul or body, will end in death, and every day draw nigher to it. Health is the means of both natural and spiritual growth."[12] "Grow or die," Wesley suggests, is the idea underlying Peter's exhortation to "grow in grace." If the principle of new life has been imparted in the new birth, then it will exercise itself in all the ways of spiritual health. Wesley goes on to consider the stark alternative while bringing in Paul's language to clarify Peter's:

> If the remaining evil of our fallen nature be not daily mortified, it will, like an evil humor in the body, destroy the whole man. But "if ye through the Spirit do mortify the deeds of the body," (only so far as we do this,) "ye shall live" the life of faith, holiness, happiness. The end and design of grace being purchased and bestowed on us, is to destroy the image of the earthly, and restore us to that of the heavenly. And so far as it does this, it truly profits us; and also makes way for more of the heavenly gift, that we may at last be filled with all the fulness of God.[13]

To grow in grace, the believer needs sustenance and nutrition, so Wesley continues by describing the daily food needed by the Christian soul. To fail in feeding the soul is to abandon the project of growth and "invert the order of God in his new creation":

> The strength and well-being of a Christian depend on what his soul feeds on, as the health of the body depends on whatever we make our daily food. If we feed on what is according to our nature, we grow; if not, we pine away and die. The soul is of the nature of God, and nothing but what is according to his holiness can agree with it. Sin, of every kind, starves the soul, and makes it consume away. Let us not try to invert the order of God in his new creation: we shall only deceive ourselves. It is easy to forsake the will of God, and follow our own; but this will bring leanness into the soul.[14]

Finally, Wesley cannot leave the subject of "growing in grace" without driving home the fact that this transformation is a real one. It is not on the

---

[12] Wesley, *Explanatory Notes upon the New Testament*, at 2 Pet. 3:18, pp. 900–901.
[13] Ibid., 900.
[14] Ibid.

level of a judicial reality known only by careful reasoning or by submission to what God has said. It can be known, encountered, experienced, and felt. Growth in grace produces real changes in the mind and real transformation in the heart. In other words, to grow in grace is to experience holiness and happiness. Wesley will not tolerate having this real transformation brushed aside, juggled away, or mocked as "just feelings." It is the very outworking in a human life and character of the great salvation given by God:

> It is easy to satisfy ourselves without being possessed of the holiness and happiness of the gospel. It is easy to call these frames and feelings, and then to oppose faith to one and Christ to the other. Frames (allowing the expression) are no other than heavenly tempers, "the mind that was in Christ." Feelings are the divine consolations of the Holy Ghost shed abroad in the heart of him that truly believes. And wherever faith is, and wherever Christ is, there are these blessed frames and feelings. If they are not in us, it is a sure sign that though the wilderness became a pool, the pool is become a wilderness again.[15]

The concreteness and the reality of this transformation must be kept in mind if Wesley's teaching about realizing the goal of sanctification is to make sense. Sanctification—growth in grace—is something that can be observed and experienced. Of course it must arise from an invisible divine action of relational change, but it becomes a process of real change. And the experience of it is not infallible; it can be counterfeited. Nevertheless, the real change of sanctification manifests itself as a heart transformed in love.

Wesley kept his focus on the real change brought about by God's Spirit in the process of growth in grace. There is a great confusion for those who fail to keep their sight focused on real transformation. They run the risk of confusing the perfection of justification with the perfection of sanctification. That is, when asked about their character or conduct, they will imagine that both are somehow perfect because the character and conduct of Christ are perfect. But that answer changes the subject from sanctification back to justification. Such confusion is widespread and easy to fall into. When Wesley preached the possibility of perfection, some people yawned and said that every Christian already has perfection by definition. Wesley puts the objection in the mouth of an imagined opponent: "But what great matter is there in this? Have we not all this when we are justified?" Wesley's

---

[15] Ibid., 901.

response is striking; he changes the subject from justification back to the real transformation of sanctification:

> What! Total resignation to the will of God, without any mixture of self-will? Gentleness, without any touch of anger, even the moment we are provoked? Love to God, without the least love to the creature, but in and for God, excluding all pride? Love to man, excluding all envy, all jealousy, and rash judging? Meekness, keeping the whole soul inviolably calm? And temperance in all things? Deny that any ever came up to this, if you please; but do not say all who are justified do.[16]

Though it seems humble and pious, and often arises from such good motives, to point away from oneself to the righteousness of Christ in this context is actually an evasion. It is Wesley's "grand pest," the antinomian impulse, showing up again. The perfect and infinite righteousness of Christ is not in question here; it is the observable and to some degree even measurable righteousness or unrighteousness of the Christian that is in question. A spiritual advisor might reply, "I know Jesus is sober and chaste; I am inquiring whether you are."

Charles Wesley expresses this theology of sanctification in his hymn "I Want a Principle Within." By focusing on the principle itself, he helps us see that our sanctification is an organic outworking of what God has put into us:

> I want a principle within
> of watchful, godly fear,
> a sensibility of sin,
> a pain to feel it near.
>
> I want the first approach to feel
> of pride or wrong desire,
> to catch the wandering of my will,
> and quench the kindling fire.
>
> From thee that I no more may stray,
> no more thy goodness grieve,
> grant me the filial awe, I pray,
> the tender conscience give.

---

[16] "A Plain Account of Christian Perfection," 355.

Quick as the apple of an eye,
O God, my conscience make;
awake my soul when sin is nigh,
and keep it still awake.

Almighty God of truth and love,
to me thy power impart;
the mountain from my soul remove,
the hardness from my heart.

O may the least omission pain
my reawakened soul,
and drive me to that blood again,
which makes the wounded whole.

Here is the hunger for holiness, the reliance on God's power imparted in regeneration, and the return to the atoning blood that alone can heal the needs of fallen people.

All the Benefits of Union with Christ

We are approaching the doctrine of *entire sanctification*, which is one of the most divisive elements of John Wesley's theology of the Christian life. Many believers who have learned a great deal from Wesley have had to part company with him at this point, grateful for what they could gather but unable to embrace the full message. "It is this doctrine which, more even than Predestination, separates the Methodist from the Calvinist-Evangelical wings of the Revival."[17]

But just before we reach that point of division, we encounter one of the greatest gifts Wesley was able to bequeath to Christians of all sorts: his emphasis on the unity of all the benefits of union with Christ. Wesley had a hunger for the fullness of salvation, and he eagerly preached each of the benefits as connected to the whole. His whole career as a preacher was a series of discovered connections between the parts of the Christian message that we are always tempted to take apart. He routinely preached on sanctification in a way that drew the mind back to justification; in his preaching, the law and the gospel interpenetrated perfectly.

---

[17] Gordon Rupp, "The Future of the Methodist Tradition," *The London Quarterly and Holborn Review* 184 (1959): 270.

Watch how Wesley concludes the constructive part of sermon 1, "Salvation by Faith," with a statement about justification that seamlessly segues into regeneration and transformation and on to perfection:

> This then is the salvation which is through faith, even in the present world: a salvation from sin, and the consequences of sin, both often expressed in the word justification; which, taken in the largest sense, implies a deliverance from guilt and punishment, by the atonement of Christ actually applied to the soul of the sinner now believing on him, and a deliverance from the power of sin, through Christ formed in his heart. So that he who is thus justified, or saved by faith, is indeed born again. He is born again of the Spirit unto a new life, which "is hid with Christ in God." And as a new-born babe he gladly receives the *adolon*, "sincere milk of the word, and grows thereby"; going on in the might of the Lord his God, from faith to faith, from grace to grace, until at length, he come unto "a perfect man, unto the measure of the stature of the fullness of Christ."[18]

Wesley was keen to make distinctions for the sake of clarity, but as a preacher he loved to elide the differences and lead an audience from one phase to another without alerting them that he was doing so: "Be of good cheer, thy sins are forgiven thee; so forgiven, that they shall reign over thee no more."[19] Free forgiveness blossoms into power over sin imperceptibly in Wesley's preaching. "Justification," he once wrote, "is sanctification begun."[20] And if John Wesley was able to do this in his sermons, Charles was able to use the medium of the hymn to blur the dividing lines even more. In his work, "redemption flows quickly and powerfully through justification toward its logical and theological completion in sanctification."[21]

In this holism, Wesley's theology is a helpful corrective to much contemporary preaching, and a preservative against the rot that inevitably sets into the popular use of theological terms. Think how degraded the average conversation about salvation becomes when it is not under the discipline of a vision that takes in the whole horizon of evangelical soteriology. "Salvation" comes to mean one particular benefit of union with Christ rather than the full range of all the benefits. In particular, it tends to mean going to heaven. When Christians today ask, "Can you lose your salvation," they

---

[18] Sermon 1, "Salvation by Faith," Burwash, 6–7.
[19] Ibid., 9.
[20] *Works*, 9:387–88.
[21] Tyson, *Charles Wesley on Sanctification*, 42.

almost always mean exclusively, "Can you fail to go to heaven?" They have singled out one of the blessings of union with Christ (glorification—admittedly, an infinite one!) and ruled all the others to be not worth considering. The other blessings apparently do not deserve the name "salvation."

But "salvation," for John Wesley, was always a more comprehensive term and always pointed to a bundle of good gifts from God. Preaching on the text "by grace are ye saved through faith" (Eph. 2:8), Wesley stressed that salvation refers not *only* to our future entrance into heaven, but also to what we possess right now. Salvation, he wrote, "is not something at a distance; it is a present thing." In fact, "the salvation which is here spoken of might be extended to the entire work of God, from the first dawning of grace in the soul, till it is consummated in glory."[22]

Perversely, some people use the promise of heaven as a way of hiding from all the other benefits of union with Christ. Wesley never made the reactionary mistake of denigrating eternal life, a tragically short-sighted error of the "imagine there's no heaven" variety. Instead, he held up the other benefits of union with Christ, and chief among them, sanctification. It is "the privilege of those who are born of God" that they are given power over sin.

To see the difference in emphasis, imagine somebody asking, "Can you lose your salvation?" and meaning by that, "can you stop having fellowship with God," or "can you lose access to God in prayer," or "can you be conquered by sin?" Wesley would point out that to suffer any of these losses in the course of the Christian life is already to lose one of the benefits of union with Christ. A person who is unperturbed by losing those benefits, but seeks assurance only of the eschatological benefit in isolation from all others is simply not thinking about reality. For this reason, Wesley always drove the conversation about salvation out the narrow grooves of habitual reductionism and into the wide field of the full gospel:

> By salvation I mean, not barely, according to the vulgar notion, deliverance from Hell, or going to Heaven: But a present deliverance from sin, a restoration of the soul to its primitive health, its original purity; a recovery of the divine nature; the renewal of our souls after the image of God, in righteousness and true holiness, in justice, mercy, and truth. This implies all holy and heavenly tempers, and by consequence all holiness of conversation.[23]

---

[22] Sermon 43, "The Scripture Way of Salvation," Burwash, 441. This sermon is widely considered Wesley's most comprehensive and mature overview of his total message.

[23] "A Farther Appeal to Men of Reason and Religion," in *The Works of the Reverend John Wesley*, ed. John Emory, 7 vols. (New York: Emory and Waugh, 1831), 5:35.

Fighting the disintegration of the idea of salvation, Wesley characteristically described salvation as both an immediate reality and a vast expanse of multiple blessings. In sermon 62 he described "real religion" in a panoramic survey of salvation history:

> Here then we see in the clearest, strongest light, what is real religion: A restoration of man by Him that bruises the serpent's head, to all that the old serpent deprived him of; a restoration not only to the favor but likewise to the image of God, implying not barely deliverance from sin, but the being filled with the fullness of God.[24]

Wesley's goal in describing salvation so fully was to awaken a hunger and thirst for more of God and more of the gospel. His impassioned plea to his hearers was for them not to settle for less, but to take all that God had promised:

> O do not take any thing less than this for the religion of Jesus Christ! Do not take part of it for the whole! What God hath joined together, put not asunder! Take no less for his religion, than the "faith that worketh by love"; all inward and outward holiness. Be not content with any religion which does not imply the destruction of all the works of the devil; that is, of all sin. We know, weakness of understanding, and a thousand infirmities, will remain, while this corruptible body remains; but sin need not remain: This is that work of the devil, eminently so called, which the Son of God was manifested to destroy in this present life. He is able, he is willing, to destroy it now, in all that believe in him. Only be not straitened in your own bowels! Do not distrust his power, or his love! Put his promise to the proof! He hath spoken: And is he not ready likewise to perform? Only "come boldly to the throne of grace," trusting in his mercy; and you shall find, "He saveth to the uttermost all those that come to God through him!"[25]

"To the uttermost" is a phrase from the King James Version of Hebrews 7:25. In his *Notes on the New Testament*, Wesley expanded "the uttermost" as "from all the guilt, power, root, and consequence of sin."[26] Wesley's doctrine of the Christian life has been called "an optimism of grace,"[27] and

---

[24] Sermon 62, "The End of Christ's Coming," in Emory, *The Works of the Reverend John Wesley,* 2:73.
[25] Ibid.
[26] Wesley, *Explanatory Notes upon the New Testament,* 829–30.
[27] E. Gordon Rupp, *Principalities and Powers: Studies in the Christian Conflict in History* (London: Epworth, 1952), 77.

Charles Wesley himself called it an "omnipotence of grace" in some of his hymns. For example:

> By faith we see our Lord descend,
> And every obstacle give place:
> He comes, He comes, our sin to end,
> With all th' omnipotence of grace![28]

John Wesley staked his view on the competence of Christ as Savior, and on God's stated will to overthrow the power of sin in the lives of his children.

In his preaching and teaching, Wesley was eager to hold together all the benefits of union with Christ. He tried to put his hearers in a position where they did not have the option of picking and choosing among the benefits, but had to take them all. This strategy of Wesley's—actually a whole bundle of integrated rhetorical, pastoral, and organizational strategies—was effective, and it led many people into a grander, more comprehensive encounter with God in salvation.

But there is one benefit of union with Christ that he left out, and he was never able to satisfy his critics about it. I mean the benefit of preservation in grace, sometimes described as perseverance. Shouldn't eternal security be reckoned as one of the great benefits of being united to Christ, and shouldn't a holistic approach like Wesley's have taken it in as well?

The New Testament describes salvation in terms of confidence, security, and the expectation of fulfillment. Wesley knew these passages, and he taught that believers could know they were justified and live a life of certainty rather than uncertainty. He carefully traced the way the witness of God's Spirit (sermons 10 and 11) connected with the witness of our own spirits (sermon 12) to produce assurance. But Wesley did also affirm that a believer could fall from grace.[29] In his *Explanatory Notes upon the New Testament*, he handles the warning passage of Hebrews 6 as "not a supposition, but a plain recitation of fact." Commenting on those who "have fallen away," and how it is "impossible to renew them again unto repentance," he says, "The apostle here describes the case of those who have cast away both the power and the form of godliness; who have lost both their faith, hope, and love, and that willfully. Of these willful total apostates he declares,

---

[28] Tyson, *Charles Wesley on Sanctification*, 164.
[29] See J. Matthew Pinson, ed., *Four Views on Eternal Security* (Grand Rapids: Zondervan, 2002), to see the Wesleyan view compared to other options.

it is impossible to renew them again to repentance."[30] This possibility of "willful total" apostasy is not something that Wesley dwells on long in his sermons. He asserts that "the great privilege of those that are born of God" is to cease from sinning (sermon 19), yet he also offers advice "On Sin in Believers" (sermon 13) and "Repentance in Believers" (sermon 14).

Above all, his great concern is to persuade his listeners that they should not settle for one isolated benefit of union with Christ, and toward this end he points out remorselessly that anybody who is living in sin has lost their salvation in the sense of having lost one of the benefits of union with Christ. Perhaps this was too tricky, an attempt at misdirection to make people stop asking the wrong question ("Have I lost my salvation?") and start asking the right one ("Am I in fellowship with God?"). And perhaps, ironically, it led Wesley to remove perseverance from the total catalog of benefits of union with Christ. Those who part company with Wesley at this point should nonetheless make good use of his guiding principles: to hold together all the benefits of union with Christ as a single package, and to trust in God's promises that he is a competent Savior and preserver.

What Christian Perfection Is and Isn't

In the introduction to an anthology of the most important readings from Wesley, Philip S. Watson summarizes John Wesley's theology "in terms of a simple fourfold formula, which, although not Wesley's own, admirably represents his mind and is rather more comprehensive than any single statement of his." Watson's formula is

(1) All men need to be saved;
(2) all men can be saved;
(3) all men can know they are saved;
(4) all men can be saved to the uttermost.[31]

These four points cover Wesley's teaching on sin, conversion, assurance of salvation, and Christian perfection, respectively. For Wesley, the fourth point flowed so naturally out of the first three that he was shocked when his fellow ministers in the revival found themselves reaching a different conclusion and sharply contradicting him. "What most surprised us," he

---

[30] Wesley, *Explanatory Notes upon the New Testament*, 824.
[31] Philip S. Watson, *The Message of the Wesleys: A Reader of Instruction and Devotion* (New York: Macmillan, 1964), 34.

reflected later, "was that we were said to 'dishonor Christ' by asserting that he saves to the uttermost; by maintaining that he will reign in our hearts alone, and subdue all things to himself."[32]

Wesley taught that sanctification could be complete, and the resulting state of entire sanctification he often called Christian perfection. He explained the sense of the term *perfection* in a 1762 letter to his brother Charles: "By perfection, I mean the humble, gentle, patient love of God and man ruling all the tempers, words, and actions, the whole heart and the whole life."[33] It was a term that made few friends, and he spent considerable time explaining it, hedging it, qualifying it, and defending it against misinterpretations. We will have to follow him through some of that work below. But first, it is possible to spell out what perfection is, according to Wesley. His clearest statement is probably the one he made in 1764 and subsequently edited into the definitive 1766 work *A Plain Account of Christian Perfection*. "Upon a review of the whole subject," Wesley boiled his teaching down into eleven "short propositions."

1. "There is such a thing as *perfection*; for it is again and again mentioned in scripture." Here we see Wesley insisting on the biblical language itself. He apparently felt obligated to have some doctrinal explanation of Christ's command for his followers to "be perfect" (Matt. 5:48) and for Paul's stated goal of "present[ing] every man perfect in Christ" (Col. 1:28). Modern translations tend to take the words for "perfect" (the *teleios* word group) and render them with a variety of words like "mature," "complete," and "fulfilled." These are all appropriate in their places, but the King James Version, which Wesley preached from, makes the word "perfect" somewhat more conspicuous. Also, Wesley had the Greek New Testament in mind. So he referred to perfection in verses where readers of English translations would not always see it. Further, he had the Greek word root in mind, which is related to a *telos*, a goal or a teleological end. "The basic meaning of *teleios* has to do with enjoying the full benefits, the end, goal, or outcome of something."[34] For a thing to be itself at all, it must be meaningfully oriented toward its *telos*.

2. "It is not so early as justification; for justified persons are to *go on to perfection* (Heb. 6:1)."

[32] "A Plain Account of Christian Perfection," 306.

[33] Letter to Charles Wesley, September 1762, in *The Letters of John Wesley*, 4:187, cited by Jason Vickers in "Wesley's Theological Emphases," in *The Cambridge Companion to John Wesley*, ed. Randy L. Maddox and Jason E. Vickers (New York: Cambridge University Press, 2010), 205, and Vickers, *Wesley: A Guide for the Perplexed* (London: T&T Clark, 2009), 102.

[34] Tyson, *Charles Wesley on Sanctification*, 165.

3. "It is not so late as death, for Saint Paul speaks of living men that were perfect (Phil. 3:15)."

Taken together, these three points are the foundation: there is some state of perfection between justification and death. John and Charles had a long-running debate about just how long before death a believer could expect to experience entire sanctification. Throughout his life, Charles increasingly came to see it as something that a victorious believer could hope for God to give him at the very moment of death. John seemed to agree, rather grudgingly, that this was the way it usually worked. But they were united in believing that there is such a thing, a kind of crowning event that consummates sanctification, and that it is a different experience from actual glorification.[35] John more than Charles continued to urge that if God could grant it on the deathbed, there is no reason he could not grant it a year earlier, or ten years, or right now. But he does not go into these details in his short account. Having established its reality, he next inquires into its character.

4. "It is not *absolute*. Absolute perfection belongs not to man, nor to angels, but to God alone." Here is where most people object to Wesley's terminology. "Perfection" immediately suggests absoluteness to us. But Wesley always intended the adjective *Christian* to draw the necessary distinction. "Christian Perfection" is not "Absolute Perfection." One expositor of the Wesleyan doctrine puts the contrast this way: "To our modern minds, the word perfection seems appropriate to describe a grade of a hundred percent on an exam, full attendance, a flawless job, or an unsurpassable standard of performance."[36] I would only add that not just "our modern minds" hear the word that way, but the minds of many of Wesley's eighteenth-century contemporaries registered the same connotation. But Wesley emphatically denied it. The next point is similar.

5. "It does not make a man *infallible*: None is infallible, while he remains in the body."

6. "Is it *sinless*?" This is a much harder question for Wesley. On the one hand, he did not like the term "sinless perfection" because it runs too close to absolute or infallible perfection. On the other hand, if sanctification is being made actually holy and righteous, then entire sanctification would exclude all sin. So in his "short proposition" he answered his own question

---

[35] For the contrast between the brothers on details of perfection, see John R. Tyson, *Assist Me to Proclaim: The Life and Hymns of Charles Wesley* (Grand Rapids: Eerdmans, 2007), 230–51.
[36] Ibid., 164.

circumspectly: "It is not worth while to contend for a term. It is *salvation from sin*." By avoiding the adjective, Wesley was probably trying to direct our attention away from the state of the saved person and toward the One whose power does the saving from (the power of) sin. But these three qualifications bring him to the point of needing to state positively what perfection consists of.

7. "It is *perfect love*. (1 John 4:18.) This is the *essence* of it; its *properties*, or inseparable fruits, are, *rejoicing evermore, praying without ceasing, and in everything giving thanks* (1 Thess. 5:16ff.)." Here Wesley strikes the main note of his teaching, and many Wesleyans have wished that he had been more consistent in emphasizing the language of 1 John, talking of perfect love more than Christian perfection. The goal of God's work in salvation is to renew the human person in his image, and the essence of that renewal is perfect love in the heart. The root of rebelliousness, the constant desire to sin, is dug out of the heart and removed in a sovereign, transforming act of God. When the heart is renewed in love, and gratitude and prayer flow unceasingly from it, sanctification has reached its goal, and the Christian is perfect. But having reached its goal, is it therefore a static condition, incapable of getting better or worse? The next two clarifications belong together: Christian perfection is improvable and amissible.

8. "It is improvable. It is so far from lying in an indivisible point, from being incapable of increase, that one perfected in love may grow in grace far swifter than he did before." This cuts across the expectations and intuitions of most people, but according to Wesley, perfection is not the end of growth in grace. It opens up new possibilities for greater growth, and even for faster growth. Once a believer enters the state of Christian perfection (after justification but before death), he is no longer held down and oppressed by the power of sin, and can therefore get serious about growth. Christian perfection, according to Wesley, is an achievement of a goal, but not the arrival at an end.

9. "It is amissible, capable of being lost." A Christian can reach this state and then fall from it. Initially, Wesley believed otherwise. But closer observation of Christian conduct over a longer course of time convinced him that it could be lost, as he says: "of which we have numerous instances. But we were not thoroughly convinced of this, till five or six years ago." With this empirical observation, Wesley turns to "how" questions, raising two issues about the method of Christian perfection.

10. "It is constantly both preceded and followed by a gradual work."

11. "But is it in itself instantaneous or not? In examining this, let us go on step by step." Wesley's understanding of the normative Christian experience was that after conversion, believers would have a gradual expansion of their knowledge and understanding of their own sin and of God's holiness. With the regenerate nature working within them, the increasing awareness of spiritual reality would produce a mounting tension, with greater grief over sin and greater desire to be delivered from it. Then, at a time and in a manner that pleased him, God would answer the Christian's faithful prayer for a deliverance from indwelling sin. Wesley thought this change happened in a moment, just like regeneration itself, although Methodists reported different levels of awareness of it: "an instantaneous change has been wrought in some believers," but "in some . . . they did not perceive the instant when it was wrought." The pattern was event-process-event-process; conversion, gradual growth, entire sanctification, then more gradual growth.

Concluding his 1764 review of the subject, Wesley wrote, "All our Preachers should make a point of preaching perfection to believers constantly, strongly, and explicitly; and all believers should mind this one thing, and continually agonize for it."[37] And in letters through the 1770s, we hear Wesley urging exactly that: "Never be ashamed of the old Methodist doctrine. Press all believers to go on to perfection. Insist everywhere on the second blessing as receivable in a moment, and receivable now, by simple faith."[38]

There are several threads woven together in the Wesleyan teaching on Christian perfection. Everything Wesley has taught about the distinction between justification and sanctification, of regeneration as initial sanctification, and about the Christian life as being normed and formed by the law comes together here. To this are joined new threads such as the idea of a second definitive work of grace subsequent to conversion, and the need to ask God for that second blessing. But the dominant theme in Wesley's teaching on Christian perfection is the renewed heart. Wesley

---

[37] Quoted in Whaling, *John and Charles Wesley*, 375.
[38] Letter to Samuel Bardsley, quoted in Kenneth Collins, *The Theology of John Wesley: Holy Love and the Shape of Grace* (Nashville: Abingdon, 2007), 281. Collins offers six examples here of John Wesley himself using the language of a "second blessing." Many Wesley interpreters have wrongly argued that it was not Wesley but the American holiness movement that began using the "second work of grace" language. The notion of a second blessing or second definitive work of grace following conversion would go on to be an important element in both holiness teaching and Pentecostalism.

was opposed to the notion that the best a mature Christian could hope for is perpetual battle against a rebellious heart, repressing sinful conduct by sheer force of will. Wesley believed that God intends to do a further work in mature Christians, a work that puts their hearts on the same side as God's heart in opposing the dominion of sin. As William Cannon wrote, "The teaching itself is simple enough" and "can be cast into a single sentence. Christian Perfection, according to Wesley, is a life every action of which issues from an uncompromised love of God and therefore of all the things of God."[39]

Charles Wesley wrote many hundreds of hymns on the subject of Christian perfection; it was not a minor point for him. He was especially good at capturing the note of the heart's yearning for holiness:

> In thee my wandering thoughts unite,
> Of all my works be thou the aim;
> Thy love attend me all my days,
> And my sole business be thy praise.[40]

Elaborations and Qualifications

Wesley was committed to this doctrine and invested considerable time and energy in its defense. "This doctrine," he reflected late in life, "is the grand *depositum* which God has lodged with the people called Methodists; and for the sake of propagating this chiefly He appeared to have raised us up."[41] Wesleyans have periodically agonized over the fact that their founder left them saddled with a *depositum* that requires so much upkeep. In his book *Wesley: A Guide for the Perplexed*, Jason Vickers notes that the doctrine "was a matter of controversy and debate for most of the latter half of his life" and "has been a matter of intense and at times acrimonious debate among his ecclesiastical descendents."[42] In an apt image, he compares talking about sanctification among Methodists and Wesleyans to defusing a bomb. In Wesley's own clarifications, it seems

> as though every word or phrase is a wire that must either be cut or left alone. One word is green, the next yellow. This phrase represents a purple

---

[39] William R. Cannon, "Perfection," *London Quarterly and Holborn Review* 184 (1959): 214.
[40] From the 1739 hymnal, 122, cited in Oden, *John Wesley's Scriptural Christianity*, 313.
[41] Letter to Robert Carr Brackenbury, September 15, 1790, in *The Letters of John Wesley*, ed. John Telford, 8 vols. (London: Epworth, 1931), 8:238.
[42] Vickers, *Wesley: A Guide for the Perplexed*, 102.

wire, that one a blue wire. Cut the wrong wire, and the consequences are devastating. The whole of Wesley's doctrine of sanctification explodes into a million pieces.[43]

The doctrine of Christian perfection may be powerful, but such power can be nerve-wracking to live with!

Of the many objections that hounded this teaching, two are especially illuminating. First, the idea of Christian perfection always suggested to some hearers a kind of spiritual self-sufficiency. That is, it seems that one who has attained Christian perfection would no longer have any need of Christ. In Wesley's 1759 tract *Thoughts on Christian Perfection*, he reported these argumentative questions: "If they live without sin, does not this exclude the necessity of a Mediator? At least is it not plain that they stand no longer in need of Christ in his priestly office?" Wesley's immediate reply was definite: "Far from it. None feel their need of Christ like these; none so entirely depend upon him. For Christ does not give life to the soul separate from, but in and with himself."[44] There are two lines of argument in this brief response. One is from the nature of perfection. If a Christian is perfect, it stands to reason he would perfectly depend on Christ. In fact, the more thoroughly sanctified one becomes, the more one moves from self-reliance to reliance on Christ. To argue otherwise would run the risk of making our active sinfulness the cement that holds us to Christ; a perverse conclusion to which Paul might respond "may it never be." Surely Christ can free us from sins without losing his grip on us. Thus "none so entirely depend on him" as do perfected Christians.

The second line of argument is from the nature of Christ's work: he saves not by remote, but by direct presence. Wesley puts this most eloquently a few lines later: "We have this grace not only *from* Christ, but *in* him." He goes on, "For our perfection is not like that of a tree, which flourishes by the sap derived from its own root, but . . . like that of a branch, which united to the vine, bears fruit; but severed from it, is dried up and withered."[45] The same question came up in 1763, and Wesley dealt with it more expansively. In particular he addressed the question of whether the entirely sanctified have any continuing need of Christ's priestly work:

---

[43] Ibid.
[44] "A Plain Account of Christian Perfection," 328. Wesley reprinted the tract *Thoughts on Christian Perfection* as part of his "Plain Account."
[45] Ibid., 329.

> The holiest of men still need Christ, as their prophet, as the light of the
> world. For he does not give them light, but from moment to moment: the
> instant he withdraws, all is darkness. They still need Christ as their king.
> For God does not give them a stock of holiness. But unless they receive a
> supply every moment, nothing but unholiness would remain. They still
> need Christ as their priest, to make atonement for their holy things. Even
> perfect holiness is acceptable to God only through Jesus Christ.[46]

Christ as prophet, king, and priest is not less necessary, but more necessary
to those who experience greater dominion over sin. But Wesley had to make
this case over and over, because everywhere he taught, some hearers left to
themselves would draw the opposite conclusion.

The other perpetual objection to examine is that the Bible does not give
many examples of entire sanctification. To defeat this objection, Wesley
makes an interesting move. He argues that Christian perfection is specifically a new covenant blessing. It has come to light because of the finished
work of Christ and the outpouring of the Holy Spirit, so it was only foreseen
in the Old Testament, to be experienced in the New. Therefore most of the
Bible would not bear witness to it directly. As for the New Testament, much
of it is addressed to a mixed body of believers occupying various positions
along the path to sanctification. So while the apostolic authors, in Wesley's
view, are constantly summoning their readers to "go on to perfection," they
are not often describing those who have done so. This line of thought can
be seen when Wesley answers the objection, "Solomon says [1 Kings 8:46],
'There is no man that sins not.'"

> Doubtless thus it was in the days of Solomon; yea, "and from Solomon
> to Christ there was then no man that sinned not." But whatever was the
> case of those under the law, we may safely say with Saint John, that since
> the Gospel was given, he that is born of God sins not. The privileges of
> Christians are in no wise to be measured by what the Old Testament re-
> cords concerning those who were under the Jewish dispensation; seeing
> the fullness of time is now come, the Holy Ghost is now given, the great
> salvation of God is now brought to men by the revelation of Jesus Christ.[47]

This appeal to the new covenant places the doctrine of Christian perfection in an eschatological context: it is a mystery not previously made

---

[46] Ibid., 350.
[47] Ibid., 307–8.

known. It is now possible because the end of the world has come in the Messiah. It is possible because God in Christ has taken the human condition into his own hands:

> He is able to save you from all the sin that still remains in your heart. He is able to save you from all the sin that cleaves to all your words and actions. He is able to save you from sins of omission, and to supply whatever is wanting in you. It is true, this is impossible with man; but with God-man all things are possible.[48]

But are there no examples in Scripture of the entirely sanctified? Wesley had a few pet theories on the subject. He admitted that "few of those to whom Saint Paul wrote his Epistles" had experienced this blessing, and he goes on to say that Paul himself was not entirely sanctified "at the time of his writing his former Epistles."[49] Apparently Paul went on to Christian perfection before writing the letters of his second imprisonment. And there is one conspicuous example of an entirely sanctified believer in the New Testament. "Saint John, and all those of whom he says, Herein is our love made perfect, that we may have boldness in the day of judgment, because as he is, so are we in this world (1 John 4:17)."[50]

These diagnoses of the levels of apostolic sanctification strike most readers as plain weird. Wesley did not build arguments on them, and they certainly never caused him to handle different sections of Scripture as having higher or lower levels of inspiration or inerrancy. Still, they show how thoroughly committed Wesley was to the truth and helpfulness of the doctrine of Christian perfection.

A sympathetic friend of Wesley's, the Irishman Alexander Knox (1757–1831), even when writing in Wesley's defense, nevertheless laid much of the blame for the ongoing controversy at his feet. Even if what Wesley meant by perfection was right, his use of the word was a mistake. "He made an injudicious use of it, so that the word became hackneyed, and the idea which it conveys perniciously misconceived."[51] J. I. Packer, who has some real differences with Wesley's view, complains about how difficult it is even to get through the two centuries of "misunderstanding and misdirected

---

[48] Sermon 14, "Repentance in Believers," Burwash, 134.
[49] "A Plain Account of Christian Perfection," 320.
[50] Ibid., 323.
[51] These remarks are from Knox's 1828 "Remarks on the Life and Character of John Wesley"; reprinted in Robert Southey, *Life of Wesley*, vol. 2 (London: Longman, 1846), 455.

criticism" provoked by "the confusing and provocative way in which Wesley expressed his view." Packer (as a nomophilic Puritan) is sympathetic to many of Wesley's concerns and appreciates "the fact that he found this vocabulary in both Scripture and tradition." But the biblical source of his terminology "cannot of itself excuse his willfulness or insensitiveness or truculence (it is hard to know which word best fits) in persisting with it when he saw what vast confusion it caused."[52] Packer catalogs examples of the confusion that arises from Wesley's decisions in this area:

> It was indeed confusing for Wesley to give the name of perfection to a state which from many standpoints was one of continued imperfection. It was yet more confusing that he should define sin "properly so called," subjectively, as "voluntary transgression of a known law," rather than objectively, as failure, whether conscious or unconscious, voluntary or involuntary, to conform to God's revealed standards. It was supremely confusing when he let himself speak of sanctified persons as being without sin (because they were not consciously breaking any known law) while at the same time affirming that they need the blood of Christ every moment to cover their actual shortcomings. Wesley himself insisted that by the objective standard of God's "perfect law," every sanctified sinner needs pardon every day; that makes it seem perverse of him also to have insisted on stating this view of the higher Christian life in terms of being perfect and not sinning.[53]

Choose Your Danger: Perfection or Anti-Perfection

When John and Charles Wesley explained their convictions about Christian perfection to Bishop Gibson in the 1740s, the Bishop replied, "Mr. Wesley, if this be all you mean, publish it to the world." But as Gordon Rupp admitted, "Alas, it was not all that Wesley did mean, for it is when we ask how this goal is to be attained and when it may be realized, that difficulties begin."[54]

We have already seen a few of the difficulties. In Wesley's own lifetime, some of his followers radicalized his teaching and became cultic, claiming to have reached angelic perfection. If we were to trace the legacy of perfection teaching from Wesley's age down through American holiness groups of various kinds, the "higher life" teaching associated with Keswick,

[52] J. I. Packer, *Keep in Step with the Spirit: Finding Fullness in Our Walk with God*, rev. ed. (Grand Rapids: Baker, 2005), 115.

[53] Ibid., 114–15.

[54] Gordon Rupp, *Religion in England 1688–1791* (Oxford: Clarendon, 1986), 425.

and the wide range of Pentecostal and charismatic varieties, we would find more than enough complications, contradictions, and spiritual casualties of perfectionism. And as other factors entered into the stream of historical influence, we could inquire whether the casualties are the logical outcome of Wesley's own teaching, or the result of defecting from his teaching or twisting it.

Again and again we have seen that Wesley's major decisions were driven by his horror at antinomianism. He suspected that it was lurking behind every tree and rock, and that it was the chasm his age was always on the brink of falling into. He presented entire sanctification, in many ways, as a massive counterweight to offset that danger. But in later times and among other subcultures, the main danger has often been legalism, and a semi-Wesleyan presentation of Christian perfection mixes with legalism in ways that are spiritually deadly. A two-tier system of elite Christians versus substandard Christians develops; works-righteousness sneaks back into the doctrine of the Christian life; behavioral expectations are taught as if they were the gospel, resulting in crushing guilt for those who cannot meet them and spiritual pride for those who believe they have done so.

But our interest here has only been to understand Wesley's own pre-sentation of entire sanctification, and perhaps to account for why it brought about many good effects in the earliest Methodist congregations. Part of the answer is that he nestled it in among his other evangelical commit-ments, which is why we have saved it for chapter 8. To do what it did for Wesley, the doctrine must be yoked to an overtly Protestant doctrine of justification, situated in a 1 John framework, ordered toward obeying God's law on the basis of the gospel, and located in regular use of the means of grace. The whole package worked for Wesley, but may come apart in the hands of less capable practitioners. Wesley was well aware that it had to be preached carefully, and one of the recurring questions he grappled with was how to present the doctrine. His classic answer was, "Scarce at all to those who are not pressing forward; to those who are, always by way of promise, always drawing rather than driving."[55] If the doctrine had always been presented in this way, drawing rather than driving, and using less objectionable ways of speaking, it would have done more good and less harm among its adherents and their victims.

Anyone who follows Wesley in the theology of entire sanctification

---

[55] "A Plain Account of Christian Perfection," 320.

needs to be careful. But critics of Christian perfection have need of equal care. Some people react with visceral revulsion to the teaching, and often need to examine their motives. Perhaps the dangers here will be more palatable if delivered in the words of J. I. Packer. In his book about sanctification, *Keep in Step with the Spirit*, Packer clearly recommends that his readers get their holiness teaching from John Calvin, John Owen, and J. C. Ryle. In other words, go shopping at the Calvinist store, or at least the Augustinian store. But Packer immediately warns about "some second-rank Augustinians who really do leave the impression that their interest is limited to orthodoxy and antiperfectionism and does not extend to holiness in any positive way."[56] There are such "second-rank Augustinians" and Calvinists abroad in our time, who are persistently allergic to any and all talk about real transformation, spiritual disciplines, and the necessity of good works in the Christian life. They dodge these realities by changing the subject to conversion, imputation, the righteousness of Christ, and the inescapability of sin in general. Mark such men and avoid them. "But," as Packer urges, "all positions should be judged by their best exponents," and there is a kind of Reformed sanctification teaching that is a law-abiding heart religion that John Wesley himself would rejoice to see, whatever other doctrinal disagreements might be present.

For his part, Packer levies four serious critiques against Wesley (taking care not to blame him for his followers) and then goes on to commend him. Even if you reject his doctrine of Christian perfection, Wesley's exposition of it sketches such a portrait of what it is to be altogether Christian that any true believer must be struck by the reality of what a Christian could be. "The nobility of Wesley's ideal of the Christian temper—all joy, thanksgiving, and love—stands as an abiding rebuke to anyone tempted to settle for anything less. . . . It exposes all shallow, self-absorbed, and self-indulgent elements in our devotion with devastating force."[57] The Wesleyan description of the heart renewed in love is the true image of a follower of Christ, and the legacy of Wesley includes thousands of pages of this description, wrought out of the words of Scripture, applied to the conscience, and sung in hymns and spiritual songs.

The final thing that Wesley's view of Christian perfection makes available to all as a kind of side effect, whether they accept his doctrine or not,

---

[56] Packer, *Keep in Step with the Spirit*, 109.
[57] Ibid., 119.

is a certain earnestness in prayer for sanctification. All Christians should pray for God to make them holy. Most do. But John and Charles Wesley, and those who learned from them, prayed these prayers with a kind of earnestness that can be shocking to overhear. The secret of their prayers is that they meant it. When they asked God to give them the gift of holiness, they had in mind a very concrete and particular change—a real change, not a relative one—which they were pleading for God to impart to them. To pray "God make me holy" without any real notion of what that would look like or expectation that God might in this very instant answer that prayer is to behave unseriously in the presence of God, to linger in the hallway while pretending one has entered into the room. The same words, on the lips of the Wesleys, meant something real, and really dangerous to "shallow, self-absorbed and self-indulgent elements in our devotions."

Wesley ends his long and (sometimes) tedious *Plain Account of Christian Perfection* with the question, "Are we your enemies because we look for a full deliverance from that carnal mind, which is enmity against God? Nay, we are your brethren, your fellow-laborers in the vineyard of our Lord." He goes on to say what is distinctive about his argument for being perfected in love: "We do expect to love God with all our heart, and our neighbor as ourselves. Yea, we do believe that he will in this world so 'cleanse the thoughts of our hearts, by the inspiration of his Holy Spirit, that we shall perfectly love him, and worthily magnify his holy name.'"[58] Wesley's fellow Anglicans would immediately recognize that he was quoting the ancient "Collect for Purity" found in the Book of Common Prayer: "Almighty God, unto Whom all hearts be open, all desires known, and from Whom no secrets are hid: Cleanse the thoughts of our hearts by the inspiration of Thy Holy Spirit, that we may perfectly love Thee, and worthily magnify Thy holy Name: through Christ our Lord. Amen." These words were prayed constantly all over England, but Wesley's theology of the Christian life equipped him to pray them in earnest, expecting an answer. Rupp asks, "Does not Wesley call all our bluff when he ends his *Plain Account* with the Collect for Purity?" After all, if he really means it, what do the rest of us mean?

> What do Christians mean when, at the altar, they pray that their hearts
> may be cleansed by the Holy Spirit, that they may perfectly love God,

---

[58] "A Plain Account of Christian Perfection," 377.

and worthily magnify his Holy Name? It would be blasphemy to suppose they mean nothing at all, that it is just a pious hope, a kind of pseudo-Augustinian "Give me to love thee perfectly—but not yet!" Better surely to say with Wesley, in the words of a modern saint, Temple Gairdner, "Let us believe the maximum!"[59]

---

[59] Rupp, *Religion in England 1688–1791*, 427.

CHAPTER 9

CATHOLIC SPIRIT

Ecumenical used to be a good word, but it has lost some of its luster. A word that used to point to the unity of all Christians now only conjures the image of mainline denominational heads congregating every few years on international junkets. *Catholic* was a good word, too, pointing to all Christians, as in the ancient formula "I believe in the holy catholic church." But now it is capitalized and points to one particular branch (Roman), which claims to be the only true one. *Inter-denominational* might help us think of all Christians, but (unlike *ecumenical* and *catholic*, with their Greek roots) it is an unbeautiful word suggesting bureaucratic jurisdictions. *Non-denominational* doesn't work at all.

How can we talk about the kind of Christian unity that spans the divisions between the various churches, the kind that reminds that us we have the central things in common, the kind that draws us together so we can stay close enough to keep arguing meaningfully? There is no single word that captures the attitude we are seeking; we have to keep using and explaining these old, compromised words. And as quickly as we invent a new one, it will suffer abuse and become unusable. The best we can do is look to examples of teachers and movements who have succeeded in negotiating those tensions.

John Wesley was such a leader. He knew that a Christian's life could not be lived out in isolation from the universal church. Wesley showed that this catholicity is not just a leisure activity, but part of what constitutes a real Christian life.

The Great Tradition of Christian Spirituality

To be a Christian means to live in the one great church founded on the apostles, rather than to follow a sectarian impulse. In a divided Christendom, living a fully and universally Christian experience will mean being open to the best in many sub-traditions, even while being persuaded of the rightness of one's own particular church. The best index of Wesley's catholicity is his wide devotional reading. In an impressive lifetime of reading spiritual writings, Wesley surveyed as much of the Christian tradition as was available to him at the time. His breadth was remarkable. Wesley lived by the Bible, of course, and claimed to be a man of one book (*homo unius libri*). But his single-minded focus on Scripture did not result from failing to read other books. It was something he achieved on the far side of wide reading and much learning. Wesley knew how to learn from Christians of all ages and denominations, and he wanted to pass that privilege along to as many people as he could.

As a result, Wesley devoted a considerable part of his ministry to editing and publishing books that he considered spiritually helpful. As his personal influence grew, he used it to recommend classic books. He wanted his people to be reading widely in the best works available, and when the best works had ceased being available, he brought them back into print himself. From the beginning of his ministry he was distributing reprints and abridgments of devotional literature. Then in 1748 he wrote to a friend that he had long been hoping to print "a little library, perhaps of fourscore or one hundred volumes, for the use of those that fear God." He gave a thumbnail sketch of his intention: "My purpose was to select whatever I had seen most valuable in the English language and either abridge or take the whole tracts, only a little corrected or explained, as occasion should require."[1] He soon set to work on his plan, and by 1755 he had brought out fifty volumes of about three hundred pages each, under the title *A Christian Library*. The subtitle was *Extracts from and Abridgments of the Choicest Pieces of Practical Divinity Which Have Been Published in the English Tongue*.

Richard Heitzenrater claims that in Wesley's *A Christian Library*, "part of his effort is to demonstrate that Christian truth is one from the beginning to his own day."[2] Wesley carried out this demonstration by the sheer

---

[1] Quoted in Thomas Walter Herbert, *John Wesley as Editor and Author* (Princeton, NJ: Princeton University Press, 1940), 25. See Herbert for a good overview of the whole *Christian Library* project.
[2] Richard P. Heitzenrater, "John Wesley's Reading of and References to the Early Church Fathers," in *Orthodox and Wesleyan Spirituality*, ed. S. T. Kimbrough Jr. (Crestwood, NY: St Vladimir's Seminary Press, 2002), 25–32.

scope of his reach, drawing from as far back as the first centuries of the church (the apostolic fathers such as Clement and Ignatius), and coming down to his own day (publishing his contemporary Jonathan Edwards). But he did not gather writers at random or in a mere attempt to be historically representative. He was evidently following some implicit set of principles that helped him trace the course of evangelical Protestant spirituality down through the centuries, even the centuries before there were evangelicals and Protestants. "Behind the diversity of men and movements in this astonishing miscellany there is a unity. With a little topping and tailing, it is true, he made them all speak one language, Scriptural Holiness, Christ, Methodism."[3] Wesley did focus on the Protestant centuries, which loom largest in the collection. He drew lightly on the church fathers and skipped over the medievals. Though he bypassed the major Reformers, some figures from the sixteenth century show up, and from that point it becomes the torrent that filled fifty volumes.

The collection is bracingly diverse and surprisingly nonpartisan. The works of Arminius are absent, though Wesley was the Arminian editor of *The Arminian Magazine*. Wesley rejected the doctrine of limited atonement, but in *A Christian Library* he included copious writings by the Puritan Thomas Goodwin (certainly in favor of limited atonement), while omitting John Goodwin (famously against limited atonement). Why would Wesley choose the Goodwin with whom he disagreed over the one who held his views? Here are two reasons: (1) John Goodwin wrote polemical, or argumentative and doctrinal, theology, while Thomas Goodwin wrote spiritual and devotional theology, and Wesley was a lover rather than a fighter. (2) Wesley had excellent taste, and it was the great Thomas Goodwin who wrote some of the "choicest practical divinity in the English tongue" (as the *Library*'s subtitle promised). Wesley could happily republish the writings of members of the Westminster Assembly, if they could write treatises as brilliant as *The Heart of Christ in Heaven toward Sinners*. There is quite a bit of writing by John Owen in these volumes as well, including his classic *Communion with God*.

From Wesley's point of view, only an anti-Calvinist bigot would refuse to recommend books so excellent on grounds that they were by Calvinists or included numerous lines of argument that were obviously Calvinist.

---

[3] Gordon Rupp, "Son to Samuel: John Wesley, Church of England Man," in *Just Men: Historical Pieces* (London: Epworth, 1977), 122.

Wesley was not hemmed in by his doctrinal positions on such matters; he knew that fifty volumes was hardly enough space to exhaust the great central core of Christian truth and its outworkings in the human heart. Wesley gathered in the greatest authors wherever he found them.

He did occasionally exercise some line-item veto authority over his authors, and he would especially strike out sentences and phrases that ran afoul of his own convictions. He especially loved the works of his contemporary Jonathan Edwards, eagerly republishing five of Edwards's books and boosting their circulation considerably. But Wesley was keen to eliminate the Calvinist elements of Edwards's work. His heavy-handed editing of Edwards's masterpiece *Religious Affections* is an extreme instance of Wesley's editorial method. "Wesley's treatment of *Religious Affections* is the most radical of all his abridgements, inasmuch as he takes the most liberties with this text."[4] In this mature work, Edwards explained the difference between true religion and false. During the revivals, many American colonists had professed faith but later abandoned it. It seemed obvious to Edwards that these people had never had true faith, and his book provided marks to confirm this judgment. But it seemed equally obvious to Wesley that these people had indeed had true faith, from which they had fallen away: they professed and then ceased to profess. Wesley asked, "What was the plain inference to be drawn from this? Why, that a true believer may make shipwreck of the Faith. How then could he evade the force of this? Truly by eating his own words, and proving, (as well as the nature of the thing would bear) that they were no believers at all!"[5]

Wesley thought that Edwards could only make the facts fit his faulty theological preconceptions by introducing a series of "curious, subtle, metaphysical distinctions" that turned his otherwise excellent book into something that would "puzzle the brain, and confound the intellects, of all the plain men and women in the universe." So Wesley as editor excised long sections and snipped many words and expressions from the text, publishing the *Religious Affections* for his readers, but in an altered form. "Out of this dangerous heap," he wrote, "wherein much wholesome food is mixt with much deadly poison, I have selected many remarks and admonitions, which may be of great use to the children of God."[6] Wesley was no textual

---

[4] Christopher M. B. Allison, "The Methodist Edwards: John Wesley's Abridgement of the Selected Works of Jonathan Edwards," *Methodist History*, 50, no. 3 (April 2012): 144–60.
[5] Ibid., 157.
[6] Ibid.

purist when it came to the distribution of theological and spiritual writings. His goal was pastoral, not bibliographic, so he filtered out what he considered harmful before passing along what he considered helpful.

Not all of Wesley's editing decisions were driven by theological judgments, though. Many were simply attempts to improve the writings. Because Wesley was a popular communicator, he had some justification for thinking that he knew the right way to put words together to reach a large audience. He seemed to enjoy the work of abridging other authors, producing shorter digests of longer works. It was his conviction that "even in the best books there was usually more said than was worth a man's time to read."[7] You can almost hear the glee with which he boasts in his journal about his day's editorial work: "I abridged Dr. Watts' pretty 'Treatise on the Passions.' His hundred and seventy pages will make a useful tract of four-and-twenty."[8] Wesley was cramming a large amount of material into a manageable fifty volumes, and much was left on the cutting-room floor.

Compiling the list of best books was a major undertaking, and Wesley asked for help from more seasoned teachers. For a starting point, he wrote to Philip Doddridge, who was only one year older than Wesley, but had long been famous for his labors as a leader of the dissenting party. "Doddridge replied with a carefully selected series. With these and other suggestions to supplement his own ideas, Wesley mapped out his table of contents."[9] Perhaps the Doddridge connection is what led some people to question whether the whole collection was really suitable for Anglican Christians. "Is not your Christian Library an odd collection of mutilated writings of Dissenters of all sorts?" was one challenge raised against it. Wesley's response was simply to recite the table of contents, which was overwhelmingly Anglican: "In the first ten volumes there is not a line from any Dissenter of any sort; and the greatest part of the other forty is extracted from Archbishop Leighton, Bishops Patrick, Ken, Reynolds, Sanderson, and other ornaments of the Church of England."[10]

This is certainly a notable list of Anglican luminaries. But when pressed, he was also happy to admit that "some of the writers he had followed were, indeed, of other denominations." Wesley stood his ground, though, and appealed to the unity that believers in Christ had, even across

---

[7] Herbert, *John Wesley as Editor and Author*, 28.
[8] From Wesley's journal, January 17, 1769, in *Works*, 4:298.
[9] Herbert, *John Wesley as Editor and Author*, 29.
[10] Ibid., 30.

those denominational boundaries. Just as he was an Arminian in the business of promoting the best Calvinist spiritual writers, his *Christian Library* was an Anglican project that maintained openness to the best from non-Anglican sources. "He was delighted with the opportunity of admitting the fact and supplementing his retort with a declaration of intellectual independence and tolerance."[11] Wesley's ecumenical scope was part of his vision of the Christian life.

"Books from time to time bowled Wesley over,"[12] and his life story is a sequence of reports on which book had most recently bowled him over. He was also an influencer, so passing along the best books was one of Wesley's most important ministries. And while his emphasis was consistently on spiritual things, Wesley also knew that the best Christian books could be read only by people whose minds had been exercised in as much literature and philosophy as possible. For this reason, Wesley's preaching, teaching, and publishing were always closely tied to an extensive educational task. His greatest successes in mass evangelism were among people considerably less educated than this fellow of Lincoln College, Oxford. He brought the simple gospel to simple people. But as soon as his influence was felt, he also tried to help the simple to begin to grow intellectually. "He was one of the few truly successful popularizers in the history of preaching," said Albert Outler. "His preaching and teaching offered both the gospel and a liberal education, as an integrated experience, to the common people who heard him gladly."[13] In his sermons, Wesley freely quoted Horace, Virgil, Ovid, and Cicero. He often misquoted them, indicating that he was working from memory. He published an abridgment of Milton's *Paradise Lost*, an act that speaks of astonishing self-assurance (to think he could improve on Milton!). The abridgment sold well, and that among people not likely to buy the whole work or to have read it at all in any form without Mr. Wesley's stamp of approval.

Bare literacy was not enough for Christians in a complex society; Wesley wanted his Methodists to be able to read critically, to think precisely, and to feel deeply the things they read. People needed their minds broadened and their intellectual powers stimulated if they were to receive biblical truth deeply. He once published an abridgment of a novel that had moved him, but had admittedly negligible spiritual value. One of the Methodist

---

[11] Ibid.

[12] Gordon Rupp, *Religion in England 1688–791* (Oxford: Clarendon, 1986), 353.

[13] Albert Outler, *Theology in the Wesleyan Spirit* (Nashville: Discipleship Resources, 1975), 6.

lay preachers, John Easton, criticized Wesley for stooping to publish mere fiction. Wesley "felt nothing but pity for those who could not enjoy a feeling of sympathy with fictional characters. . . . Wesley listened to [Easton's objections] patiently, then quizzed him about two episodes in the book."

> Wesley:　Did you read Vindex, John?
> Easton:　Yes, sir.
> Wesley:　Did you laugh, John?
> Easton:　No, sir.
> Wesley:　Did you read Damon and Pythias, John?
> Easton:　Yes, sir.
> Wesley:　Did you cry, John?
> Easton:　No, sir.
> Wesley, lifting up his eyes, and clasping his hands, exclaimed,
> 　　　"O earth—earth—earth!"[14]

Wesley's ardent spirit attracted fiery young men to join him in ministry. Some of them, perhaps like John Easton, were in grave danger of growing narrow in their sympathies, their outlook, and their abilities to enter into common life. Not everyone had the advantage of the robust, classical education Wesley had enjoyed. But insofar as it was in his power, he would transmit to them the benefits of a broad and deep study of the best that had been thought and said.

The Catholic Spirit, and a Caution against Bigotry

Especially as Wesley's movement grew and gained self-confidence, Wesley found that he needed to preach against narrowness and triumphalism. Two of his sermons on the subject were classics, and he included them among the *Standard Sermons*. The first one, "Catholic Spirit," describes the attitude Christians ought to have toward those they disagree with. The second, "A Caution Against Bigotry," explores the way Christians from different churches should cooperate in ministry.

Sermon 39, "Catholic Spirit," is on the text from 2 Kings 10:15, in which Jehu says to Jehonadab, "Is thine heart right, as my heart is with thy heart? . . . If it be, give me thine hand." Wesley abstracted from this line the principle that Christians whose hearts are in one accord, who share the same

---

[14] Quoted in Herbert, *John Wesley as Editor and Author*, 96.

intention with regard to bringing the message of Jesus to the world, ought to join hands. Not surprisingly, the emphasis for Wesley fell on the heart. The text does not say: "Are you of my church, of my congregation? Do you receive the same form of church government, and allow the same church officers, with me? Do you join in the same form of prayer wherein I worship God?"[15] Nor does it go on to say, "If it be, be of my opinion." It offers one criterion: heart agreement. And it gives one image of the right attitude: "Give me thy hand." Joining hands, Wesley explained, symbolizes love. "Give me thy hand" means,

> first, love me: and that not only as thou lovest all mankind; not only as thou lovest thine enemies, but as a brother in Christ, a fellow citizen of the New Jerusalem, a fellow soldier engaged in the same warfare, under the same Captain of our salvation. Love me as a companion in the kingdom and patience of Jesus, and a joint heir of his glory.[16]

Just as it means coming alongside each other and joining in the common warfare, it also means praying: "Commend me to God in all thy prayers." And finally, joining hands symbolizes that Christians from different churches should exhort one another to do good works. Wesley pleaded with his audience:

> Provoke me to love and to good works. Second thy prayer, as thou hast opportunity, by speaking to me, in love, whatsoever thou believest to be for my soul's health. Quicken me in the work which God has given me to do, and instruct me how to do it more perfectly. Yea, "smite me friendly, and reprove me," whereinsoever I appear to thee to be doing rather my own will, than the will of him that sent me. O speak and spare not, whatever thou believest may conduce, either to the amending my faults, the strengthening my weakness, the building me up in love, or the making me more fit, in any kind, for the Master's use.[17]

"Join with me," said Wesley, "in the work of God; and let us go on hand in hand."

In sermon 38, "A Caution Against Bigotry," Wesley went even further in arguing for full fellowship with other Christians. This sermon is on Mark

---

[15] Sermon 39, "Catholic Spirit," in *Wesley's 52 Standard Sermons*, ed. N. Burwash (Salem, OH: Schmul, 1988), 392.
[16] Ibid., 396.
[17] Ibid., 397.

9:38–39, in which John tells Jesus, "Master, we saw one casting out devils in thy name, and he followeth not us: and we forbad him, because he followeth not us." Jesus gives the striking answer, "Forbid him not." Wesley preached earnestly from this text, insisting that his listeners open their hearts to the work that God was doing among other Christian groups. In a later description of why he began preaching this message, Wesley said, "The thing which I was greatly afraid of all this time, and which I resolved to use every possible method of preventing, was, a narrowness of spirit, a party zeal . . . that miserable bigotry which makes many so unready to believe that there is any work of God but among themselves."[18] Wesley devised a possible cure for this creeping narrowness and sectarianism: "I thought it might be a help against this, frequently to read, to all who were willing to hear, the accounts I received from time to time of the work which God is carrying on in the earth, both in our own and other countries not among us alone, but among those of various opinions and denominations."[19] He apparently scoured the news reports to find exciting stories of God doing great things among Baptists and Calvinists, and then made it a point to read these reports to his Methodist Anglicans. It was not a weekly event, but it was often enough:

> For this I allotted one evening in every month; and I find no cause to repent my labour. It is generally a time of strong consolation to those who love God, and all mankind for his sake; as well as of breaking down the partition-walls which either the craft of the devil or the folly of men has built up; and of encouraging every child of God to say, (O when shall it once be) "Whosoever doeth the will of my Father which is in heaven, the same is my brother, and sister, and mother."[20]

This is an interesting strategy for keeping the heart rightly aligned while living in a divided Christendom. Wesley knew that we are stuck with the problems caused by Christian denominational diversity for the foreseeable future. There are "so many several parties . . . infinite varieties of opinion." The English in particular "have been continually dividing from each other, upon points of no moment, and many times such as religion had no concern in." With so many groups, Wesley noted, it was highly likely "that whenever we see any 'casting out devils,' he will be one that, in this

---

[18] Sermon 38, "A Caution Against Bigotry," Burwash, 379.
[19] Ibid., 380.
[20] Ibid.

sense, 'followeth not us'—that is not of our opinion." When you see some-body doing great and liberating work in the name of Christ, you should rejoice and encourage him—even, notes Wesley, if he is not Anglican: "He may have many objections to that Liturgy which we approve of beyond all others; many doubts concerning that form of church government which we esteem both apostolical and scriptural." But the command of Christ is clear: "Forbid him not." Wesley had an expansive view of all the ways we might be tempted to forbid such a person:

> Beware how you attempt to hinder him, either by your authority, or argu-ments, or persuasions. Do not in any wise strive to prevent his using all the power which God has given him. If you have authority with him, do not use that authority to stop the work of God. Do not furnish him with reasons why he ought not any more to speak in the name of Jesus. Satan will not fail to supply him with these, if you do not second him therein. Persuade him not to depart from the work. If he should give place to the devil and you, many souls might perish in their iniquity, but their blood would God require at your hands.[21]

Wesley knew that fiery Methodists eager to enforce their doctrines and practices would have a host of objections. Should they not take up the case against Dissenters, Calvinists, and others? If these other doctrines were wrong, why not keep the crowds from going to hear them? Should Meth-odists not make it a point to argue publicly against them? Wesley's answer was stark: "If you do any of these things, you are a bigot to this day." In fact, Wesley wanted his followers to emulate his example in celebrating the work God was pleased to do outside their communion:

> But be not content with not forbidding any that casts out devils. It is well to go thus far; but do not stop here. If you will avoid all bigotry, go on. In every instance of this kind, whatever the instrument be, acknowledge the finger of God. And not only acknowledge, but rejoice in his work, and praise his name with thanksgiving. Encourage whomsoever God is pleased to employ, to give himself wholly up thereto.[22]

Wesley had one last caution, one more safeguard against bigotry. "Think not the bigotry of another is any excuse for your own." And here

---

[21] Ibid., 386.
[22] Ibid., 388.

he imagined a theological opponent not only casting out devils, but also forbidding Wesleyans from doing so. "But beware of retorting. It is not your part to return evil for evil. Another's not observing the direction of our Lord, is no reason why you should neglect it. Nay, but let him have all the bigotry to himself. If he forbid you, do not you forbid him." As a closing *coup de grace*, Wesley proposed a role model for his Methodist listeners: John Calvin. When Calvin heard that Luther had a low opinion of Calvin's work, Calvin replied, "Let Luther call me a hundred devils; I will still reverence him as a messenger of God."[23]

Nevertheless, Wesley did declare some boundaries beyond which the "catholic spirit" of toleration and Christian cooperation could not go. As we will see in the next chapter, any form of anti-Trinitarianism was simply beyond the pale, a non-Christian view of God and salvation. By drawing some boundaries so clearly, Wesley showed that his principle of Christian cooperation is a completely different thing from simply not caring about doctrine. As he said:

> a catholic spirit is not speculative latitudinarianism. It is not an indifference to all opinions: this is the spawn of hell, not the offspring of heaven. This unsettledness of thought, this being "driven to and fro, and tossed about with every wind of doctrine," is a great curse, not a blessing, an irreconcilable enemy, not a friend, to true catholicism.[24]

While Wesley did not quite describe Roman Catholicism as non-Christian, he did allude to the challenge presented by "such a Church as we account to be in many respects anti-scriptural and anti-Christian," and he went on to describe it as

> a Church which we believe to be utterly false and erroneous in her doctrines, as well as very dangerously wrong in her practice; guilty of gross superstition as well as idolatry,—a Church that has added many articles to the faith which was once delivered to the saints; that has dropped one whole commandment of God, and made void several of the rest by her traditions; and that, pretending the highest veneration for, and strictest conformity to, the ancient Church, has nevertheless brought in number-

---

[23] Wesley's quotation from Calvin is inexact. He was probably citing from memory the line from Calvin's 1544 letter to Bullinger, "I have frequently said, that, were he to treat me as an incarnate demon, I would still not the less rank him as a great servant of Christ." Quoted in J. M. V. Audin, *History of the Life, Works, and Doctrines of John Calvin* (Louisville: Webb, 1850), 405.

[24] Sermon 39, "Catholic Spirit," Burwash, 397.

less innovations, without any warrant either from antiquity or Scripture. Now, most certainly, "he followeth not us," who stands at so great a distance from us. What of them?[25]

These are, of course, simply the standard Anglican critiques of the Roman Catholic Church, stated with Wesley's characteristic decisiveness. Elsewhere he said of Roman Catholics, "I pity them much, having the same assurance that Jesus is the Christ, and that no Romanist can expect to be saved according to the terms of his covenant."[26] What Wesley certainly opposed and rejected was the system of doctrines that were distinctive to the Roman Catholic Church. He admitted that many "Romanists" would be saved in spite of that system of theology. "Persons may be truly religious, who hold many wrong opinions," he said. In fact, he took devout Roman Catholics to be evidence of this, and even Calvinists:

> Can any one possibly doubt of this, while there are Romanists in the world? For who can deny, not only that many of them formerly have been truly religious, as Thomas a Kempis, Gregory Lopez, and the Marquis de Renty; but that many of them, even at this day, are real inward Christians? And yet what a heap of erroneous opinions do they hold, delivered by tradition from their fathers! Nay, who can doubt of it while there are Calvinists in the world,—assertors of absolute predestination? For who will dare to affirm that none of these are truly religious men? Not only many of them in the last century were burning and shining lights, but many of them are now real Christians, loving God and all mankind.[27]

It seems that Wesley may have placed Roman Catholics just inside the line of Christians with whom he could cooperate. "What of them?" His answer was the same: having rehearsed his grievances with the Roman system, he said, "If thy heart be as my heart, give me thy hand." In his "Letter to a Roman Catholic," Wesley asked, "can nothing be done, even allowing us on both sides to retain our own opinions, for the softening our hearts towards each other, the giving a check to this flood of unkindness, and restoring, at least, some small degree of love among our neighbours and countrymen?"

---

[25] Sermon 38, "Caution Against Bigotry," Burwash, 385.
[26] From Wesley's journal, August 1759, in *Works*, 3:151.
[27] Sermon 55, "On the Trinity," in *The Works of the Reverend John Wesley*, ed. John Emory, 7 vols. (New York: Emory and Waugh, 1831), 2:20.

Do not you wish for this? Are you not fully convinced that malice, hatred, revenge, bitterness, whether in us or in you, in our hearts or yours, are an abomination to the Lord? Be our opinions right or be they wrong, these tempers are undeniably wrong. They are the broad road that leads to destruction, to the nethermost hell.[28]

The catholic spirit and the warning against bigotry were John Wesley's attempt to stay rightly oriented toward all that God was doing in the world. The key, predictably for Wesley, was the attitude of the heart. Equally predictably, Charles Wesley captured the main idea in a hymn:

> Weary of all this wordy strife,
> These notions, forms, and modes, and names,
> To Thee, the way, the Truth, the Life,
> Whose love my simple heart inflames,
> Divinely taught, at last I fly,
> With Thee and Thine to live and die.
>
> Forth from the midst of Babel brought,
> Parties and sects I cast behind;
> Enlarge my heart, and free my thought,
> Where'er the latent truth I find
> The latent truth with joy to own,
> And bow to Jesus' name alone.
>
> Redeem'd by Thine almighty grace,
> I taste my glorious liberty,
> With open arms the world embrace,
> But cleave to those who cleave to Thee;
> But only in Thy saints delight,
> Who walk with God in purest white.[29]

Grounded in the great tradition, and with the right attitude in his heart, Wesley carried out his ministry with his eye on Christian unity. But he was born into a fractious time, and had to do the best he could with the situa-

---

[28] "Letter to a Roman Catholic," reprinted in *John Wesley*, ed. Albert Outler (New York: Oxford University Press, 1964), 493.
[29] This is the hymn entitled "Catholic Love," often printed after the sermon "Catholic Spirit" in most editions of Wesley's sermons, though it is curiously omitted in the Burwash edition. It is also available in Charles Wesley, "Catholic Love," *Poetical Works of John and Charles Wesley*, vol. 6 (London: Wesleyan-Methodist Conference Office, 1869), 71–72.

tion he found. Sometimes the most ecumenical thing you can do is dig in your heels and stay in your own church, and that is what Wesley did. He remained Anglican even when the easier thing to do would have been to spin off a new denomination. But remaining Anglican was no easy matter, because Wesley had to make it clear what kind of Anglican he was remaining.

There Are Anglicans, and Then There Are Anglicans

Wesley's grandparents had been Dissenters and Puritans, but both of his parents had converted as adults to Anglicanism. Wesley endorsed their decision and clung tenaciously to the established church. But the revival movement was constantly exerting centrifugal force on the established church. Wesley's most ardent admirers were constantly pushing him to start a new church. And to make matters much worse, the Anglican churches themselves began opposing various aspects of Wesley's ministry and shutting him out of ministry there. This rejection came early and was the very thing that launched Whitefield and Wesley on their new methods of preaching outdoors. For several crucial years, everything the established church did seemed like an invitation for John Wesley to leave it and start a new religious community. Gordon Rupp sketches the dangerous situation into which Anglicanism put itself during these years:

> More important than 1784 is 1739, when the London churches closed their doors on John Wesley, and when, following Whitfield, he did in Bristol what he had already done in Georgia and preached in the open air. The real manifesto is indeed the phrase in the letter to Hervey that the world was his parish, when he set out on his tremendous itinerancy like a human sputnik, a Don Quixote for Christ's sake. The troubles of those years, the antagonism of magistrates, of the mobs, of the local clergy, arose because for such men the parish was their world, and at that time each new parish boundary required another Act of Parliament and the Church machine, rigid and inflexible, was unable to undertake either the evangelism or the pastoral care of the unchurched multitudes.[30]

Without ever leaving the church, Wesley and his people set up a complete alternative system within the church, meeting the spiritual needs of the people directly:

---

[30] Gordon Rupp, "The Future of the Methodist Tradition," *The London Quarterly and Holborn Review* 184 (1959): 266.

Through John Wesley and his little band of helpers there came into exis-tence companies of men and women living by rule, singing their hymns and praying together with a simple fervour the like of which England had perhaps not seen since the first coming of the friars. They were at first wholly encompassed by the Church of England. They still went to the parish church for baptisms, weddings, funerals, Holy Communion and, when Bishops did their duty, confirmation. And yet in an amazingly short time they had their own framework of edification, intended not to supersede but to supplement the ordinances of the Church of England, their fasts, vigils, watch-nights, love feasts, and their band, class and society meetings.[31]

And all this time, Wesley was learning how to articulate the spiritual transformation that had reoriented his own life. He had been confused by Roman Catholic mystics, and then had learned much from the Moravians, and finally heard the voice of Luther explaining biblical salvation to him. These were exotic voices. Once again, all roads seemed to lead anywhere but to Anglicanism. But in 1738, Wesley set himself "more narrowly to in-quire what the doctrine of the Church of England is concerning the much controverted point of justification by faith," and he found his answer in the Thirty-Nine Articles and the Elizabethan Homilies of the Church of England. It turned out that the revolutionary theology of salvation that had gripped him had been right there in his Anglican formularies all along. He found justification and regeneration right under his nose, "and the sum of what I found in the Homilies I extracted and printed for the use of oth-ers." The result was a twelve-page pamphlet called *The Doctrine of Salvation, Faith, and Good Works*.

To his shock, Wesley was told by his establishment enemies that this was not properly Anglican and that he was at odds with the Church of England. He appealed to a bishop and received a very strange answer:

> When your adversaries tax you with differing from the Church, they cannot be supposed to charge you with differing from the Church as it was a little after the Reformation, but as it is at this day. And when you profess great deference and veneration for the Church of England, you cannot be sup-posed to profess it for the Church and its Pastors in the year 1545, and not rather in the year 1745. If, then, by the "the Church of England" be meant

---

[31] Ibid.

(as ought to be meant) the present Church, it will be no hard matter to show that your doctrines differ widely from the doctrines of that Church.[32]

All at once Wesley found that his greatest weapon, his appeal to true Anglicanism, had been taken from him. But he immediately realized that the Bishop had inadvertently shifted the burden of proof. If Wesley was in fact being true to the Church of England circa 1545, then he was in the right, and it was the Church of England circa 1745 that was wrong for opposing him. "Well, how blind was I!" he responded.

> I always supposed, till the very hour I read these words, that when I was charged with differing from the Church, I was charged with differing from the Articles or Homilies. And for the compilers of these, I can sincerely profess great deference and veneration. But I cannot honestly profess any veneration at all for those Pastors of the present age, who solemnly subscribe to those Articles and Homilies which they do not believe in their hearts. Nay, I think, unless I differ from these men (be they Bishops, Priests, or Deacons) just as widely as they do from those Articles and Homilies, I am no true Church-of-England man.[33]

In his struggle against narrowness, Wesley had encountered an unexpected variety: the liberal narrowness that will not tolerate tradition. Undeterred, Wesley continued digging deeper and deeper into his Anglican heritage, and found there more and more grounds for the robust evangelicalism of the revival.

According to Wesley's contemporary William Grimshaw (1708–1763), the rise of Methodism should be understood as nothing but the revival of real Anglicanism. "The disuse, I say, of the Homilies and Thirty-Nine Articles of our Religion is certainly the chief occasion of all this mischief in our Church." From his perspective, it was the neglect of true Anglican spiritual theology for several generations that had been the disaster. As the people of England began to experience the awakening, many of them looked around for better churches; in places where the Dissenters had strong presences, the Methodist revival was in danger of emptying out the Church of England and turning the people into Baptists. Grimshaw again pointed to the Anglican documents that had been underused for so long:

[32] Rupp, *Religion in England 1688–1791*, 63–64.
[33] Ibid., 64.

Had they been constantly read, 'tis very probable that all these evils had not only been effectually prevented, but Methodism also, which is nothing else but the revival of the doctrines contained therein, had never appeared, those books and what the Methodists preach being all one. This, let me add, some few of our clergy are so well advised of, that they purposely evade the reading of them to the people for fear of increasing Methodism, a term very likely made use of by the art of the Devil to prevent the true end of their ministry, I mean, the making of good Christians.[34]

Grimshaw told the same story from another perspective: "A certain old clergyman of my acquaintance, lately deceased, being asked by his curate if he might read the Homilies in the church, answered, No; for if he should do so, all the congregation would turn Methodists."[35] Wesley wanted Anglicans to remain Anglican. But he also intended to deliver the theology of the Anglican Homilies, the Book of Common Prayer, and the Thirty-Nine Articles to his generation. When he did so, he created Methodism. On his watch, however, it was not a breakaway denomination. It was his attempt to be the best Anglican he could be, a 1545-style Anglican. Wesley wanted an ecumenism that reached back across time, through the great tradition.

Cooperating across the Calvinist-Arminian Divide

For anybody outside the Anglican communion, it may seem unimportant that John Wesley chose to stay inside it. Besides, as his brother Charles would point out, John did take some steps, like appointing lay preachers and ordaining American bishops, that eventually made possible "the Methodist schism" away from the Church of England. John Wesley is hardly the icon of Christian unity! But the point is not to present him as more than he was; it is to show how an instinct for maximal Christian unity was integral to his view of the Christian life. His commitment to the unity of the church caused him to hold things together at any point that happened to come within his sphere of influence. For Wesley, that meant staying put when the easiest thing to do would have been to start a new church.

Similarly, when it comes to Calvinism, Wesley is hardly an advertisement for evangelical unity. He is the figurehead of one side of the two-party

---

[34] William Grimshaw writing in 1749 on Wesley, quoted in Richard P. Heitzenrater, *The Elusive Mr. Wesley*, 2nd ed. (Nashville: Abingdon, 2003), 274.
[35] Ibid.

system that split the great awakening down the middle. From Whitefield's point of view, Wesley broke the unity of the movement when he began making an issue of promoting Christian perfection and rejecting Reformed theology. That is to tell the story from only one side, of course; from Wesley's perspective, it was Whitefield who disrupted unity by beginning to preach predestination aggressively. But whoever pushed whom first, it became obvious that there were two wings of the evangelical revival with very different commitments on these issues. If we take the theological chasm between Calvinism and Arminianism as a given, what we can learn from Wesley's conduct is that he knew how to stay centered on the gospel and found ways to cooperate with evangelicals whose theology differed on some important points.

Wesley was Arminian and therefore necessarily a non-Calvinist. But he was not quite an anti-Calvinist. In describing his doctrine of justification by faith, he did "not differ from [Calvin] an hair's breadth." He did see five-point Calvinism as a problem, and he indulged in some contemptuous talk about it. But in his public preaching and teaching, he emphasized the evangelical doctrines that Calvinism and Arminianism hold in common. And even when he said nasty things in private about Calvinism ("Satan threw it in our path"), he was usually focusing on the antinomianism with which Calvinism too often kept company in the eighteenth century. Antinomianism is of course not properly part of Calvinism, any more than legalism is properly part of Methodism.

Wesley was able to cooperate across the Calvinist-Arminian divide because he had perspective. He knew the great tradition of Christian theology, and he had a large view of the gospel. With these massive realities in place, he could turn to the dispute with Calvinism and see it as a relatively small matter. However important the issues involved may be in their own right, they are relativized by the greatness of the gospel. One of the most beautiful expressions of this understanding was voiced by Charles Simeon (1759–1836), who, as a young clergyman, met the elderly John Wesley. He recorded the following exchange:

Simeon: Sir, I understand that you are called an Arminian; and I have been sometimes called a Calvinist; and therefore I suppose we are to draw daggers. But before I consent to begin the combat, with your permission I will ask you a few questions. Pray, Sir, do you feel yourself a depraved creature, so depraved that you would never have thought of turning to God, if God had not first put it into your heart?

Wesley: Yes, I do indeed.

Simeon: And do you utterly despair of recommending yourself to God by anything you can do; and look for salvation solely through the blood and righteousness of Christ?

Wesley: Yes, solely through Christ.

Simeon: But, Sir, supposing you were at first saved by Christ, are you not somehow or other to save yourself afterwards by your own works?

Wesley: No, I must be saved by Christ from first to last.

Simeon: Allowing, then, that you were first turned by the grace of God, are you not in some way or other to keep yourself by your own power?

Wesley: No.

Simeon: What then, are you to be upheld every hour and every moment by God, as much as an infant in its mother's arms?

Wesley: Yes, altogether.

Simeon: And is all your hope in the grace and mercy of God to preserve you unto His heavenly kingdom?

Wesley: Yes, I have no hope but in Him.

Simeon: Then, Sir, with your leave I will put up my dagger again; for this is all my Calvinism; this is my election, my justification by faith, my final perseverance: it is in substance all that I hold, and as I hold it; and therefore, if you please, instead of searching out terms and phrases to be a ground of contention between us, we will cordially unite in those things where in we agree.[36]

Wesley and Simeon could put up their daggers because they genuinely had so much in common, but also because they made a habit out of dwelling on those truly central realities of the gospel. Today, some Calvinists routinely think of Calvinism as the opposite of Arminianism. They would be on better historical ground if they defined it as the opposite of Roman Catholicism.

C. H. Spurgeon, whom we quoted above as recommending Wesley and Whitefield as the best candidates to fill up the ranks of missing apostles, gave a lecture entitled "The Two Wesleys," at the Metropolitan Tabernacle

---

[36] Simeon tells the story obliquely, but Handley Carr Glyn Moule identifies Simeon more directly as the Calvinist participant in his biography, *Charles Simeon* (London: Methuen, 1892), 79f.

on December 6, 1861. In that message, he used the exact same trick recommended by Wesley in his remarks about "Catholic Spirit": he praised
the work that God had done through someone who did not belong to Spurgeon's own camp, and then warned his Calvinist supporters not to indulge
in bigotry:

> To ultra-Calvinists his name is as abhorrent as the name of the Pope to a
> Protestant: you have only to speak of Wesley, and every imaginable evil is
> conjured up before their eyes, and no doom is thought to be sufficiently
> horrible for such an arch-heretic as he was. I verily believe that there are
> some who would be glad to rake up his bones from the tomb and burn
> them, as they did the bones of Wycliffe of old—men who go so high in
> doctrine, and withal add so much bitterness and uncharitableness to it,
> that they cannot imagine that a man can fear God at all unless he believes
> precisely as they do.

Spurgeon went on to say, on the other hand, that Wesley fans can be annoy-
ing: "Unless you can give him constant adulation, unless you are prepared
to affirm that he had no faults, and that he had every virtue, even impossible virtues, you cannot possibly satisfy his admirers." Nobody said living
together would be easy.

Bishop J. C. Ryle, in his book on evangelical leaders of the eighteenth
century, gets the warnings out of the way right up front: "He was an Arminian in doctrine. I fully admit the seriousness of the objection. I do not
pretend either to explain the charge away, or to defend his objectionable
opinions."[37] But he goes on to his main point, saying, "We must beware
that we do not condemn men too strongly for not seeing all things in our
point of view, or excommunicate and anathematize them because they do
not pronounce our shibboleth."[38]

What is to be found in Wesley, according to Ryle? For all Wesley's devia-
tions from the Calvinist line, Ryle says:

> But if the same man strongly and boldly exposes and denounces sin,
> clearly and fully lifts up Christ, distinctly and openly invites men to be-
> lieve and repent, shall we dare to say that the man does not preach the
> gospel at all? Shall we dare to say that he will do no good? I, for one, can-

---

[37] J. C. Ryle, *Christian Leaders of the Last Century; or, England a Hundred Years Ago* (London: T. Nelson, 1869), 85.
[38] Ibid.

not say so, at any rate. If I am asked whether I prefer Whitefield's gospel or Wesley's, I answer at once that I prefer Whitefield's: I am a Calvinist, and not an Arminian. That Wesley would have done better if he could have thrown off his Arminianism, I have not the least doubt; but that he preached the gospel, honored Christ, and did extensive good, I no more doubt than I doubt my own existence.[39]

And like so many other Calvinistic Wesley fans, Ryle goes on to caution against bigotry:

Finally, has any one been accustomed to regard Wesley with dislike on account of his Arminian opinions? Is any one in the habit of turning away from his name with prejudice, and refusing to believe that such an imperfect preacher of the gospel could do any good? I ask such a one to remould his opinion, to take a more kindly view of the old soldier of the cross, and to give him the honour he deserves. . . . Whether we like it or not, John Wesley was a mighty instrument in God's hand for good; and, next to George Whitefield, was the first and foremost evangelist of England a hundred years ago.[40]

There is a famous story about one of Whitefield's followers, who, after a discussion about how un-Calvinist Wesley was, asked Whitefield what he took to be a hard question: Will we see John Wesley in heaven? Whitefield's answer was that the Calvinists of his generation were unlikely to see John Wesley in heaven. "I fear not," said Whitefield. But then he delivered the punch line: "He will be so near the throne, and we shall be at such a distance, that we shall hardly get a sight of him." Spurgeon reports this Whitefield story, and comments, "In studying the life of Wesley, I believe Whitefield's opinion is abundantly confirmed—that Wesley is near the eternal throne, having served his Master, albeit with many mistakes and errors, yet from a pure heart, fervently desiring to glorify God upon the earth."

An earlier generation of Reformed thinkers and ministers were revived and awakened by Wesley's teaching. Spurgeon knew that an awakener was not someone to take lightly, that God didn't often send people with that ability to revive and stir up the church. We always have to keep an eye on the main danger, and Spurgeon was quite sure that Wesleyanism wasn't the main danger of his, or any, age. The main danger is Christians failing to be

---

[39] Ibid., 86.
[40] Ibid., 104–5.

wide awake, failing to be fully Christian. Wesley was a strong stimulant, and Spurgeon wanted more, not less, of that from Wesley:

> I am afraid that most of us are half asleep, and those that are a little awake have not begun to feel. It will be time for us to find fault with John and Charles Wesley, not when we discover their mistakes, but when we have cured our own. When we shall have more piety than they, more fire, more grace, more burning love, more intense unselfishness, then, and not till then, may we begin to find fault and criticize.

Taking a moment to compare his own ministry to that of Wesley's, Spurgeon thought the comparison was like a little candle held up in the sun: "For my part, I am as one who can see the spots in the sun, but know it to be the sun still, and only weep for my farthing candle by the side of such a luminary."[41]

We began with Wesley cautioning against bigotry and requiring his people to listen at least once a month to good reports of God's work among other kinds of Christians. We have closed with good reports of Calvinists behaving without bigotry toward their Wesleyan brethren.

---

[41] C. H. Spurgeon, "John Wesley," *Banner of Truth*, July–August 1969, 58.

CHAPTER 10

THE TRINITARIAN THEOLOGY OF JOHN WESLEY

You can talk about the Christian life for a long time without ever really rising to the level of talking about God. There is so much to say about the spiritual dynamics of the experience of salvation, and so many things to attend to, that it is possible to lose the big picture. But the big picture is that Christian salvation is reconciliation with God, and a theology of the Christian life ought to make constant, detailed reference to the Father's gift of the Son and the Spirit. The doctrine of the Christian life has to reach its climax with a definite reference to the God who saves us by giving himself to us. John Wesley's theology of the Christian life succeeded in doing that. It kept a skylight open at all times to the living God, the triune God.

Decidedly Trinitarian

Wesley's Trinitarianism has not always been adequately appreciated, or even noticed. Not long ago, a Methodist bishop wrote, "Overall, the doctrine of the Trinity in Methodism plays a subordinate role. Of course, its articles of faith make reference to the basic assertions concerning the doctrine of the Trinity, and John Wesley dedicated a sermon to that theme, which frankly has more the character of an exercise of duty."[1] While this may be a true and disheartening judgment on Methodism, it misses the mark by a

---

[1] Walter Klaiber and Manfred Marquardt, *Living Grace: An Outline of United Methodist Theology* (Nashville: Abingdon, 2001), 56.

great distance as a description of John Wesley's Trinitarianism. The sermon in question, number 55, "On the Trinity," hardly assigns the doctrine of the Trinity a subordinate role. Wesley says that "what God has been pleased to reveal upon his head, is far from being a point of indifference, is a truth of the last importance. It enters into the very heart of Christianity: It lies at the heart of all vital religion." Indeed, "the knowledge of the Three-One God is interwoven with all true Christian faith," and as Wesley explains its connection with salvation, he marvels that anybody could think of the doctrine as anything but central:

> But I know not how any one can be a Christian believer till he "hath," as St. John speaks, "the witness in himself"; till "the Spirit of God witnesses with his spirit, that he is a child of God"; that is, in effect, till God the holy Ghost witnesses that God the Father has accepted him through the merits of God the Son: And, having this witness, he honours the Son, and the blessed Spirit, "even as he honours the Father."[2]

Furthermore, Wesley preached several other sermons that, not having *Trinity* in the title, nevertheless are devoted to the doctrine and its connection to "vital religion." Sermon 114, "The Unity of the Divine Being," for example, discusses the Trinity, as does sermon 77, "Spiritual Worship." And Wesley weaves Trinitarianism into so many of his other sermons that it is hard to understand how it could be ignored. Perhaps the problem is that only in one sermon does Wesley announce the Trinity as his topic. In all the others (and actually even in "On the Trinity"), he is primarily talking about salvation and the Christian life. But that is the genius of Wesleyan Trinitarianism: its connection to the gospel and the Christian life. If that has the disadvantage of enabling some interpreters to overlook the pervasively Trinitarian character of Wesley's theology, it makes up for it by being more practical, and more like the New Testament.

We have already seen repeatedly that Wesley thinks of justification and sanctification—those two central structural elements of the Christian life—in Trinitarian terms: "The one implies, what God 'does for us' through his Son; the other, what he 'works in us' by his Spirit."[3] Everything about our salvation is given its shape by this coordinated action of the Father accom-

---

[2] Sermon 55, "On the Trinity," in *The Works of the Reverend John Wesley*, ed. John Emory, 7 vols. (New York: Emory and Waugh, 1831), 2:20.
[3] Sermon 5, "Justification by Faith," in *Wesley's 52 Standard Sermons*, ed. N. Burwash (Salem, OH: Schmul, 1988), 45.

plishing our salvation in the Son and applying it in the Spirit. No wonder Wesley claims that Trinitarianism "is interwoven with all true Christian faith," and no wonder he wrote this prayer: "Glory be to thee, O holy, undivided Trinity, for jointly concurring in the great work of our redemption, and restoring us again to the glorious liberty of the sons of God."[4]

As Geoffrey Wainwright has pointed out in an article entitled "Why Wesley Was a Trinitarian," it was not self-evident that an Oxford-trained young intellectual pastor would be Trinitarian in the mid-eighteenth century. All sorts of anti-Trinitarian systems were abroad at the time, and it was not hard to find respectable living advocates of deistic, Socinian, or even Arian options. Wesley knew these options and rejected them; he was not Trinitarian by default, but *chose* to be Trinitarian. "Even at his most 'catholic spirited,' he refused his hand to Arians, Socinians, and Deists, for their heart was not right with his heart."[5] How could he join forces with them, when the encounter with the triune God was at the center of his understanding of salvation? Wainwright summarizes Wesley's Trinitarian theology in these terms:

> Our salvation is for Wesley the differentiated but united work of the Three Persons of the Godhead; it sets us into an appropriate relation to each Person, and it gives us, as will shortly be insisted, a share in their divine communion. The Holy Trinity appears, therefore, as both the origin and goal of soteriology.[6]

The Trinity is the origin of soteriology (the doctrine of salvation) because it is the Father, Son, and Holy Spirit who summon us to reconciliation. Even when describing the invisible stirrings of prevenient grace, Wesley casts them in terms that identify the work of each of the three persons. The vague rumblings of "natural conscience" are in fact better understood to be

> all the drawings of the Father; the desires after God, which, if we yield to them, increase more and more;—all that light wherewith the Son of God "enlighteneth every one that cometh into the world"; showing every man "to do justly, to love mercy, and to walk humbly with his God";—all the convictions which His Spirit, from time to time, works in every child of man."[7]

---

[4] "Forms of Prayer," in Emory, *The Works of the Reverend John Wesley*, 6:378.
[5] Geoffrey Wainwright, "Why Wesley Was a Trinitarian," *Drew Gateway* 59, no. 2 (1990): 26–43, quoting 27.
[6] Ibid., 35.
[7] Sermon 43, "The Scripture Way of Salvation," Burwash, 441.

It is striking that Wesley would describe this work of God in such personal, Trinitarian terms, because as a work of God on the unregenerate soul, it does not yet have the character of personal communion. Yet even this phase of God's work has the fingerprints of all three persons on it. Charles Wesley emphasizes that when the actual gospel call goes out, we see the coordinated work of the three persons even more. See how the three stanzas of this gripping gospel hymn work through the call of the Creator, the Savior, and the Spirit:

> SINNERS, turn, why will ye die?
> God, your Maker, asks you why?
> God, who did your being give,
> Made you with himself to live—
> He the fatal cause demands,
> Asks the work of his own hands,
> Why, ye thankless creatures, why
> Will ye cross his love, and die?
>
> Sinners, turn, why will ye die?
> God, your Saviour, asks you why?
> God, who did your souls retrieve,
> Died himself, that ye might live;
> Will you let him die in vain?
> Crucify your Lord again?
> Why, ye ransomed sinners, why
> Will you slight his grace, and die?
>
> Sinners, turn, why will ye die?
> God, the Spirit, asks you why?
> He who all your lives hath strove,
> Wooed you to embrace his love:
> Will you not his grace receive?
> Will you still refuse to live?
> Why, ye long-sought sinners, why
> Will you grieve your God, and die?[8]

And the Trinity is the goal of soteriology because there is no other salvation but life in the Trinity. In his sermon "The New Creation," Wesley

---

[8] *Hymnal of the Methodist Episcopal Church* (New York: Easton and Mains, 1878), 129.

exclaims that in heaven, "to crown all, there will be a deep, an intimate, an uninterrupted union with God; a constant communion with the Father and his Son Jesus Christ, through the Spirit; a continual enjoyment of the Three-One God, and of all creatures in him!"[9]

Experiencing the Trinity

Wesley's Trinitarianism was resolutely gospel-centered. While it was a teaching about the eternal nature of God, the whole point for Wesley was that God as he exists in his eternal nature has saved us for fellowship with him. Wesley's Trinitarianism was also uniquely experiential. It terminated not in an objective or factual declaration about the gospel, but in personal experience of the three persons. Wainwright points out, "Wesley starts with the available experience of the Holy Spirit" and moves on to explore the way the Spirit brings about our communion with the Father and the Son: "The 'adoption' of believers is, for Wesley, a major soteriological category."[10]

Sermon 77, "Spiritual Worship," is on a text from 1 John, which led Wesley to sing the praises of his favorite book. One reason it was his favorite is that 1 John "does not treat directly of faith, which St. Paul had done; neither of inward and outward holiness, concerning which both St. Paul, St. James, and St. Peter, had spoken"; instead, 1 John is permitted to teach about "the foundation of all,—the happy and holy communion which the faithful have with God the Father, Son, and Holy Ghost."[11] We have already seen that Wesley considered 1 John the capstone of biblical revelation, and one reason for that is the clarity and density of the letter's presentation of the believer's experience of the Trinity.

When Wesley said that the Trinity lies at "the heart of all vital religion," he did not mean that every believer has a special consciousness of the three persons entering into relationship with him. He meant that the Father has saved the Christian through the Son and Spirit, whether the Christian knows it or not. The Trinitarian reality is going on, with or without human consciousness of what is happening, and the ordinary Christian experience is an engagement with the triune reality.

On the other hand, Wesley did believe that it was possible to have a clear and distinct experience of each of the three persons. He routinely

---

[9] "The New Creation," in *Works*, 2:510.
[10] Wainwright, "Why Wesley Was a Trinitarian," 33.
[11] Sermon 77, "Spiritual Worship," in Emory, *The Works of the Reverend John Wesley*, 2:177.

cited the Roman Catholic mystic Gaston de Renty (1611–1649), whose testimony about this special experience fascinated him. De Renty said, "I have
generally within me an experimental realization and a plenitude of the
presence of the most Holy Trinity." He went on, in words that Wesley came
back to again and again:

> All things are blotted out of my mind as soon as they are done; nothing re-
> mains except God, by a naked faith, which, causing me to abandon myself
> to our Lord Jesus Christ, imparts to me much strength and great confidence
> in the Divine Trinity, because the operation of the Three Divine Persons is
> distinctly shown to me therein: the love of the Father, who reconciles us
> through His Son, and the Father and the Son, who give us life by the Holy
> Spirit, who causes us to live in communion with Jesus Christ, which com-
> munion effects in us a marvellous alliance with the most Holy Trinity, and
> at times produces in hearts sentiments which are inexplicable.[12]

Of this kind of experience, Wesley said,

> The knowledge of the Three-One God is interwoven with all true Chris-
> tian faith; with all vital religion. I do not say that every real Christian
> can say with the Marquis de Renty, "I bear about with me continually an
> experimental verity, and a plenitude of the presence of the ever-blessed
> Trinity." I apprehend this is not the experience of babes, but, rather,
> "fathers in Christ."[13]

All Christians experience the Trinity, but Wesley hoped that spiritually
mature Christians might have a clear understanding of what they were experiencing.

In fact, Wesley remained alert and on the lookout among his own people for such spiritual experiences as de Renty had reported. By 1788, Wesley
reported to a friend that he had interviewed a handful of Methodists who
had been granted some sort of experiential grasp of "the ever-blessed Trinity." "I have as yet found but a few instances," he wrote, "so that this is not,
as I was at first apt to suppose, the common privilege of all that are 'perfect
in love.'"[14] A holy woman nicknamed "Praying Nanny" had a kind of vision

---

[12] *The Life of the Baron De Renty; or, Perfection in the World Exemplified*, ed. Edward Healy Thompson (London: Burns & Oates, 1873), 372.
[13] Sermon 55, "On the Trinity," 20.
[14] Quoted in Geoffrey Wainwright, "Trinitarian Theology and Wesleyan Holiness," in *Orthodox and Wesleyan Spirituality*, ed. S. T. Kimbrough Jr. (Crestwood, NY: St Vladimir's Seminary Press, 2002), 76.

of the three persons distinctly, and wrote down, "I have union with the Trinity thus: I see the Son through the Spirit, I find the Father through the Son, and God is my all in all." With these visions among the early Methodists, we are back in the territory of the exotic, and in constant risk of hallucinatory enthusiasm. But John Wesley was always pleased to hear of what God could do with his people, so he gathered these stories eagerly. He had also learned some hard lessons by 1790, and he wrote to Nanny:

> My dear Sister: There is something in the dealings of God with your soul which is out of the common way. But I have known several whom He has been pleased to lead exactly in the same way, and particularly in manifesting to them distinctly the three Persons of the ever-blessed Trinity. You may tell all your experience to me at any time; but you will need to be cautious in speaking to others, for they would not understand what you say. Go in the name of God and the power of His might.[15]

Peculiar as they may be, these experiences were, for Wesley, simply more concrete signs and manifestations of a spiritual reality that was the common property of every believer: salvation as coming into communion with the Father, Son, and Spirit.

Hymns to the Trinity

By this point it should be no surprise that Charles Wesley wrote hymns about every subject we have just discussed in John's teaching. Charles wove the Trinitarian theology of Methodism into intricate rhymes and meters, and invested his hymns with dense and concentrated meditations. Here is a prayer to the Father for the Trinitarian blessings of the gospel:

> Thee that I may my Father know,
> A grain of faith impart,
> The Spirit of Thy Son bestow
> To witness in my heart;
> That Thou in Christ art reconciled,
> My conscience certify,
> And then Thy dear adopted child,
> I Abba Father cry.[16]

---

[15] Ibid., 78.
[16] Quoted in John R. Tyson, *Charles Wesley on Sanctification: A Biographical and Theological Study* (Grand Rapids: Francis Asbury, 1986), 96.

Charles also used the theology of the three persons as a template upon which to stretch out the fullness of salvation. Here he puts revelation, justification, sanctification, and sealing together in one prayer for the Spirit:

> Send us the Spirit of Thy Son,
> To make the depths of Godhead known,
> To make us share the life Divine;
> Send Him the sprinkled blood t'apply,
> Send Him, our souls to sanctify,
> And show, and seal us ever Thine.[17]

Here he explores how the Holy Spirit is not simply a gift of God, but the consummate gift, the gift in person, who unlocks all the others:

> God on us His Spirit bestow'd
> That we His other gifts may know,
> A pardon bought with Jesu's blood,
> A taste of glorious bliss below:
> The Spirit our conscience certifies
> That God to man hath freely given
> Wine without money, without price,
> Forgiveness, holiness, and heaven.[18]

And here he meditates on how the entire Trinity indwells the believer:

> Jesus, with thy Father come,
> And bring our inward Guide,
> Make our hearts Thy humble home,
> And in Thine house abide,
> Show us with Thy presence fill'd,
> Fill'd with glory from Thy throne,
> And perfected in one.[19]

Many more Charles Wesley hymns on the Trinity could be cited here. Indeed, if it is admitted that John preached only one sermon on the Trinity, Charles made up for it by writing hundreds of hymns on the subject. He published an entire volume of hymns on the Trinity, taking a theology

---

[17] Ibid., 130.
[18] Ibid., 143.
[19] Ibid., 172.

textbook on the subject and versifying every argument.[20] Many of the resulting hymns are beautiful summaries of Christian doctrine; many more are profound testimonies to the spiritual reality that underlies all Christian experience. Some, however, have been called "theological hooliganism" because of their didactic way of cramming as much doctrine as possible into a few rhymes, whether the subject was poetic or not:

> Men who Arians' blasphemies
> > Dare to scripture-doctrine name,
> Let their dire delusions cease,
> > Sink to hell from whence it came.[21]

Even this "to hell with anti-Trinitarianism" doggerel is evidence that "the Wesleys took their Trinitarian theology seriously."[22] Furthermore, it makes sense that Charles's hymns would carry more of the burden of Trinitarianism than John's sermons. The hymns were intended for the guidance and edification of the congregation, and the Wesleys wanted to guide them into orthodox theology and spirituality. "Both Wesleys thought perhaps the best way to combat the Unitarian heresy was through the hymnal, not through declarations from the pulpit. The pulpit was used to convert. The hymnal was used to instruct in Christian doctrine in order to influence the lives of the Methodists."[23] The hymnal was also used, of course, to form the hearts of the worshipers and to guide them in loving God properly and fully.

Knowing the One True God

There is one final use that John Wesley made of the doctrine of the Trinity, and it runs parallel to the way John Calvin used the doctrine in book 1 of his *Institutes*. Calvin raises the question of how we can know that we are worshiping and serving the true God rather than an idol of our own making. He provides a carefully constructed answer, weaving together a discussion of general and special revelation, and of God's speaking to us in Scripture. But Calvin's ultimate answer culminates in chapter 13, on the

---

[20] J. Ernest Rattenbury, "The Holy Trinity," in *The Evangelical Doctrines of Charles Wesley's Hymns*, 3rd ed. (London: Epworth, 1954), 137–51.
[21] Barry E. Bryant, "Trinity and Hymnody: The Doctrine of the Trinity in the Hymns of Charles Wesley," *Wesley Theological Journal* 25 (Fall 1990): 66.
[22] Ibid.
[23] Ibid.

Trinity. The concreteness of the Father, Son, and Holy Spirit revealed in salvation history and reported in Scripture is what secures our minds from wandering off to fashion gods in our own image.

Wesley does something strikingly similar in one of his last sermons. "On the Unity of the Divine Being" (1789)[24] argues that true religion is Trinitarian. Wesley works his way up through various possible idolatries before reaching the final one: false religion. False religion is, first of all, "any religion which does not imply the giving of the heart to God." One such false religion is "a religion of opinions; or what is called orthodoxy." Wesley warns, "Into this snare fall thousands of those who profess to hold 'salvation by faith'; indeed, all of those who, by faith, mean only a system of Arminian or Calvinian opinions." Another false religion is "a religion of forms; of barely outward worship, how constantly soever performed; yea, though we attend the Church Service every day, and the Lord's Supper every Sunday." A third false religion is "a religion of works; of seeking the favour of God by doing good to men." And finally, the "religion of Atheism; that is, every religion whereof God is not laid for the foundation."[25]

Wesley then defines true religion as "right tempers towards God and man." It can be stated "in two words, gratitude and benevolence; gratitude to our Creator and supreme Benefactor, and benevolence to our fellow creatures. In other words, it is the loving God with all our heart, and our neighbor as ourselves." So far all of this is classic Augustinianism, with an extra emphasis on heart religion. But after a few more meditations on the relation of holiness and happiness, Wesley takes a sudden, explicitly Trinitarian, turn: the happiness for which we were made "begins when we begin to know God, by the teaching of his own Spirit. As soon as the Father of spirits reveals his Son in our hearts, and the Son reveals his Father, the love of God is shed abroad in our hearts; then, and not till then, we are happy."[26] Everything Wesley has taught about the heart renewed in love and in the image of God, about happiness and holiness, is consummated here in the way he anchors our happiness in the true, triune God. He strikes the same Trinitarian notes one more time as the fitting climax to his vision of the Christian life, describing how our fellowship with the three persons is the ultimate fulfillment of our lives:

---

[24] Sermon 118, "On the Unity of the Divine Being," in *Sermons on Several Occasions* (London: Tegg, 1829), 508–15.
[25] Ibid., 512.
[26] Ibid., 512–13.

We are happy, first, in the consciousness of his favour, which indeed is better than life itself; next, in the constant communion with the Father, and with his Son Jesus Christ; then, in all the heavenly tempers which he hath wrought in us by his Spirit; again, in the testimony of his Spirit, that all our works please him; and, lastly, in the testimony of our own spirits, that "in simplicity and godly sincerity we have had our conversation in the world." Standing fast in this liberty from sin and sorrow, wherewith Christ hath made them free, real Christians "rejoice evermore, pray without ceasing, and in everything give thanks." And their happiness still increases as they "grow up into the measure of the stature of the fullness of Christ."[27]

---

[27] Ibid., 513.

APPENDIX

VOLUMES CITED FROM *THE BICENTENNIAL EDITION OF THE WORKS OF JOHN WESLEY*

References cited simply as *Works*, followed by the volume and page numbers, are from *The Bicentennial Edition of the Works of John Wesley*, ed. Frank Baker and Richard P. Heitzenrater (Nashville: Abingdon, 1976–). Corresponding volume titles are the following:

Volume 2: *Sermons II (34–70)*
Volume 3: *Sermons III (71–114)*
Volume 4: *Sermons IV (115–51)*
Volume 7: *A Collection of Hymns for the Use of the People Called Methodists*
Volume 9: *The Methodist Societies: History, Nature, and Design*
Volume 10: *The Methodist Societies: The Minutes of Conference*
Volume 20: *Journal and Diaries III (1743–1754)*
Volume 24: *Journal and Diaries VII (1787–1791)*
Volume 26: *Letters II (1740–1755)*

GENERAL INDEX

SCRIPTURE INDEX

GAINING WISDOM FROM THE PAST
FOR LIFE IN THE PRESENT

Other volumes in the Theologians on the Christian Life series

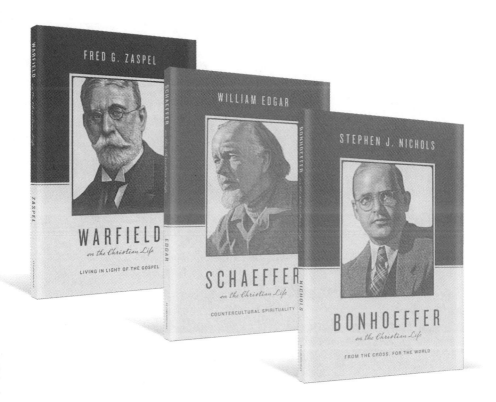